WHY
WATERGATE?

Why Watergate?

EDITED BY

PAUL J. HALPERN
UNIVERSITY OF CALIFORNIA, LOS ANGELES

PALISADES PUBLISHERS
PACIFIC PALISADES, CALIFORNIA

Library of Congress Catalog Card Number: 74-21037

International Standard Book Numbers:

0-913530-03-4 (paper)
0-913530-04-2 (cloth)

Palisades Publishers
P. O. Box 744, Pacific Palisades, California 90272

Printed in the United States of America

Contents

Part Three

The Personality in the White House

Preface

Understanding the causes of the various affairs called Watergate is important to the general public, the student, and the scholar. The Watergate experience has led to calls for numerous reforms of the American political system, but its implications for political reform depend very much on the causes of Watergate. If Watergate was primarily the result of Richard Nixon's personality, this interpretation would point us in a different direction of change than if Watergate were the natural outgrowth of a too powerful presidential institution or the inevitable aftermath of some societal change such as the decline of respect for law and order in the 1960s.

The series of essays that makes up this volume attempts to answer these questions—Why did Watergate occur and what is its significance? This book differs from other publications about Watergate because it focuses on interpretation rather than on narration of the facts, discussion of the legal and normative issues involved, or prediction of its effects on the political system. Thus we have taken an approach to the study of Watergate similar to the perspective toward the McCarthyism of the 1950s found in Daniel Bell's *The Radical Right*.

Although the various explanations of Watergate that have appeared are not mutually exclusive, considerable disagreement also exists about how much weight should be given to personality factors as compared to institutional or societal causes. This book is organized so as to highlight these differences and therefore sharpen the issues for the reader. The essays are grouped into three categories: (1) those stressing situational factors, such as the shifts in societal attitudes toward social change; (2) those focusing on the state of the presidency as an institution (the growth of the so-called imperial presidency); and (3) those emphasizing the personal importance of Richard Nixon and also attempting to explain the actions of the President and his staff in terms of their personalities.

The essays, including two original pieces by the editor and many others that initially appeared elsewhere, cover much of the political spectrum. Eleven were authored by academicians and seven were prepared by journalists and free-lance writers. In selecting essays for this volume the editor has passed over some interpretations that appear in book-length form and instead has often chosen high-quality writings that are not as readily available. Many of these essays were written before Richard Nixon resigned the office of President, which explains why some authors speak of President Nixon and the Watergate controversy in the present tense. In one sense Watergate may fittingly be referred to in the present tense because controversy over the handling of criminal cases and pardons stemming from Watergate-related events may continue for many months, and memoirs by former members of the Nixon administration could contain new revelations in the future. However, the essays in this collection are broadly interpretive and are not likely to be outdated by new disclosures.

An introductory essay by the editor discusses the conceptual framework of the book, the literature on Watergate and political reform, and the methodological problems involved in studying the Watergate events. Because discussion of Watergate varies with how broadly the phenomenon is conceived, the introduction also defines the term, Watergate. A selected bibliography of works on Watergate, Richard Nixon, and the Nixon administration concludes the volume.

The editor expresses appreciation to Marie-Catherine Artaud and Kathleen Fischer for editorial assistance and to Professor John C. Bollens, his colleague at UCLA, for editorial guidance. The editor naturally accepts all responsibility for the contents.

P.J.H.

Introduction

Paul J. Halpern

The phrase "Watergate scandals" has different meanings to various commentators who use the term. The definitions range from the narrow one of the break-in at the national headquarters of the Democratic Party and the subsequent cover-up to the broadest which tends to equate Watergate with the entire presidency of Richard M. Nixon. For our purposes it is best to conceive of Watergate somewhere between those two extremes.

WHAT IS WATERGATE?

This book is about the causes of the events that eventually led to an investigation by a special Senate committee (the Ervin Committee), an impeachment inquiry by the House Judiciary Committee, and the resignation of a president. Those initiatives were not limited to burglaries and wiretapping of the opposition party. Watergate now symbolizes a multitude of things which can be divided into three categories of activity—partisan, policy, and financial.

Partisan Initiatives

The *partisan* happenings consisted of a host of domestic intelligence activities, such as the break-in at the office of Daniel Ellsberg's psychiatrist; the wiretapping of newsmen, government officials, and former administration staffers; the proposal for the establishment of a massive domestic intelligence operation (the Huston Plan); and the actual setting up of a White House intelligence unit, the "Plumbers." Also included were other actions relating to the handling of "enemies"—the use of the Internal Revenue Service for political purposes; the inappropriate approach to the judge in the Ellsberg trial about his possible appointment to head the Federal Bureau of Investigation; the harassment of the press and mass media, including the unwarranted investigation of CBS correspondent Daniel Schorr; the forging of State Department cables attempting to link President Kennedy with the death of President Ngo Dinh Diem in Vietnam; and the numerous "dirty tricks" used against Democratic presidential candidates in the 1972 primaries, most notably the phony "Canuck" letter accusing Senator Edmund Muskie's aides of voicing ethnic slurs critical of Americans of French descent. Had it occurred in isolation, probably none of these partisan provocations would have been enough to bring down a president. Together, however, they were cause for alarm. In addition, the range of activities of the Nixon White House which ultimately became the subject of congressional investigation went beyond the category of what we call partisan pursuits involving domestic intelligence, dirty tricks, and other forms of harassment of enemies.[1]

Policy-Related Initiatives

In a second area, *public policy* activities, President Nixon stretched presidential power to its limits, engaging in many practices of questionable legality. Some of them were impoundment of massive amounts of money appropriated by Congress for domestic programs; attempted dismantling of community action programs authorized by Congress (with the argument, in effect, that the President's budget message had the force of law); waging a secret air war in Cambodia without informing most of the members of Congress much less seeking their approval; and asserting that the executive privilege of members of the administration not to testify before Congress was absolute and without limits. Other questionable actions were using the pocket-veto power during a five-day Christmas recess of Congress to kill a bill authorizing federal grants for family medicine; conferring new powers on the Subversive Activities Control Board by executive order although Congress had not authorized such a move; and deciding not to enforce a section of the Civil Rights Act of 1964 which called for the federal government to stop funding schools that continued to engage in racial discrimination. The courts eventually declared some of these actions illegal, and the Nixon administration generally did not defy court orders. But the political damage had already been done.

Financial Initiatives

Finally, in a third area, *financial transactions,* the Nixon administration and the President found themselves in legal and political troubles on several fronts. These included the President's personal problems over irregularities in his income tax deductions; questionable "security" improvements in his California and Florida residences which were paid for out of the public treasury; and ownership disputes involving gifts by foreign dignataries to the United States. There were also bribery issues raised concerning the selling of ambassadorships by the President's personal representatives; the acceptance by the Republican Party of a four hundred thousand dollar gift by the International Telephone and Telegraph Corporation as an anti-trust suit against it was being settled; and the decision by the President to increase milk price supports after a promise by the milk producer lobbyists to supply two million dollars to the President's re-election effort. Those in charge of financing the President's reelection war chest were also called extortionists and several corporate executives pleaded guilty to making illegal campaign contributions.

Although numerous observers have accurately noted that the Watergate scandals differed from most previous episodes of corruption in American history because of the absence of personal financial enrichment as a motive, the President himself is at least a partial exception to this generalization. If one views Watergate as we do here, broadly enough to encompass all three aspects of the impeachment inquiry, parts of it do share some of the characteristics of the more traditional forms of corruption.

Central Issues

The dominant theme of Watergate, however, was certainly on partisan actions to discredit the suspected political enemies of the White House and on the retention of political power at any cost. If one looks at consequences rather than motives, it is not difficult to reach the conclusion (as some scholars of solid reputation have done) that these activities, in effect, constituted an attempted coup d'état.[2] As Arthur Schlesinger points out, Richard Nixon really did give us a "revolutionary presidency" — not the New American Revolution he spoke of but revolutionary in terms of his attempts to create a plebiscitary presidency which paid relatively little attention to the separation of powers and congressional prerogatives.[3] In offering this characterization, Professor Schlesinger focuses more on the policy components of Watergate than the partisan aspects. But the efforts to eliminate political opposition were equally distinctive in their methods. The two sets of activities are united in their common focus on the aggrandizement of political power.

Ironically, it was the symbolic moral issue of lying about the cover-up that finally caused the President's downfall, not the partisan initiatives of the Plumbers nor the policy actions of the Nixon White House although they certainly played a part. To those who argue that the Watergate break-in and associated events are trivial compared to the substantive policy achievements of the Nixon administration in some areas of foreign policy, Arthur Schelsinger suggests that Watergate took on importance to the American people because

> . . . it brought to the surface, symbolized and made politically accessible the great question posed by the Nixon administration in every sector — the question of presidential power . . . [which] ran through the whole Nixon system, was bound, if repressed at one point, to break out at another. This, not Watergate, was the central issue.[1]

Quoting the analysis of British historian Hugh Trevor-Roper, Schlesinger draws a parallel between Watergate and the resistance by some Englishmen to paying ship-money to King Charles I in 1636, " 'Those who opposed the king's aims, and disliked his ministers, saw well enough that unless they could halt this process [of misrule], the whole system of English government might be permanently changed.' Ship-money 'was seen as the Achilles heel of an otherwise invulnerable enemy.' "[5] The analogy may be a good one. Both political leaders with the help of their aides systematically alienated the bases of their support and ultimately all were deposed (and in the case of Charles I and his henchmen beheaded). But if Trevor-Roper's interpretation of the era of Charles I is accurate, they share another somewhat frustrating feature. In both instances large segments of the public were willing to tolerate misrule for a substantial period of time because of their satisfaction with the substance of policy. As Professor Schlesinger comments, given the reluctance of Congress, large parts of the press, and the American working class to challenge the President's policies,

> Had Nixon confined executive aggrandizement to such visible fields as the war-making and treaty-making powers, impoundment and executive privilege and the pocket veto, he might have carried his revolution against the separation of powers very far indeed.[6]

Like the Watergate literature in general, most chapters of this book place primary emphasis on explaining the partisan initiatives of the Nixon White House to find and "get" its "enemies." Hopefully this will not draw attention away from the equally important questions raised by the policy-related actions of the Nixon administration and the public reaction to them.

INTERPRETATIONS OF WATERGATE

In the analysis of any historical phenomenon there will always be debate about how much to attribute to the influence of individuals and how much to attribute to general historical forces of a material or ideal nature. Watergate is no different. The tension between these two kinds of explanation exists throughout this book. Neither type of causal theory is sufficient by itself. Individuals do not affect history in a vacuum; they interact with a particular set of historical circumstances. And broad trends in historical development are certainly affected by the actions of specific persons. This book tries to encompass both factors and show how they interact. Some chapters focus on the historical setting in which Watergate occurred while others emphasize the role of the President and his assistants, and still others try to integrate the different levels of explanation.

Societal Explanations

The various theories of Watergate have been organized into three groups. The first group focuses on what we shall call societal explanations and is found in Part One of this book. Included are essays that stress *systemic* causes of Watergate, such as the corrupt nature of American national character and political culture (Chapter 4) or the pervasiveness of the "game theory" mentality in American society (Chapter 3). Although no chapters are devoted to elaborating them, other systemic theories point to the state of modern communications technology that has made investigative and intelligence work a growth industry; the nature of conservative thought in the United States that lacks the historical traditions of its European counterpart; and the emergence of controlled capitalism in which government regulation of business makes inevitable centralization of power in society and economic corruption.[7] The Marxist version of the controlled-capitalism approach adds that the rise of the modern capitalist state also inevitably leads to the development of techniques of repression to be used against its internal enemies.[8]

Obviously some of these perspectives are oriented more toward elucidating the policy-related aspects of Watergate, while others narrow in on the partisan or financial areas. One set of societal explanations is concerned with understanding not so much Watergate itself, but the changes which have taken place in the state of the presidency as an institution over the last decade, changes that some writers feel made Watergate possible if not inevitable. These approaches are found in Part Two of this book, which is devoted to the state of the presidency as an institution. Examples are the decline in the strength of American political parties which serve as a check on the President (Chapter 9), the changes in public demands on government which make it difficult for presidents to get credit for domestic programs (Chapter 11), and the constitutional structure which joins the functions of head of state and head of government in one office, thereby creating an institution of such status that it cannot operate properly (Chapter 8).

A second type of interpretation also listed under the general heading of societal theories are *situational* explanations, which emphasize specific political events and thus unlike long-term systemic trends are of relatively short duration. Chapter 1 highlights the societal changes of the 1960s which caused status anxieties for those who felt threatened by social change and ultimately led to the conspiracy theory logic of Watergate. Chapter 2 argues that the Republican Party had an unresolved confrontation with the New Deal and its aftermath which was bound to cause trouble for the next Republican administration regardless of its political style. Other such situational perspectives suggest that Watergate is the legacy of the Cold War mentality, the result of the Vietnam War which became a political albatross around the neck of President Nixon, or the not so surprising consequence of the decline of respect for the legal order which affected social groups and even some judges in the 1960s.[9] It has also been suggested that the end of the Cold War is responsible for Watergate because it forced President Nixon to find a domestic equivalent so that he could rule in the same style as his predecessors.[10]

A third set of interpretations which fall into the societal category are those that analyze the *social groups* actually endorsing the domestic intelligence activities of the White House or at least continuing to support the President after Watergate and the exposure of the cover-up. As the late historian Richard Hofstadter noted in regard to the phenomenon of McCarthyism, knowing the political situation which accompanied a particular historical event does not tell one anything about who supported that event or why.[11] ("What puzzled us was how to account for the complex of forces in the structure of American society, in American traditions, that made it possible for men and women who were sharing the same experience and same disorders to call for drastically different types of remedies" p. 98.) The differential support of political events by various social groups is a matter of percentages. Some socio-economic and political groups supported President Nixon during the Watergate period more than others. Although evidence of this exists in the various opinion surveys done by commercial polling agencies, there is not yet much published work on the subject by social scientists. In Chapter 5 the reader will find the results of a public opinion poll conducted by an academician, which indicates that in the fall of 1973 those who thought the President was not guilty of wrongdoing tended to be older, wealthier, and of greater Republican Party affiliation than the general population. Students of elites have also noted that the Nixon administration received much of its financial and political support from the newly wealthy "cowboys" of the Southwest who resented the influence in public affairs of the Eastern Establishment.[12]

Institutional Explanations

The second broad category of theories of Watergate views the extralegal activities of the Nixon administration as an extension or culmination of trends in the development of the presidential institution. Elaborated in Part Two of the present work, these tendencies are often summed up in the phrase "the imperial presidency" which is the title of Arthur Schlesinger's book on the subject. Schlesinger emphasizes the growth of presidential power particularly in the areas of foreign policy and war-making.[13] Other matters encompassed by this term "imperial presidency" include the kingly life style and rhetoric of the chief executive (Chapter 6); the increasing power and physical size of the White House staff (Chapter 7); the isolation of the president from political realities because of the extraordinary deference shown him by other government officials (Chapter 8); the neglect of domestic politics for the more glamorous world of foreign affairs (Chapter 10); and the greater attention paid to public relations rather than substantive policy development (Chapter 11). Each of these particulars in turn has a root cause in the societal factors mentioned above, some of which are noted by the authors. But the emphasis in Part Two is on the state of the presidency as an institution and the precedents that made Watergate seem less an aberration than an extreme extension of the logic of presidential growth.

Psychological Explanations

The third and final category of theories stresses the role of Richard Nixon in the initiation of the various activities associated with Watergate. The argument is that President Nixon, like any other president, set the tone for his administration. Even in those pursuits in which he was not personally involved, the President was responsible for selecting his staff and creating the atmosphere in which it worked. If White House aides run to a type (and not a very attractive type), it is because the President finds this desirable and compatible with his needs. In his May 22, 1973, statement on Watergate, President Nixon made a direct reply to those espousing these notions when he said of the extra-legal events, "to the extent that I may in any way have contributed to the climate in which they took place, I did not intend to; to the extent that I failed to prevent them, I should have been more vigilant."

In their statements before the Senate Select Committee on Campaign Practices, some former members of the Nixon White House staff have, themselves, testified to the influence that the President had in setting the tone of the place. Most notable among them is Jeb Stuart Magruder whose biography, *An American Life: One Man's Road to Watergate,* seems especially credible since it makes no attempt to exonerate the author from wrongdoing.[14]

The personality theories of Watergate can be divided into three groups. First are those that focus on Richard Nixon's character and his behavior over the years in political life. They point to his early red-baiting congressional election campaigns against Jerry Voorhis and Helen Gahagan Douglas and his California gubernatorial race against Edmund G. "Pat" Brown in 1962 in which a California court proceeding showed that Nixon and his top aides (including Haldeman) had established a phony "Democrats for Nixon"-type committee. From these examples and other historical materials they conclude that Nixon has always played dirty politics and that his troubles as president stemmed from defects of character.[15]

A second approach makes use of depth psychology arguing, in effect, Nixon has a neurotic personality which lacks feelings of security and self-assurance and is full of self-hate at the unconscious level.[16] Focusing on the personal style of Mr. Nixon as much as on political substance, the advocates of this viewpoint feel that his isolated decision-making apparatus, his difficulties in engaging in interpersonal confrontations, and his sporadic outbursts of anger at his opponents indicate that Mr. Nixon possesses the kind of personality ill-suited to politics and the presidency. The exponents of this perspective often devote as much time to finding the roots of Richard Nixon's personality in his early years as they do to demonstrating the effects his personality has had on public affairs during his presidency. The personality approach could be extended to the public supporters of Nixon after the Watergate cover-up was exposed, but so far no one, to this author's knowledge, has done so.[17]

The third variety of personal interpretations places more emphasis on the character of Mr. Nixon's White House staff. Some suggest that the central problem was that none of the President's closest aides had ever run for elective office or could be considered a politician in terms of his background. Others note that the Nixon White House was top heavy with assistants whose backgrounds were in business and public relations, professions that sometimes have different codes of ethics than what is required in the presidency.[18]

PROBLEMS OF EVALUATION

In assessing the interpretations of Watergate one should keep in mind certain methodological considerations. By focusing on one cause of the extra-legal actions of the Nixon administration, a writer may over-emphasize its importance. This does not necessarily mean, however, that the factor discussed is without some significance. For instance, in the personality area, some in-depth analyses of Richard Nixon's psyche are fairly speculative and difficult to prove either right or wrong. This does not mean that personality is a minor factor in trying to explain Watergate. The same is true for George Reedy's sweeping generalizations about the isolation of the presidency.

Interaction of Causes

The reader should also remember the interrelatedness of Watergate theories. Most interpretations are not mutually exclusive. The distinctions between approaches outlined by the editor are not absolute. In addition, the various factors that brought about Watergate have interacted with one another. If Richard Nixon had become President in 1960 or 1955 he would have faced a different set of political circumstances, in a different stage of his own career and personal development, and in a different institutional setting. Those who have written about Watergate have sometimes obscured this fact out of their desire to focus more attention on one aspect of the phenomenon. This is a legitimate scholarly enterprise. But it should not lead one to think solely in terms of single-factor theories.

Historical Perspective

Another matter that may affect the way we view Watergate is our limited knowledge of the behind-the-scenes activities of previous presidents. One does not have to accept Richard Nixon's assertion that "they all do it." But in denying the Nixon defense, one should still retain a healthy skepticism about the actions of other administrations. It was the pervasive pattern of the Nixon initiatives which was the cause for concern. It may still be true that, taken individually, some of these practices have occurred in the presidencies of Mr. Nixon's predecessors. The significance of this possibility remains to be seen.

This problem of historical perspective is particularly apparent in evaluating the policy-related initiatives of the Nixon administration that extended presidential power. Richard Nixon was not the first president to stretch presidential power to its limits. Some have called Watergate

a constitutional crisis. Perhaps it was. But if so, it was not the greatest
one we have had by any means. The President did not defy court orders
either after the firing of Special Prosecutor Archibald Cox or after
the Supreme Court ruled against him on the executive privilege issue
involving the tapes of June 23, 1972. Presidents Abraham Lincoln and
Franklin D. Roosevelt were at least as strong wielders of presidential
power and challengers of the prerogatives of other institutions of
government. Arthur Schlesinger is one of the few commentators who
has pointed out that we do not judge the use of presidential power in
the abstract.[19] What is distinctive about the Nixon presidency is not
the number of technical violations of the law but the failure to wed
presidential power to legitimate and necessary purposes and the sweeping nature of the legal justifications provided by the White House for
its actions. This distinction is important to remember since the time
may come again (as it did in 1861) when we will want to condone the
exercise of extra-constitutional powers by a president.

A. Schles

Effects

There are other issues of historical accuracy involving Watergate
itself. Some of these involve its impact. We hear, for instance, that
the Watergate burglaries were ineffective and gained the Nixon team
no valuable information. On the other hand, it has been observed that
the dirty tricks perpetrated on Senator Edmund Muskie's presidential
election campaign had a devastating impact. How important were the
"Canuck" letter and other such provocations in destroying the Muskie
campaign? Would a different kind of personality have been able to
turn the "Canuck letter" incident to his own advantage? Was the
Muskie campaign doomed to fail for other reasons anyway?

It has also been said that if it were not for the discovery of the
piece of tape on the door of the Watergate complex, the "White House
horrors" would not have been discovered. Perhaps this is so but what
about the President's activities in the area of public policy? The courts
not only stood up to Mr. Nixon in the matter of the cover-up, they
declared illegal a number of the President's initiatives in public policy
fields. Presumably this would have happened regardless of the discovery
of the Watergate burglary. The role of the courts in disclosing domestic
intelligence and other partisan pursuits has overshadowed some significant actions by judges in other areas.

A final area of interest on the impact of Watergate concerns whether
the experience will ultimately turn out to have benefits in terms of
political reform and political change greater than the costs of this
aspect of the Nixon presidency. There are three areas in which political

change is being urged. First, in the realm of theory, some social scientists are suggesting that we reassess our attitudes toward bureaucratic autonomy and executive-legislative relations.[20] Until recently the independence of bureaucratic agencies from the White House was looked upon unfavorably by many students of government. Bureaucracies were conservative institutions that resisted the programs of liberal presidents. Now, with Watergate, some bureaucracies are heroes. The same transformation has taken place with Congress. Students of politics cannot have it both ways. If social science is to avoid being merely the servant of ideology, a normative theory of government institutions must be developed that is equally valid for both liberal and conservative administrations, for both Democrats and Republicans.

The attitude of the public toward political leaders is a second field where changes are recommended. It is suggested that the American people show less reverence for their presidential institution and demand higher ethical standards from their politicians, even if it means electing to high office men or women with less manipulative skill. If the alterations in public attitudes towards political leaders turn out to be the ones recommended, we can assume that the effects will be salutary. But what if the result of Watergate is the election of politicians who are moral purists and demagogues who manipulate the public by using moral issues? If public expectations change, it is not yet clear that the consequences will be for the good of the nation.

The same is true of the proposed reforms in our government institutions that are now receiving much attention. Sometimes there is an inverse relationship between the importance of a factor in our politics and our ability to directly control that variable. This appears to be the case with personality. Nothing is more important to the impact of the presidency than the personality and character of the individuals who hold the office. But it is very difficult to find a way to regulate the kinds of personalities that obtain the office without causing even worse problems than those occasionally presented by the accidents of political success.[21] The Founding Fathers had a healthy skepticism about the possibilities of finding people with the proper temperament to rule. In the words of Benjamin Franklin at the Constitutional Convention:

> And of what kind are the men that will strive for this profitable preëminence, through all the bustle of cabal, the heat of contention, the infinite mutual abuse of parties, tearing to pieces the best of characters? It will not be the wise and moderate, the lovers of peace and good order, the men fittest for the trust. It will be the bold and the violent, the men of strong passions

and indefatigable activity in their selfish pursuits. These will thrust themselves into your government, and be your rulers [June 2, 1787].

It is because of this philosophy that we have a system of checks and balances. Supplementing that system with good laws is certainly a goal we should try to achieve. But even the best of laws is useless unless it is enforced and supported through political action. There is no way that law by itself can guarantee us good government. It is worth keeping these thoughts in mind as we consider some of the structural reforms that have been proposed for our political system in the post-Watergate period. In addition, a student of politics recently observed that just as military planners have a tendency to develop strategy to win the last war rather than the next, so writers on the presidency address themselves inflexibly to present conditions.[22] Advocates of structural reforms should consider whether the changes they suggest would be beneficial if the future were conceived of as unpredictable as the past rather than merely as an extension of the present. It would be most ironic if the final cost of Watergate were the passage of a series of structural reforms that ultimately caused more harm than good. We can only hope that the cure will not be worse than the disease.

NOTES

1. "Partisan" as it is used here refers not only to actions taken against opposition political parties but also to activities of harassment directed at anyone perceived as an enemy.

2. Hans J. Morgenthau, "The Aborted Nixon Revolution," *The New Republic,* August 11, 1973, pp. 17-19; Malcom Moos, Commencement Address at Notre Dame University, May 20, 1973, *Congressional Record,* May 29, 1973, as quoted in Arthur M. Schlesinger, Jr., *The Imperial Presidency* (Boston: Houghton Mifflin, 1973), p. 268.

3. Schlesinger, *The Imperial Presidency,* chap. 8. This is not the first presidency to have revolutionary implications. Michael Novak has argued that the Nixon administration was not revolutionary in *constitutional* terms since other presidents have also exercised great power, but that its actions did have revolutionary implications in *political* terms because their ultimate goal was to establish "a new Republican majority." Regardless of the factual issues involved, it is possible for both interpretations to be correct as a matter of logic. See Michael Novak, "The Presidency and Professor Schlesinger," *Commentary,* February, 1974, pp. 74-78.

4. Schlesinger, *The Imperial Presidency,* p. 275.

5. Hugh Trevor-Roper, "Nixon—America's Charles I?", *Spectator,* August 11, 1973, as quoted in Schlesinger, *The Imperial Presidency,* p. 276.

6. Schlesinger, *The Imperial Presidency,* p. 266.

7. James A. Reichley, "Getting at the Roots of Watergate." *Fortune,* July,

1973, p. 92; Morgenthau, "The Aborted Nixon Revolution," p. 19; Arthur I. Waskow, "Impeachment Is Only A Crossroads," *The Nation,* February 9, 1974, p. 174ff. Each of these references refers to a different theory.

8. Noam Chomsky, "Watergate: A Skeptical View," *The New York Review of Books,* September 20, 1973, pp. 3-8.

9. David Halberstam as quoted in Andrew St. George, "The Cold War Comes Home," *Harper's,* November, 1973, p. 69; David Landau, *Kissinger: The Uses of Power* (New York: Thomas Y. Crowell, 1974, pb ed), p. ix; Alexander M. Bickel, "Watergate and the Legal Order," *Commentary,* January, 1974, pp. 19-29. Each reference refers to a different theory in the order presented in the sentence of the text.

10. St. George, "The Cold War Comes Home."

11. Richard Hofstadter, "Pseudo-Conservatism Revisited: A Postscript (1962)," in Daniel Bell, ed., *The Radical Right* (Garden City, N.Y.: Doubleday, 1963), pp. 97-98.

12. Kirkpatrick Sale, "The World Behind Watergate," *The New York Review of Books,* May 3, 1973, pp. 6-19; Waskow, "Impeachment Is Only A Crossroads," p. 176ff.

13. Schlesinger, *The Imperial Presidency,* passim.

14. Jeb Stuart Magruder, *An American Life: One Man's Road to Watergate* (New York: Atheneum, 1974).

15. Frank Mankiewicz, *Perfectly Clear: Nixon from Whittier to Watergate* (New York: Quadrangle, 1973).

16. Frank Fox and Stephen Parker, "Why Richard Nixon Did Himself In: A Behavioral Examination of His Need to Fail," *New York Magazine,* September 9, 1974, pp. 26-32; Elis Chesen, *President Nixon's Psychiatric Profile* (New York: Wyden, 1973). See also Bruce Mazlish, *In Search of Nixon* (New York: Basic Books, 1972) and James David Barber, *The Presidential Character* (Englewood Cliffs, N.J.: Prentice-Hall, 1972).

17. For previous efforts using this approach, see T. W. Adorno, E. Frenkel-Brunswick, Daniel J. Levinson, and R. Nevitt Sanford, *The Authoritarian Personality* (New York: Harper, 1950); Herbert McClosky, "Conservatism and Personality," *American Political Science Review,* March, 1958, pp. 27-45.

18. Robert Bendiner, "A Word for the Old Pols," *New York Times,* July 15, 1973; Joseph Bensman, "Watergate: In the Corporate Style," *Dissent,* Summer, 1973, pp. 279-280.

19. Schlesinger, *The Imperial Presidency,* esp., chaps. 7, 8.

20. Ithiel de Sola Pool, "Inquiries Beyond Watergate," *Society,* September-October, 1973, pp. 24-25.

21. For a good analysis of the proposal that psychiatrists screen presidential candidates, see Arthur Schlesinger, Jr., "Can Psychiatry Save the Republic?", *Saturday Review/World,* September 7, 1974, pp. 10-16.

22. David L. Paletz, "Perspectives on the Presidency," *Law and Contemporary Problems,* Summer, 1970, p. 434.

Part One
The Political Situation in the Nation

1 | An Appointment With Watergate

Seymour Martin Lipset and *Earl Raab*

Numerous commentators have remarked on the conviction in the Nixon White House that organized opposition to Nixon policies in Vietnam was part of a conspiracy engineered by foreign governments and that Daniel Ellsberg might be another Alger Hiss despite CIA conclusions to the contrary. In this essay Lipset and Raab explain the social situations that lead to the development of conspiracy theory logic. Although they see the extralegal activities of the Nixon administration as a situational response or "backlash" to the social changes of the 1960s, they do not place the "blame" for Watergate on the activism of that period as some observers have done. This does not prevent Lipset and Raab, however, from noting that Mr. Nixon's reelection was aided by the nomination of a Democratic candidate with an extremist image.

As the witnesses testified before the Ervin Committee, one could hear the rustling of a two-hundred-year-old American ghost. The Watergate affair, standing as it does for the whole bag of "White House horrors," was not just the creation of evil men; it was the symptomatic rumbling of a deep strain in American society, of which Richard Nixon has come to seem the almost perfect embodiment. To characterize the behavior which has emerged as "dirty tricks" is to minimize it. To characterize it as "fascist" is to evade its specific American meaning. The United States, and the Nixon administration, had an appointment with Watergate. The form this appointment has taken is significant because of its similarity to certain episodes in America's past; and

Seymour Martin Lipset is Professor of Government and Sociology, Harvard University. Two of his books are *Political Man* and *The First New Nation*. He is co-author of *The Politics of Unreason: Right-Wing Extremism in America, 1790-1970*. Earl Raab is Executive Director, Jewish Community Relations Council of San Francisco. He is co-author of *The Politics of Unreason*.

also significant because of the ways in which it departs from those characteristic episodes.

Watergate begins with the idea, first expressed in the testimony of James McCord and Bernard L. Barker, that the people involved were engaged in a holy mission to combat the secret internal enemies of the United States. Throughout the testimony before the Senate Committee, there runs a self-justifying description of the background of the Watergate horrors: disruptive demonstrations, violence, trashing, bombings, burnings, civil disobedience—much of it conducted by shadowy figures who were never apprehended. And against that background, there was the failure, as the Watergate conspirators saw it, of large segments of the American public to understand the danger fully and the frustrating need this bred to submit to constraints in fighting it.

John Mitchell, who had come to volunteer nothing, said that the Nixon mission was so important that Mitchell would have done anything "short of treason and high crimes" to insure the President's re-election. Jeb Stuart Magruder, who had come, clean-cut, to volunteer everything, was more explicit. He said that "because of that atmosphere that had occurred, to all of us who had worked in the White House, there was that feeling of resentment and frustration at being unable to deal with them on a legal basis." And about the clandestine activities of various members of the Nixon team—the break-in and bugging which gave Watergate its name, the Ellsberg break-in, the proposed raid on the Brookings Institution, the "enemies list," the plans for a new intelligence unit, and so forth—he said: ". . . Although I was aware they were illegal, we had become somewhat inured to using such activities in accomplishing what we thought was a cause, a legitimate cause."

There is a direct line between the rhetoric of the Watergate conspirators and the statement in 1799 of a prominent Bostonian, Jedediah Morse, who said that the new country had internal

> enemies whose professed design is to subvert and overturn our holy religion and our free and excellent government. . . . Among those fruits of their endeavors may be reckoned our unhappy and threatening political divisions; the increasing abuse of our wise and faithful rulers; the virulent opposition to some of the laws of our country; and the measures of the Supreme Executive; . . . the industrious circulation of baneful and corrupting books, and the consequent wonderful spread of infidelity, impiety, and immorality.

But what links Jedediah Morse to Jeb Stuart Magruder is more than a matter of conspiracy theory. It is also a matter of circumstance. In detail, of course, the circumstances of 1799 were different from those of the late 1960's, but their essential nature was remarkably similar, just as both were similar to those in the 1920's. In each case, an important segment of the American population felt that it was being displaced in power and status; in each case this feeling generated a cultural and moralistic "backlash" among the segment in question; and in each case a conspiracy theory was developed to provide ideological justification for the backlash.

THE BACKLASH OF THE 1920's

American history is rich in examples of movements fostering some complex conspiracy-theory explanation for the subversion of American morals and institutions by a foreign-linked cabal. These include the anti-Illuminati agitation of the 1790's, the anti-Masonic party of the Jacksonian era, and assorted anti-Catholic movements such as the Native Americans and Know Nothings of the pre-Civil War period and the American Protective Association of the 1890's.[1] In trying to understand Watergate, however, it is especially instructive to look at the backlash of the 1920's which was not only typical of such episodes in American history but also had a direct relationship to current events.

In 1920 the Census Bureau reported that, for the first time, urban population was larger than rural population. The metropolitan areas, which were becoming the power sites of the nation, were numerically dominated not by Protestants, but by immigrant Catholics and Jews. And even among the Protestants of the city, those denominations which formed the backbone of the traditional Protestantism of the small towns and rural communities of the Midwest and the South—the Methodists and Baptists—were poorly represented.

For this population the shift of power and status was symbolized and dramatized by defections from the "traditional way of life." The Scopes trial held the old-time religion up to national ridicule, and the rise of "modernist" morals and manners seemed to signal an even larger cultural decline. In response, Henry Ford's anti-Semitic Dearborn *Independent* flayed away at those who were undermining the morality of the country by the spread of pornography in Hollywood, the corruption of baseball by gambling, and the deafening cacophony of jazz. In addition to individual efforts like Ford's there also developed a substantial backlash organization, the second Ku Klux Klan. Like its older namesake of Reconstruction days, this KKK was certainly racist, but promoting racism was not its primary purpose. As one historian has pointed out:

> The 1920's meant "modernism." And "modernism" among other things meant the waning of church influences, particularly over

younger people, the breaking down of parental control, the discarding of the old-fashioned moral code in favor of a freer or "looser" personal one, which manifested itself in such activities as purchasing and drinking contraband liquor, participating in ultra-frank conversations between the sexes, wearing skirts close to the knees, engaging in various extreme forms of dancing in smoke-filled road houses, and petting in parked cars. A host of Americans were unwilling, or unable, to adapt themselves to this postwar culture. In the Klan they saw a bulwark against the hated "modernism," an opportunity to salvage some of the customs and traditions of the old religio-moralistic order.

At its height this KKK had a membership of somewhere between three and six million. Some historians estimate that it included a quarter or more of the adult male Protestant population. At various times it virtually ran a number of states, including Oregon and Indiana.

The KKK clothed its cultural backlash with a rich conspiracy theory. Secret collusion and conspiracy are of course a constant in political life but conspiracy theory goes far beyond the perception of that simple truth. It is comprehensive in nature. It posits a broad network of conspiracy—and it holds that the conspiracy is *decisive* in shaping the course of history. Several decades after the KKK, and a century-and-a-half after Jedediah Morse, Senator Joseph McCarthy restated the basic assumption of conspiracy theory, which rejects the possibility of honest error and disregards the independent effect of social change on history:

> How can we account for our present situation unless we believe that men high in this government are concerting to deliver us to disaster? This must be the product of a great conspiracy. . . . What can be made of this unbroken series of decisions and acts contributing to the strategy of defeat? They cannot be attributed to incompetence.

And finally, conspiracy theory holds that the conspiratorial forces are secret because they are evil, and would lose if they fought out in the open. As one post-World War II conspiracy theorist, William Guy Carr, put it:

> History repeats itself because there has been perfect continuity of purpose in the struggle which has been going on since the beginning of time between the forces of Good and Evil to decide whether the Rule of Almighty God shall prevail, or whether the world shall literally go to the Devil. The issue is just as simple as that.

For the KKK, the sources of the Great Conspiracy were ". . . Bolsheviks . . . Foreigners . . . Jesuits . . . and descendants of Abraham." But the KKK was a fairly loose organization, and different branches would emphasize different centers of conspiracy. The most prominent Northern KKK leader, a former Socialist party organizer named D. C. Stephenson, argued that the Jewish international bankers were responsible for World War I and the deterioration of America. Others made the Jews responsible for the Bolshevik revolution. The *Searchlight,* the national organ of the KKK, suggested that a secret Catholic army was preparing to take over the country. KKK spokesmen contended that Warren G. Harding had been murdered by Catholic plotters. (Similar charges had been made by earlier extremist movements concerning the assassinations of Lincoln, Garfield, and McKinley.) And some Klan leaders specifically proposed that the Catholics and Jews were united in the Great Conspiracy.

However, it is important to note that this ethnic bias was a subsidiary element of the conspiracy theory of the 1920's which, like all modern right-wing conspiracy theories, had a more basic and universal "enemy" at its center: the "intellectuals"—writers, journalists, professors, college students, and the educated class in general. (Even the ethnic targets of the KKK were made to fit this basic image of the enemy as intellectual; hence the emphasis on Jesuits and Elders of Zion.)

The intellectuals were secretly conspiring to steal the country from its rightful owners and rulers, and the rightful rulers were fighting back. Thus Hiram Evans, the Grand Wizard of the KKK, expressing a 1926 version of the Middle American backlash:

> We are a movement of the plain people, very weak in the matter of culture, intellectual support and trained leadership. We are demanding, and we expect to win, a return of power into the hands of everyday, not highly cultured, not overly intellectualized, but unspoiled and not de-Americanized, average citizens of the old stock. . . . This is undoubtedly a weakness. It lays us open to the charge of being "hicks" and "rubes" and "drivers of second-hand Fords." We admit it.

But if there is a hidden conspiracy, if the enemy is winning by not playing fair, if indeed, he has subverted the very weapons of persuasion, then the ordinary rules of fair play must be broken in fighting him. As one KKK leader put it (prefiguring Barry Goldwater's "Extremism in the pursuit of liberty is no vice"):

> In a nation, toleration becomes a vice when fundamentals are in danger. . . . The American liberals . . . have extended their liberality till they are willing to help the aliens tear at the foundations of the nation. They have become one of the chief menaces of the country, instead of the sane intellectual leaders they should be. . . .

The backlash of the 1920's, accordingly, was marked by severe violations of democratic procedure. A restrictive and racist immigration law was passed. A General Intelligence Division was established in the Attorney General's office to investigate domestic radical activities. It gathered and indexed the histories of 200,000 people for its suspect files, while the Department of Justice conducted raids which resulted in the arrest of 10,000 people. All this was done without benefit of supporting legislation by Congress. Then state and local governments followed suit, as did private vigilante groups which hounded prostitutes and adulterers as well as political offenders. Some were lynched; many others were tarred and feathered.

NIXON AS PROVINCIAL

The displacing developments of the 1920's were interrupted by the Depression and the war, but galloping megalopolization brought them back in the 1960's, and in force. In addition, of course, those who had previously been ruled out of America's "achieving society," the blacks, now declared themselves in. America's closed frontiers were closing in even further with the evident decline of American power and expansion abroad. Huge, highly-taxing welfare programs were concocted in Washington. The still resentful non-metropolitans, the entrenched labor forces in the cities, the postwar *nouveaux riches,* all began to feel insecure about their old or newly-won power and status.

This feeling was reinforced and given body by all those activities of the late 1960's ticked off by the Watergate witnesses: disruptive demonstrations, riots, violence, bombings, flag-burnings, civil disobedience. The attack on the culture was made explicit by the drug revolution, the sexual revolution, the gay revolution, and so forth. The moralists of the 1920's had complained bitterly about knee-length skirts; how were their descendants to feel about another eight inches of elevations? And most humiliating of all was our inability to defeat a small and underdeveloped Communist enemy in Southeast Asia. How was all this possible except as a consequence of demoralization and betrayal in high places?

When George Wallace received the support of a quarter of the American people in the opinion polls, he was clearly expressing the virulence of their backlash sentiments. Nevertheless, while everybody (including Henry Kissinger) waited breathlessly anticipating a repressive right-wing movement like the KKK of the 20's, no such movement ever developed. Instead of the KKK, we got Watergate. Why? The answer to that question lies to a considerable extent in the political career of Richard Nixon and the complex relation of that career to America's backlash tradition.

It has often been pointed out that Nixon was originally the product of provincial America. He was raised in the backwater environments of Yorba Linda and Whittier in the 1920's, an area in which the Klan was relatively strong. Of course, most people in the area did not support the KKK, but they were affected by the same anxieties of displacement which lay behind the Klan. In a latter-day TV interview, Nixon himself said that the fundamental cause of unrest in this country is not war, poverty, or prejudice but "a sense of insecurity that comes from the old values being torn away." And not only did Nixon grow up in this area; it was also here that he first ran for political office immediately after World War II.

The backlash "package" of the 1920's included anti-radicalism; and after World War II, with the quick outbreak of the cold war, the revelation of widespread Communist espionage, and then the Korean war, militant anti-Communism became a leading backlash staple. Since almost all Americans were anti-Communist in one degree or another, and since there was a real Communist threat in Berlin, Czechoslovakia, Korea, China, and Western Europe, it is perhaps more accurate to say that anti-Communism was often used as the centerpiece of a backlash syndrome. Thus, to many on the political Right, Communism was made to symbolize the immoralities of "modernism" in general. As Senator Joseph McCarthy put it: "The great difference between our Western Christian world and the atheistic Communist world is not political . . . it is moral."

In this environment Nixon ran against Jerry Voorhis for Congress; and a few years later, against Helen Gahagan Douglas for Senator. In the Voorhis campaign he charged that his opponent had the support of radical groups, and that a vote for Nixon was a vote "to preserve the American way of life." To an American Legion post he declared that "the infiltration of Communists into public office is part of a design to impose a Communist form of government on the American people." This kind of public antagonism to Communism was a standard part of the temper of the times; indeed it was Jerry Voorhis himself who had authored the law requiring Communists (and any other left- or right-wing subversive group) to register with the Department of Justice. The fact that Nixon could attack the author of such a bill as soft on Communism helped give him his reputation as "Tricky Dick." And it also began Nixon's identification with the ideological backlash syndrome.

Nationally this identification was established for Nixon by his prominent role in the Congressional investigations and especially in the prosecution of Alger Hiss. In that role, he conducted himself with dogged persistence, but without any marked McCarthy-like excesses. Nevertheless he was pictured as the heavy villain by everyone who

refused to accept the fact that Hiss was guilty. Nixon himself, in his
Six Crises, pointed to the underlying support for Hiss as

> the symbol of a considerable number of perfectly loyal citizens
> whose theaters of operation are the nation's mass media and
> universities, its scholarly foundations, and its government bur-
> eaucracies. . . . They are not Communists, they are not even
> remotely disloyal. . . . But they are of a mind-set, as doctrin-
> aire as those on the extreme Right, which makes them
> singularly vulnerable to the Communist popular-front appeal
> under the banner of social justice. . . . As soon as the Hiss case
> broke and well before a bill of particulars was even available,
> much less open to close critical analysis, they leaped to the
> defense of Alger Hiss—and to a counter attack of unparalleled
> venom and irrational fury on his accusers.

By becoming an enemy to this group, Richard Nixon became a
hero to the backlash ideologues—a position he consolidated by con-
ducting a slashing anti-Communist campaign against Helen Gahagan
Douglas for the Senate in 1950. To be sure, her own Democratic
opponents in the primary had referred to her as one of a "small
subversive clique of red-hots conspiring to capture, through stealth
and cunning, the nerve centers of our Democratic party," and the
like. But Nixon did no less, distributing the famous Pink Sheet hand-
bills. which pointed out that Helen Gahagan Douglas had voted 354
times the same way as the Communist party-liner Vito Marcantonio.
Most of those votes, of course, had nothing to do with any Communist-
related issues, yet such, again, was the temper of the times that Helen
Gahagan Douglas ended up publicly accusing Nixon of giving "aid and
comfort to the Communists. On every key vote Nixon stood with
party-liner Marcantonio against America in its fight to defeat Com-
munisim." In any case, Nixon won and in the process earned additional
love from the Right and additional hatred from the Left.

NIXON AS COSMOPOLITAN

However, if Nixon's reputation as a prime defender of Americanism,
the old American virtues, sat well in his Orange County constituency,
in the nation's other backlash regions, and in his own mind as a winning political stance, he was also a flawed defender in the eyes of
backlash extremists like the leaders of the John Birch Society—flawed
by a tendency to cosmopolitanism. In the first place, he had always
been an internationalist. From the beginning of his Congressional
career, he was deeply committed to and gratified by his work on the

Herter Committee which set up the first foreign aid plans, even though the concept of foreign aid received a negative poll in his own district. Worse, still, he argued during the age of McCarthyism that the Republican party must avoid extremism, a position which he expressed later in these words:

> It is as wrong for the Republican party to become a far-right party as it is for it to become a radical party. As a matter of principle it can never look back and it must never put itself in the position of dividing Americans into classes. To take the far-right viewpoint would destroy it as a national party.

Of course this attitude was partly a function of political acuity. But cosmopolitanism among political conservatives is, in general, just that: a function of acuity, of enlightened self-interest based on a history-wise understanding of the necessity not just to "look back," but to accept and even promote certain types of social change. The "Eastern Republican establishment," often the educated descendants of the old robber barons, became increasingly cosmopolitan on precisely that basis. Moreover, the cosmopolitan understands that political victory cannot be won in America by a fringe party or an ideologically pure faction, and he understands that majorities only accrue to coalition parties which can engage in political enterprise, which can deal comfortably with some element of change (or with some element of resistance to change, as the case may be: the cosmopolitans in the Democratic party saw that when the McGovern provincials took over from them: and the cosmopolitans in the Republican party saw it when the Goldwater provincials took over from them).

Conspiracy theories and their attendant political implications are obviously not in the cosmopolitan style. Political cosmopolitans usually know that most grand conspiracy theories have, in fact, been old wives' tales. (Some become so "sophisticated" that they resist accepting even routine little conspiracies when they are proved, such as the Communist party spy rings in Washington which were related to the Alger Hiss case.) They know too that history is being changed by social forces which are not in any prime way subject to manipulation, let alone dependent on conspiratorial master-direction. And they know that the kind of departure from democratic process encouraged by extremist thinking is dangerous and normally does not serve their enlightened self-interest.

To be sure, none of this has prevented cosmopolitans from aligning themselves temporarily under certain circumstances with extremist movements and tendencies. During the early 1950's, for example, just such a marriage of covenience took place between establishment Republicans and Joseph McCarthy, although they always basically disapproved of his extremist provincialism and the methods which flowed therefrom.

Nixon was among those who disapproved. Apparently making a distinction between the way he himself conducted electoral campaigns, and the way he conducted government business, Nixon in office constantly pulled back from McCarthy-like statements. Even when armed during the Hiss investigation with clear evidence that high Democratic officials had, for various political reasons, failed to act on information of espionage activities, Nixon said: "There are some who claim that Administration officials failed to act because they were Communist or pro-Communist. But the great majority of our officials were not in this category, and I cannot accept this accusation as a fair one."

It was in fact Nixon who as Vice President finally engineered the confrontation which sank Joe McCarthy. With the Republican party now in power, McCarthy had, of course, become an embarrassment to it, while Nixon had become a full-fledged member of the cosmopolitan Eastern Republican establishment which had chosen Eisenhower over Taft and had (if somewhat reluctantly) accepted Nixon as Eisenhower's running mate. The result was that Nixon now became an object of attack by the extreme ideologues of the backlash.

Commenting on Nixon's bid for the Presidency in 1960, Robert Welch, the head of the Birch Society, explained that "the Insiders [the conspirators] think they can accomplish far more for the Communist movement, far more safely, with an Eisenhower-type administration, this time under Richard Nixon, than they would with a Kennedy or a Humphrey as President." When Nixon met privately with Nelson Rockefeller in the latter's Fifth Avenue apartment on the Saturday before the 1960 Republican convention, Phyllis Schlafly, a leading Goldwater pamphleteer, denounced him for making "himself acceptable to the New York kingmakers." Goldwater himself predicted that the alliance between Nixon and Rockefeller, who seconded Nixon's nomination at the convention, would "live in history as the Munich of the Republican party." Later, in the California campaign, Joseph Shell, Republican leader of the California Assembly, charged Nixon with being "soft on Communism."

For his part, Nixon denounced the Birch Society, and seemed to settle down as part of the cosmopolitan Republican establishment. He was booed by the California Young Republicans when he said he wanted to study an anti-Communist proposition before endorsing it, and told them: "The American Constitution has to apply even when you're fighting Communism."

TOWARD WATERGATE

For all this, however, Nixon never quite lost his favorable reputation among the ideologues of backlash. To many of them he was a strayed soul, perhaps reclaimable, rather than an ancestral enemy. Conversely, to many cosmopolitan Republicans, he remained suspect for the same reason — in addition to remaining subject to the normal dosage of snobbery against the provincial from Whittier, the same kind of snobbery which some of the Democratic elite directed at Lyndon Johnson.

But most important of all in affecting his future role was the fact that while at his cosmopolitan peak, Nixon suffered two demoralizing defeats: for President in 1960, and for Governor of California in 1962. At the end of that last disaster, he gave vent to one of the least controlled outbursts of his public life, possibly his most quoted words:

> . . . as I leave the press, all I can say is this: for sixteen years, ever since the Hiss case, you've had a lot of fun . . . you've had an opportunity to attack me . . . I leave you gentlemen, now, and just think how much you're going to be missing. You won't have Nixon to kick around anymore. . . .

That speech had been festering for a long time. Once, during his campaign for Vice President, when a heckler shouted something about the "secret fund" story which had just broken, in another unprepared outburst, Nixon heatedly replied:

> You folks know the work that I did investigating Communists in the United States. Ever since I have done that work, the Communists, the left-wingers have been fighting me with every smear that they have been able to. Even when I received the nomination for the Vice Presidency, I want you to know — and I'm going to reveal it today for the first time — I was warned that if I continue to attack the Communists and the crooks in this government they would continue to smear me. . . .

But the forces he saw unfairly arrayed against him were not restricted to Communists. "The Hiss case," he later wrote,

> brought me national fame, but it also left a residue of hatred and hostility toward me—not only among the Communists but also among substantial segments of the press and the intellectual community . . . who have subjected me to a continuous utterly unprincipled and vicious smear campaign.

Nixon's ultimate triumph, his election to the Presidency in 1968, occurred in a sequence of events which could only have served to reinforce his sense of the power of his interlocking opposition. When Hubert Humphrey left the disastrous Chicago convention, he was 16 percentage points behind Nixon in the polls, in a three-candidate race. Yet by election day, the gap had closed spectactularly, and Humphrey's popular vote was almost equal to that of Nixon. Since polling began in 1936, no Presidential candidate had ever experienced such a precipitous decline. Just as in 1960—so it must have seemed to Nixon—the liberal establishment had again demonstrated its marvelous ability to turn public opinion against him. Little wonder, then, that immediately after taking office in 1969 the administration's chief ideological spokesman, Spiro Agnew, undertook to attack the "effete corps of impudent snobs who characterize themselves as intellectuals," and to complain about news commentators and producers who "to a man . . . live and work in the geographical and intellectual confines of Washington, D.C., or New York City, the latter of which James Reston terms the 'most unrepresentative community in the entire United States.' " The depth of sentiment in high White House circles was expressed even more strongly when Attorney General John Mitchell, after complaining in a press interview in September 1970 about the "stupid kids," feelingly said: "The professors are just as bad, if not worse. They don't know anything. Nor do the stupid bastards who are running our educational institutions. . . ."

Thus while Nixon stood against and resisted blatant backlash extremism, and while he repudiated comprehensive conspiracy theories such as were held by the KKK and then by the Birch Society, he did have a markedly adversary relationship to those elements which have always formed the central core of conspiracy theories: the "intellectual community," the journalists, the Ivy League elite, the "liberals." Furthermore, Nixon explicitly put these elements together into a connected network, which he had indicated was hostile toward him and toward traditional American values. It was ironic that this man, one of whose main political purposes was to contain the excesses of right-wing extremism which he saw as inimical to the Republican party and to his Presidency, should have carried the atmosphere and the logic of that very extremism right into the White House and into the heart of the Republican establishment. Once in the White House, however, it became easy for the logic of that extremism to unfold, especially given the circumstances which the Nixonites found in Washington.

For the Washington they entered was still a Democratic town. Democrats not only held a majority in Congress, they clearly retained the sympathies of the potent civil service, including its upper echelons — not to mention the press corps, particularly those representing the most influential papers and the national TV news programs. The bulk of consultants were heavily liberal, as were the largely government-financed "think tanks," from Brookings to Rand. (Brookings was to be the target of a planned break-in, and Henry Rowen, the then president of Rand, appeared on the enemies list.) And then the evidence began to pile up, in the form of leaks and pilfered documents, that persons in high places in government were in collusion with this elite to expose and frustrate the new administration. As John Erhlichman described the way the administration people saw their situation:

> There were a number of holdovers in the executive branch who actively opposed the President's policies . . . These people conducted a kind of internal guerilla warfare against the President during his first term, trying to frustrate his goals by unauthorized leaks of part of the facts of a story, or of military and other secrets, or by just plain falsehood. The object was to create hostility in the Congress and abroad and to affect public opinion.

Meanwhile, outside government, there was the anti-war movement. Even though the New Left was obviously exhausted, even though the campuses had begun to quiet down by the fall of 1969 in response to troop withdrawals and the disappearing draft, many in the White House, finding confirmation in the May 1970 demonstrations on Cambodia, persisted in believing that the same "extra-parliamentary" forces which had destroyed Lyndon Johnson would, if left unchecked, destroy Richard Nixon too.[2]

It was also believed in the White House that the disruptive forces were being supported by foreign funds. When the FBI and the CIA reported that they could unearth no evidence of significant foreign involvement in the domestic New Left or in the anti-war movement, the White House staffers concluded that a new intelligence operation, controlled by the White House itself, was needed. Arguing for such an operation which would include proposals he himself described as "clearly illegal," a young White House aide, Tom Huston, wrote in a September 1970 memo to Haldeman:

> The biggest risk we could take, in my opinion, is to continue to regard violence on the campus and in the cities as a temporary phenomenon. . . . I believe we are talking about the future of this country, for surely domestic violence and disorder threaten the very fabric of our society. For eighteen months we have watched people in this government ignore the President's orders, take actions to embarass him, promote themselves at his expense, and generally make his job more difficult.

The original plans, though initially approved by the President, were killed by the opposition of J. Edgar Hoover, who apparently saw the scheme as reflecting a negative evaluation of the FBI by the White House. And he was correct in this.

For now even Hoover was suspect. Huston told Haldeman in August 1970 that Hoover "has become totally unreasonable and his conduct is detrimental to our domestic intelligence operation." He particularly singled out FBI campus coverage as inadequate. And in March 1973, Nixon apparently reiterated to Richard Moore the curious myth which had become the in-house explanation, that Hoover could not be relied on to investigate Daniel Ellsberg properly since Ellsberg's father-in-law was a friend of Hoover's, a statement which, though also spread by Ehrlichman and others, was false.

To be sure, the situation with the FBI is clearly complex. Given the enormous number of terrorist bombings and other illegal acts in the late 60's and early 70's, there can be little doubt that the FBI and the assorted state and local police groups which sought to deal with them were largely unsuccessful. Few of the guilty were apprehended. Rarely did the law-enforcement agencies give advance notice of terroristic acts. As compared, for example, to the Israeli secret police, Shin Beth, which seems to know everything about Arab terrorism, the Americans were a failure. And this fact seemingly justified administration proposals to change procedures, and even to create new agencies, the secret domestic intelligence evaluation group, under Robert C. Mardian, located in the Justice Department, and the covert "special investigation unit," under Egil Krogh, in the White House.

Placing blame on the FBI or other investigative agencies for failing to uncover the terrorists, however, ignored the nature of the protests of the 1960's. Unlike the Communist party of earlier decades, or the Arab terrorists today, both with centralized leadership, the recent American "Movement" was composed of literally hundreds, if not thousands, of separate, independent "cells," many bitterly hostile on ideological grounds to one another. There were few national organizations. Most of those which existed — the SDS, the Young Socialist Alliance, the Progressive Labor party, the Spartacus Leagues — did not take part in terrorism, either for ideological or practical reasons. The bombings, the arson, the raids on government offices, were largely conducted by small local groups, often comprising a handful of people. It was quite impossible for the FBI or even the local police to penetrate these cells. And most of them evidently were clever enough not to let anyone in the above-ground anti-war organizations know who they were.

There was, then, no single large conspiracy, there were thousands of small conspiracies. Few of those were in a position to secure foreign funds or help, although some probably did. Alien subversive forces would have had as little luck in locating the American terrorists as did the FBI; and Mardian and Krogh were later equally unsuccessful in finding them. Hence, both the CIA and the FBI were undoubtedly correct in reporting to the White House that foreign-supported conspiracies did not explain the continuation and spread of terrorism.

But such reports did no good, for conspiracy-theory logic had enveloped the White House. Much as extremists, both of the Left and of the Right, found it impossible to accept the fact that Lee Harvey Oswald was a loner linked neither to the CIA nor to Castro, so the White House could not accept a non-conspiratorial interpretation of Daniel Ellsberg's turn-about. Faced with the "betrayal" of a once-trusted supporter of the Vietnam war, they refused to see Ellsberg as a man who has always shown a need for passionate commitment, who, in the words of the CIA psychological profile which they rejected, had always been "either strongly for something or strongly against," and who had now reached a time of life when many men, especially very ambitious ones, "come to doubt their earlier commitments, and are impelled to strike out in new directions." The CIA profile asserted that "There is no suggestion that [Ellsberg] thought anything treasonous in his act. Rather, he seemed to be responding to what he deemed a higher order of patriotism." But in the White House view Ellsberg *had* to be part of a broader conspiracy, and anyone who doubted this — even the CIA or so reliable an ally as J. Edgar Hoover — must either have been misled or somehow corrupted.

THE TWO SIDES OF WATERGATE

In short, the behavior summed up in the name Watergate was typical, at least in form, of American backlash extremism. But if this is so, two important questions still have to be answered. First, how did this syndrome get seated so directly in the White House and in the Republican establishment? There had been other backlash administrations in Washington, but such administrations had usually taken care to separate themselves from extremist behavior while sympathizing with or tolerating it. Even after World War I, when the U.S. Attorney General's office was directly involved in a Watergate-type pattern, the activist-extremist centers like the KKK or the American Defense League were outside the government exerting pressure. Here the activist extremist center was the White House itself, and it was evidently self-starting. But secondly, why, emanating as it did from the highest places, should Watergate have been so pale and tepid an expression of extremist action?

    The first question seems troubling, the second comforting—but they
are both finally the same question, and the answer to both lies in
Richard Nixon's remarkable personification of the American split: convincingly enough provincial, convincingly enough cosmopolitan. Because for enough people he stood for the backlash, while for enough
people he stood for the resistance to factional extremism, he managed
to reach the White House, and he also managed to prevent the formation of a classic extremist movement. He certainly defused George
Wallace, who complained bitterly about it many times. Wallace told
a national television audience: "I wish I had copyrighted or patented
my speeches. I would be drawing immense royalties from Mr. Nixon
and especially Mr. Agnew." In order to defuse the backlash, however,
Nixon had to represent it himself, and it was this that brought the
extremist syndrome right into the White House. Yet at the same time
the "cosmopolitan" climate in which the backlash now had to operate
also blunted and made it relatively ineffectual. After World War I
Attorney General A. Mitchell Palmer set up an extra-legal intelligence
agency, and promptly swept many thousands of people into jail. Nixon's
first attempt to set up an extra-legal intelligence agency was shot down
by a cross word from Hoover, and he fell back to a "plumbers" operation which was neither massive nor very efficient. Second-story men
all over the nation must still be chuckling over the ineptitude of the
Watergate break-in itself. The plumbers found out nothing in the office
of Ellsberg's psychiatrist, and indeed managed only to guarantee Ellsberg's acquittal. Enemies lists were prepared, but for the most part
they ended up in John Dean's files without being acted on. The proposal to deny government research grants to MIT because of the objections of its president, Jerome Wiesner, to administration military
and foreign policies was never carried through, apparently because of
opposition from the Pentagon and other government agencies. In order
to harass people through their income tax, White House staff had to resort to sending anonymous "citizens" letters to the IRS, with scarcely
impressive results. They bugged the wrong phones. They tried to "get
something" on Daniel Schorr of CBS, but succeeded only in alerting
him. Nor did they have a "chilling" effect on anyone, in the way that
Joseph McCarthy so often did with an essentially one-man operation.
    This is not to minimize the seriousness of these activities, nor to
dismiss them as merely inept. Presumably, with more practice, the
Watergate group could have improved its skills. In any case, a botched
burglary is still a burglary, an unsuccessful assault on constitutional
liberties is still an assault. But the point is that the Watergate horrors
were perpetrated covertly, in the dark of night, whereas in the 1920's,
the illegal activities of the government were carried out in the open,

and apparently with the overwhelming approval of the American people. In the Nixon administration, by contrast, the most elaborate operation was the cover-up, which is itself a measure of the restraining power of the cosmopolitan climate not only within the administration but in the nation at large—in, that is, the growing cosmopolitanization of the American people.

Thus, as compared with the 1920's, for example, the American people today are more willing to accept cultural and political differences. All three Presidents of the 1920's—Harding, Coolidge, and Hoover—publicly expressed themselves in racist terms. Harding supported the immigration restrictions on the basis of inherent "racial differences" and the unassimilability of anyone but Northern Protestants. Coolidge, in an article in *Good Housekeeping,* argued that "biological laws show us that Nordics deteriorate when mixed with other races." Herbert Hoover declared that "immigrants now lived in the United States on sufferance . . . and would be tolerated only if they behaved." Today no major party politician or officeholder could possibly air such views, and racists who hope to be elected are forced to mute their appeal.

On another front, the public receptivity to charges that liberals are "soft on Communism" has declined considerably, and even during the Vietnam war—a war, after all, against Communism—various restrictions of the rights of Communists were struck down by the courts, by universities, and by trade unions, without a serious murmur from the public. Perhaps the best indication of the growth in cosmopolitanism has been Nixon's foreign policy and its acceptance by the bulk of the American population. A quarter of a century of cold-war anti-Communism in which Richard Nixon himself played a key role simply went out the window in the face of its failure to meet the test of reality in Vietnam and in connection with Sino-Soviet relations.

None of this means that fanatical anti-Communism or bigotry has disappeared. What it does mean is that more and more Americans have learned to lace their biases with democratic restraint. *That* is the nature of the cosmopolitan impulse, and its growth in the past fifty years seems to be related to the spread of formal education. The 60's taught us that education can breed a cultural intolerance of its own, but for people coming out of a traditionally anti-modernist milieu, education is still likely to encourage a greater readiness to accept diversity, if only on grounds of enlightened self-interest. On that score, of course, the difference between the American population of the 1920's and that of the 1970's is statistically spectacular. Between 1920 and 1970 the proportion of the college-age population enrolled in higher education jumped from 8 to almost 50 per cent. There were 600,000 college students in 1920; there are 9 million today. College professors alone now constitute a major occupational group, over half-a-million, almost as many as there were students in 1920.

But democratic restraint is not an absolute commitment. It describes a threshold, which in turn relates to level of provocation, level of desperation. Political extremism may be more difficult to make overt than it was in the 1920's but the dynamic is always there, never expunged. Massive unmet aspirations on the left—or, as has more often happened in America, unattended status backlash on the Right—can obviously overwhelm democratic restraint under certain conditions, and thus a major function of pragmatic politics in America has always been to prevent those conditions from prevailing. This is why the possibility of a more narrowly ideological national politics seems so ominous.

What Watergate suggests is that just such a withdrawal from cosmopolitan politics may be in store for America. The electorate in general has grown more cosmopolitan largely because of education, but education has also helped to create more ideological fervor at both ends of the political spectrum. According to a study by Everett Ladd, college-educated Democrats are more ideologically liberal and college-educated Republicans are more ideologically conservative than less educated party partisans. And abundant data indicate that well-educated ideologues are the most likely of all to be active in party affairs and to vote in primary elections. When the conservative ideologues captured the Republican party in 1964, the mass of Republicans was in effect disenfranchised, as was the mass of the Democratic electorate when the liberal ideologues captured their party in 1972. To imagine an entirely disenfranchised electorate, we need only imagine a Goldwater-McGovern contest for the Presidency. Watergate has now revealed that we were much closer to such a situation than many thought. McGovern, like Goldwater before him, lost by a landslide because he was seen as a factionalist, an extremist. Nixon, on the other hand, was perceived as a former factionalist who had turned into a pragmatist, a coalition leader, a cosmopolitan. To some extent, this was certainly true of Nixon, but we now know that the provincial, factional, ideological, extremist element in Nixon was also still alive, restrained by his cosmopolitan side but clearly not squelched.

If, then, American society, torn between provincialism and cosmopolitanism, indeed had an appointment with Watergate, it could scarcely have chosen a more likely person to keep that appointment than Richard M. Nixon. The corollary is that if American society is to avoid backlash extremism in the future, it will have to find ways of preventing the disenfranchisement of the electorate by ideological factionalists, and of making the politics of pragmatism and democratic restraint prevail once again on the national scene.

NOTES

1. No better analysis of these movements has ever been written than the late Richard Hofstadter's *The Paranoid Style in American Politics.* Hofstadter should have lived to interpret Watergate for us.

2. As noted earlier in S. M. Lipset's *Rebellion in the University,* surveys of college students in 1969 indicated that "a majority accepted the new Nixon administration policy of Vietnamization as a means of getting out. The administration was able to co-opt some of the campus opposition. Thus a Gallup survey of college students taken in May 1969 reported that when asked: 'Do you approve or disapprove of the way Nixon is handling his job as President?' 57 per cent approved, 37 per cent disapproved, and 6 per cent had no opinion. A second Gallup national student poll taken in the fall found that students were seemingly losing interst in protest, though they remained heavily against the war, *Newsweek,* in reporting the survey, concluded that 'the mood of the American campus is apparently undergoing a striking change: militancy and violence are in good measure giving way to passivity and personal introspection, and the revolutionary impulse seems—for a while at least—to have largely spent itself.' "

This situation changed drastically, of course, during the Cambodian events of May 1970, which stimulated the largest wave of student protest ever. But summer vacation and the withdrawal of American troops from Cambodia ended the demonstrations. The fall of 1970 witnessed a quiet campus, and surveys taken indicated a drop in support for radicalism. Increased campus conservatism was suggested in surveys taken in the spring of 1971.

Participants in the "Movement" agree with the import of these surveys. The high point in membership in SDS occurred in 1968-69. By the summer of 1969, it was a bitterly divided, shrunken organization. And the decline in SDS and other New Left groups continued from then on, the Cambodian protest interlude apart. The FBI reported these changes, noting that the anti-terrorist Trotskyist Young Socialist Alliance, with a few thousand members at most, had become the strongest radical youth group.

Thus those in the White House concerned with evaluating the strength of the "extra-parliamentary" opposition misread the signs. They thought the revolutionary "conspiracy" was growing at the very time their politics were undercutting the appeal of the radicals. They were, of course, not alone in this misjudgment. George McGovern's campaign was also premised on the assumption that the "revolution" of the 60's was continuing and even escalating.

2 | # The Republican Party Confronts the New Deal

Paul J. Halpern

The Nixon administration may have exaggerated the dangers posed by its "enemies" but not all its problems were imaginary. The Nixon economic and social policies included the impoundment of funds for social programs (particularly housing), the attempted dismantling of community action agencies, non enforcement of certain civil rights legislation on school funding (until the courts reversed the practice), and the redesign of numerous other domestic policies. Paul J. Halpern discusses why these shifts in domestic programs were opposed and what methods federal bureaucracies and the White House have employed in attempts to manipulate each other. Ironically, domestic spending generally was not lower in the Nixon years than in previous administrations and the Republican White House ran deficit budgets just as its Democratic predecessors had done. Spending, however, was not always for the types of programs desired by the constituents of New Deal and Great Society bureaucracies nor for the amounts authorized by Congress.

Many analyses of Watergate suggest that the behavior of the Nixon administration was a predictable consequence of the personality and character of Richard Nixon. There is considerable merit in the psychological approach to both the presidency in general and the Nixon administration in particular. The manner in which the Nixon White House responded to its adversaries certainly caused the President as much trouble as his opponents. The psychological perspective, however, is not without its limitations. We may be paying so much attention to the way the Nixon administration perceived and responded to political problems that we do not sufficiently appreciate what those problems were. As Henry Kissinger reportedly said, "Even paranoids have real enemies." The objective political conflicts confronting the

An original essay.

Paul J. Halpern is Assistant Professor of Political Science, University of California, Los Angeles.

first Republican administration after the Great Society were bound to be large. The intensity of conflict was not due simply to the personality of Mr. Nixon.

The most basic problem of the Nixon administration is faced by every administration—how to bend the government, particularly the federal bureaucracies, to its priorities. This is fundamentally a problem of control and is a headache for every chief executive. Given the size of the federal government, the existence of independent regulatory agencies, the maintenance of a civil service system, the lack of disciplined political parties, and the limited time of a president, the White House cannot hope to exercise complete control over the government. A remark by Jonathan Daniels, an aide to Franklin Roosevelt, captured the dimensions of the problem:

> Half of a President's suggestions, which theoretically carry the weight of orders, can be safely forgotten by a Cabinet member. And if the President asks about a suggestion a second time, he can be told that it is being investigated. If he asks a third time, a wise Cabinet officer will give him at least part of what he suggests. But only occasionally, except about the most important matters, do Presidents ever get around to asking three times.[1]

Perhaps this is for the better, but the normative issue is beyond the scope of this essay. What is maintained here is that the changes in American politics and society which occurred during the last decade made it nearly inevitable that the next Republican administration would have greater problems of control than any administration since World War II. One of the most important changes was the rapid growth of inflation in the mid-1960s due to the war in Vietnam and the way it was funded. To Republican politicians who have traditionally been more concerned than Democrats with maintaining the value of the dollar and less concerned with employment levels and welfare programs, even a mild inflation is cause for alarm. In general, the situation since 1968 has been far from mild. Circumstances may not have dictated that any president taking office in 1968 would try to reorder priorities. This is subject to debate, but sooner or later a Republican president with Republican preoccupations would do so. Whoever it would be would have a more difficult time than Eisenhower did in the 1950s.

THE EISENHOWER YEARS

We tend to forget that many Republicans (and Democrats for that matter) expected a full-scale political war between the Eisenhower administration and the New Deal bureaucracies and their constituents. That war never really took place. Eisenhower did give priority to the prevention of inflation over spending for domestic programs, and bitter political battles developed in the 1950s over such issue as the sale of government-owned natural resources to private interests. But the political situation facing the President tended to reduce the conflicts between the Eisenhower White House and the rest of the government. The whole point of Eisenhower's "Modern Republicanism" was to legitimize in the Republican Party the idea of federal intervention in economic affairs (and international affairs). Within his party the main problem the President encountered was to resist those who wanted to dismantle the government. In the words of Eisenhower's biographer Herbert S. Parmet,

> . . . when he faced his Cabinet, with its conservatives eager to begin a counter-revolution, he cautioned them to discard their pet notions about limiting the role of the federal government in public welfare matters because, he explained, whether they liked it or not, the American people had accepted such responsibilities as necessary and proper and the matter had gone beyond any further consideration.[2]

To be sure Eisenhower's personality was also an important factor in ameliorating conflict. He would occasionally rage in private about his frustrations with Congress or agency heads, but Ike was not inclined to public confrontations or pushing presidential power to its limits. Although his critics thought this was due to limitations of temperament, training, and intelligence, some recent biographies and memoirs of Eisenhower indicate that regardless of other causes, his behavior was very much a matter of strong intellectual conviction.[3] But differences between the Eisenhower and Nixon administrations are not limited to the personalities of these two chief executives. They faced very different political situations.

When Nixon took office in 1969 the battle between the inflation-minded Republican Party and the "permanent government" was renewed. But the times had changed in several important ways. First, the legitimacy of federal intervention in economic affairs had been established within all but the most reactionary parts of the Republican Party. Second, the number of domestic programs with vested interests in expansion had increased. For an administration that wanted to limit federal expenditures for domestic programs, this made less manageable the problem of bureaucratic imperialism. Third, the underprivileged groups in society had been politicized with the aid of middle-class reformers and the poverty program. The number of middle-class professionals devoted to lower-class interests and willing to champion their cause had also increased. In addition, the Democratic Party which had created and staffed most of these bureaucracies controlled both houses of Congress from the start of Nixon's first term. Fourth, the study of program effectiveness was growing. In the aftermath of the Great Society, disenchantment with bureaucratic solutions to social problems was no longer limited to rigid conservatives. There was less faith in the New Deal notion that money would solve all social problems. Finally, no consensus existed about the correct political agenda, as large segments of the public backed efforts to curtail street crime, drug abuse, and other problems of law and order.

RESULTS OF POLITICAL CHANGE

Taken as a group these developments meant two things. More incentives were present for centrist Republicans to try to limit domestic spending or to change its direction because of inflation and the problems with the Great Society. Also, greater political support from growing clientele groups had developed for those bureaucracies that wanted to expand their budgets and to resist any efforts to change priorities in domestic policy. A good deal of "bad blood" between the White House and the rest of the government was a likely result of this set of circumstances irrespective of the incoming president's political style. In foreign affairs a Republican conservative's "hard-line" image may make it easier for him to change outdated Cold War policies, but in domestic politics the opposite is true. A liberal, were he so inclined, would have encountered less resistance in turning away from the social policies of the 1960s and the bureaucratic legacy of the New Deal.

Bureaucratic resistance to the Nixon White House, of course, was not limited to domestic policy nor to liberals. In certain areas of foreign policy (the China initiatives and the strategic arms talks, for example) where the administration was moving toward more liberal positions, it had to worry about leaks from the State Department and the Defense Department. On domestic issues, where the administration often shifted toward what are conventionally considered more conservative positions, the opposition came from liberals such as the group of young lawyers in the Justice Department who publicly protested the administration's civil rights policies in 1969. But opposition also extended to the Federal Bureau of Investigation, where the case of J. Edgar Hoover is particularly interesting. As columnist Joseph Kraft pointed out several years ago,[1] bureaucratic rather than ideological interests often motivated Mr. Hoover's positions on policy issues. He was an excellent player of bureaucratic politics who was not adverse to taking a liberal stance when it would help promote his career or protect the bureaucratic interests of the FBI. Hoover's resistance to the White House efforts to establish a domestic spy network probably stemmed more from his concern for the political risks involved for the Bureau than from any great concern about civil liberties.

In the struggle for control of government policy, bureaucracies have developed many techniques to use against presidents. As noted earlier, one method is simply to ignore or delay in carrying out White House policies and raise the costs to the president of one's compliance. Another approach is to try to sabotage new policy by leaking its contents to allies in the press and mobilizing opposition before support for the policy is consolidated. The Nixon administration complained that it is precisely this kind of sabotage which was on the increase and was used against the President . Although one can disagree with the administration's attempt to link bureaucratic opposition with threats to national security (and strongly condemn some of the methods the White House used to counter opposition), the assertion that policy leaks and other bureaucratic resistance were growing was probably valid. At least this much was not a reflection of White House paranoia. It is just what one would expect when a Republican president and his successor try to alter domestic and foreign priorities. The more a president threatens the interests of bureaucracies, the more those bureaucracies and their constituents fight back. Whether one approves of such bureaucratic guerilla warfare usually depends on how one feels about the policy changes. Because most liberals opposed Nixon policy they saw no reason to get excited . But it is unfair to deny that a bureaucratic civil war was taking place and may continue if President Ford pursues Nixon's policies.

METHODS OF PRESIDENTIAL CONTROL

Presidents have experimented with various ways of countering the problem of bureaucratic resistance. Franklin Roosevelt created new bureaucracies where old ones could not be trusted. John Kennedy used direct personal communications with lower- and middle-level bureaucrats as his favorite way to get information or give orders in difficult situations. Lyndon Johnson greatly expanded the use of *ad hoc* task forces largely composed of professionals outside government in an effort to bypass departmental opposition to new program development.

Not surprisingly, Richard Nixon was very concerned with this problem. In fact, future presidents from both parties eventually may imitate his innovations in this area once their association with Watergate is forgotten. Nixon used two approaches. First, he attempted to create his own White House bureaucracies in areas of high priority where he found the departments inadequate. In the words of one White House official:

> The President found that some segments of the bureaucracy were unresponsive to presidential directives, slow moving, or unreliable. He decided to get around all this by building his own system of control, command and policy making at the White House level. . . .
> The White House is dealing with 60 or more old-line departments with agencies. Each one is its own advocate. Not one of them can turn out an objective program. Each one is thinking of its own existence. The White House, we have found, is the only place where policy can be made objectively.[5]

Political scientist Thomas Cronin has referred to this phenomenon of White House growth as "the swelling of the presidency" [see chapter 7 below]. In the Nixon administration it applied not only to the area of secret and extra-legal intelligence gathering but also to domestic policy formation, drug abuse, press relations, and foreign economic policy. As the shockingly abusive and destructive drug raids on two innocent Illinois families demonstrated in 1973, this approach was no more successful in the area of drug control than in the field of domestic espionage. Even before the Watergate disclosures discredited some of these White House operations, evidence indicated that President Nixon was not satisfied with the results. At the beginning of his second term, the President asserted that the number of employees working at the White House level would be reduced.

During his second term Mr. Nixon put more reliance on a second strategy of command which involved infiltration of the regular departments. Rather than leave the appointment of top agency personnel in the hands of celebrity-name Cabinet members, the President chose department secretaries like HUD's James Lynn who had little national reputation and no independent political standing and assigned Nixon loyalists as deputies to them. The Nixon team began operating on the theory that placing "loyalists" in the various departments was the solution to the problem of governmental control. Before we conclude that this concern with loyalty was solely a personal aberration of the President and of members of the White House staff, it should be remembered that often in human history governments which have tried to change the direction of affairs have been preoccupied with the loyalty of subordinates. History suggests that this approach also has its limits, as Henry II of England found out when he tried to solve his problems with the Church by appointing his friend Thomas Becket as Archbishop. Institutional role has a way of altering personal loyalties. The Nixon White House discovered this when it tried unsuccessfully to get a newly-appointed CIA official, General Vernon Walters, to cooperate in getting that agency to take the blame for Watergate. The experience of L. Patrick Gray as acting director of the FBI illustrates the dangers of putting personal loyalty above bureaucratic interests regardless of the situation.

In 1960 political scientist Richard Neustadt wrote that presidential power was the power to persuade. In his words, "The essence of a President's persuasive task is to convince [officials] that what the White House wants of them is what they ought to do for their own sake and on their own authority."[6] A few years ago Neustadt was criticized for neglecting other forms of influence such as formal commands and personal loyalty. The experience of the Nixon administration demonstrates that these forms of influence also have limits. Although practitioners and theorists alike have tried to find a "final solution" to the problem of governmental control, it is unlikely that there is one. The activities of the Nixon White House, however, can be viewed as the latest attempt to solve, once and for all, the problem of governance. Every American president dabbles in this sort of thing but most administrations exercised more restraint. It took a Republican White House with new priorities, determined to rule, and largely staffed at its upper reaches with businessmen new to government, individuals not resigned to bureaucratic pessimism, to show the limits of presidential influence over the bureaucracies. Even though personality played a key role in setting the mood and in determining the character of the Nixon administration's response to its problems, the historical circumstances suggested that plenty of political friction would emerge when a Republican president resumed his party's unresolved confrontation with the New Deal and its aftermath.

NOTES

1. Jonathan Daniels, *Frontier on the Potomac* (New York: Macmillan, 1946), pp. 31-32, as quoted in Richard E. Neustadt, *Presidential Power* (New York: Wiley, 1960), p. 41.

2. Herbert S. Parmet, *Eisenhower and the American Crusades* (New York: Macmillan, 1972), p. 174.

3. See, for instance, Emmet John Hughes, *The Ordeal of Power: A Political Memoir of the Eisenhower Years* (New York: Atheneum, 1963).

4. Joseph Kraft, "J. Edgar Hoover—The Complete Bureaucrat," *Commentary,* February, 1965, pp. 59-62, and reprinted in his *Profiles in Power* (New York: New American Library, 1966).

5. *U.S. News and World Report,* April 24, 1972, p. 72 as quoted in Nelson W. Polsby, ed., *The Modern Presidency* (New York: Random House, 1973), p. 231.

6. Neustadt, p. 34.

3 | What's Wrong With Politics

Josiah Lee Auspitz and *Clifford W. Brown, Jr.*

Unlike the two previous essays that emphasize the roots of Watergate in specific historical events, this selection discusses a broader historical trend—the tendency of politicians to think more in terms of manipulation and strategy and less in terms of loyalty and principle. Auspitz and Brown do not believe this "hyperstrategic" mentality is limited to the personalities of the Nixon White House. Tracing its origins to certain intellectual and social developments during and after World War II, they argue that in some form such thinking now permeates all the professions as well as politics. This essay expands some themes in The Jaws of Victory *where the same authors suggest that by pursuing the logic of strategic thinking in the extreme, the Nixon administration undercut the moral basis of its power and "systematically undermined the authority and power of the presidency."*

At a loss to explain the Watergate foul-ups, Gen. Alexander Haig conjured up a "sinister force" at work in the White House. The General was closer to the truth than even he suspected. There is a sinister force at work, not only in the White House but throughout the American political community. And it is nothing less than a fundamental change in the way many of us—particularly the educated and those they recruit to political leadership—think about government. It is a shift in attitudes that underlies the flowering of the New Politics as much as the criminality of Watergate, the voters' celebrated independence of mind at the polls as much as their alarming-contempt for politicians.

The change consists in a movement away from a *representative* ideal and toward a *strategic* ideal of politics.

At the heart of constitutional government is a spirit of representation.

Reprinted with permission of the authors from *Harper's,* May, 1974, pp. 51-61. Copyright © 1974 by Josiah Lee Auspitz and Clifford W. Brown, Jr.

Josiah Lee Auspitz is completing his doctorate at Harvard University. He is a former president of the Ripon Society. Clifford W. Brown, Jr. is Assistant Professor of Political Science, State University of New York at Albany. He is coauthor of *Jaws of Victory.*

This spirit ties the politician to his constituency. Whether he interprets their interests broadly or narrowly, he conceives of his relationship to the voters as a personal one. He is loyal to them: he delivers, he seeks to further their goals. They reciprocate: they support and reelect him. He deals with them intuitively. He learns the value of compromise, of persuasion, of being civil to an opponent, of keeping his promises. The representative ideal discourages him from seeking power directly, for the most direct road to power has always been that of bribery, assassination, force, and fraud. Instead he must channel his ambition to the tamer goal of winning elective office, an office charged with well-defined duties, checked by other offices, regulated by procedure, and dependent on a sense of public trust. The whole system is designed not to eliminate the baser passions but to harness them and set them against each other in a way that advances the public good, disciplines the behavior of the politician, and ensures a regime of liberty and moderation.

In recent years, however, there has emerged a class of politicians who disdain these conventional practices. When they attend a funeral, it is not to fulfill debts of friendship or loyalty but to get media coverage. When they hold hearings on a bill, it is not to draft legislation but to "make news." Even when they appeal to conscience and principle, their real goal is to win the moral upper hand.

These new politicians are fascinated with the logic of conflict and the tools of strategic wargaming: the heady concepts of deterrence, contingency planning, outcome analysis, and minimax decision-making. They eschew the representative ideal in favor of a seemingly more rigorous strategic one.

Under the strategic ideal, considerations of procedure, duty, trust, and purpose give way to short-term ploys to yank public opinion in whatever direction seems profitable at the moment. The representative ideal focuses on service and performance, the strategic ideal focuses on power plays and office-hopping. The representative politician uses words to inform or lead a constituency, the strategic politician uses words to manipulate or generate one. The representative politician understands strategic calculation as a necessary expedient in politics, the strategic politician treats it as the essence of politics. For him winning is the name of the game. And when the game is merely winning, the result is a political community composed not of participants or worthy opponents, but of winners and losers in the abstract pursuit of power.

Pitting the two ideals against each other in this way makes the strategic politician seem less than an idealist. But for those who believe in it—and they include a large portion of the Washington political community—strategic politics *is* an ideal. It seems tough, vigorous, and unsentimental. It transcends the plodding pettiness of building roads for people, cleaning their air, and fixing their teeth. It possesses an intellectual purity absent from the smoke-filled minds of practical politicians. It excites and enthralls.

"Power," as Henry Kissinger once put it, "is the greatest aphrodisiac." "The more determinedly a President seeks power," writes Harvard political scientist Richard Neustadt, "the more he will be likely to bring vigor to his clerkship." And Theodore H. White has been inspired by "the romantic glow . . . of men who are transfixed by their participation in the thrill of power." It's an easy step from these breathless incantations, by thoughtful men who have written better, to the immortal words of Vince Lombardi on a poster at the headquarters of the Committee to Re-Elect the President: "Winning isn't everything; it is the only thing."

Today every Presidential contender's staff is dominated by strategists of one sort or another—in fund-raising, media, advertising, direct mail, turnout, organization, and electioneering. To be sure, they often express lofty goals, but these are not so much commitments to policy as chants to excite those citizens, especially the college educated, whose minds are most easily swayed by liturgical formulas. Such words without deeds lead to deceit, just as deeds without words lead to violence. At bottom, the new strategists are simply the obverse of a group of Latin-American army officers plotting to seize first the Presidential Palace and then the radio station. In the U.S., the radio station comes first.

TWO USES OF STRATEGY

As employed in politics, strategic thinking is not very difficult to master. It makes precise our everyday ideas of prudence. Do you look at the world around you as a series of decisions, options, and probable outcomes? Do you view your role in the world as making choices based exclusively on assessment of possible scenarios? Do you seek to maximize gain, minimize loss, and avoid what is counterproductive? If so, you have gone a long way toward becoming a strategic thinker. There is a strategic voice in each of us; it is part of our common sense. But it is not the sum total of common sense. For it is not possible or desirable to base all decisions on projected outcomes.

If, for example, you had been silly enough to offer a bribe to former Sen. John Sherman Cooper of Kentucky, a very successful politician —and no mean strategist—he would have thrown you out, not because he would calculate the possible costs and benefits of accepting or refusing a bribe but because Senator Cooper did not accept bribes at all. It was not even a matter of policy for Senator Cooper to refuse bribes—it was a matter of principle.

There are, after all, two basic dimensions to the use of strategic thinking in politics. The first is the use of strategy within a framework of morals and tradition to *attain* objectives; this is strategy as used under the representative ideal. The second is the use of strategy outside such a framework to prescribe objectives, notably winning as an end in itself.

Though this use of strategy prides itself on its icy realism, in politics it results in a crackpot naiveté. For strategic thinking can be effecive only when objectives are provided from the outside. When it is allowed to dominate politics, an activity whose whole purpose is to define objectives, it subverts the entire basis of lasting political power. It poses, moreover, a direct threat to the constitution and to any authority based on the rule of law. The politician who wrestles with his conscience about how best to uphold the Constitution and to serve his constituency is very different from the strategist who sees the legal system as just another object of manipulation. When political leaders, in full public view, start calculating the pros and cons of breaking the law, it becomes difficult for the rest of us to respect it.[1]

A NEW SET OF RULES

As the collapse of the McGovern candidacy, the Nixon Presidency, and the national political morale suggest, the strategist can scarcely claim to hold the keys to enduring success in democratic politics. He can offer only a few pieces of advice, which, if followed rigorously, will destroy his authority even though they may temporarily advance his fortunes. These can be summarized in a new set of rules of prudence for winning office and climbing the ladder of power.

Focus on fluidity, wherever you find it. The logical target of a strategic campaign is the unstable voter, the ticket-splitter, the "swing voter." After all, it makes little tactical sense to pay attention to those who are solidly with you or against you. In the campaign, therefore, you should ignore party loyalists just up to the point where they will dump you, and concentrate on potential swing voters. "Ignore anybody who has no place else to go" is a good strategic maxim.

This practice is not new, but the preponderant emphasis on it is. In traditional politics the focus was on turning out the faithful rather than on influencing the fluid voter. Ignoring anybody was considered bad policy, since the candidate's intention was not merely to maximize votes but to create a climate of accommodation in which no major interest would feel hopelessly left out.

If you cannot find fluidity, use pseudo-issues to create it. Because a minority candidate or party cannot rely entirely on independent voters, the strategists in both major parties do their best to annihilate loyalties in the other party.

There are always issues that will pry voters loose from the opposing camp. Occasionally these involve real changes in policy; more often they are pseudo-issues. President Nixon's use of the busing controversy after the Florida primary in 1972 was a case in point. He had no intention of challenging the Supreme Court guidlines on this question, as a close reading of his statements revealed, and as his subsequent dropping of the issue also showed. Kennedy's 1960 alarms about a missile gap were a similar fraud, designed to win Cold Warriors and defense-oriented interests in the South and Southwest from Nixon. The gap was forgotten after the election, until Nixon revived it in the 1968 campaign. Is it any wonder that politicians lack credibility?

Keep your options open. One never knows a year or even six months before an election what pseudo-issue may be useful. Hence the best strategic counsel to a candidate is to keep his options open so that he can move in any direction.

A policy of open options, of course, is the exact antithesis of a commitment. Whenever commitments are made, the result is a closing of some options and a loss of some bargaining power. Every commitment requires the generosity to see others succeed at their own commitments. The strategic politician's whole being, however, is devoted to beating others. His maxims are those of preemption, escalation, and deterrence: get him before he can get you. All this distracts him from true achievements, such as drafting a good law or serving his constituents, to say nothing of the nation.

Ignore your own party's organization. In 1972 both Nixon and McGovern set up campaign organizations entirely separate from the party structure. Collections of free-lance experts are the current substitutes for the traditional coalition-building of a national campaign. And when tension arises between the strategic specialist and the party loyalist, as it inevitably does, the strategist wins. His skills are considered more important to victory.

But the retribution comes later. If the party is ignored, it won't back up a leader when he is in trouble. If loyalists are shunted aside, where does the candidate get cadres for governing once his consultants go off to other lucrative clients? And if there are loyalists who remain, despite all the evidence that staying on is foolish, they are driven to ever more frenzied ideological phantasms, like the political groupies who hailed Agnew in California just before he resigned. Thus, within the party the strategist clears the field for the ideologue, and the two of them march side by side combining the cold pursuit of success with manic self-righteousness.

Govern as if you were still campaigning. Government by Gallup poll is a logical result of game-plan thinking. Having made few commitments to attain victory, the strategic politician has generated support that is broad but not deep. He has won the marginal preference of the fluid voter and weakened the devotion of the loyal party voter. Hence, he has no solid base of support to tide him over short-term reverses in public opinion. His aim, then, will logically be to avoid such reverses, and he can do this most efficiently by the same manipulation of appearances and verbal formulas that served him so well in his campaign. He concentrates not on performance but on taking credit for the things that go well and shifting blame for those that don't. The massive media exposure available to the Presidency makes this type of governing possible; but the reason it is *plausible* is that it seems to put the politician outside party and politics. He seems to be governing as an independent leader responsive only to the people, not the captive of partisan interests. This pleases the same fluid voter who holds the balance of power in elections. But without allies and coalitions, a leader cannot control the legislature or the bureaucracy. An isolated executive cannot perform effectively.

THE HYPERSTRATEGIC PERSONALITY

The dominance of these rules in our politics evokes a peculiar temper in public men. As the White House enemies list reminds us, the strategic politician becomes paranoid as a result of perceiving all competitors as potential foes. He also lacks tenacity in fighting for any objective that does not directly involve his power and survival. Consider Nixon's lack of support of his own Family Assistance Plan and by contrast (in an area where he is more than a mere strategist) the steadfast dedication to his course in Vietnam as part of a coherent approach to foreign policy. Without the long-range perspectives of men committed to causes, constituencies, and stable objectives, the strategic politician is convulsed in extremes of bullishness or bearishness. His commitment to issues and people is fickle. But he will do anything to stay in the game.

Futhermore, there is a certain juvenility about the hyperstrategist. His abstract view of conflict, his depersonalization of opponents, the paramilitary aspects of his trade, the defiantly unsentimental view of custom, law, and tradition—all these appeal to boys who have not yet grown up. To the strategic politician loyalty and friendship, for example, do not mean what they usually mean to adults, but are very similar to the restless and insecure liaisons of troubled adolescents. Shifting alliances replace friendships. Loyalty is replaced by orthodoxy. There can be no such thing as loyal opposition or friendly cricitism, since any movement from the party line of the moment may be a sign of apostasy. To the paranoiac hyperstrategist any member of the crew who is too critical may seem about to jump ship (and if he, too, is a game planner, this is probably an accurate assessment).

But the voter, too, can become a strategic politician. He also can begin to bargain and to focus on the fluid. He, to, can keep his options open and withhold his loyalties. If the politican does not deliver to him, why should he remain loyal to the politician?

This backlash is already well advanced. The electorate is fast learning that if the fluid get the spoils then it makes sense to be fluid. Black and Chicano leaders have publicly adopted this line in many regions of the country. George Wallace has used it extensively in the South. The suburbanite, the working-class Democrat, and the Jew are all beginning to behave much more independently in the voting booth. For strategic politics makes political alignment irrational, counterproductive, and ultimately impossible. Ticket-splitting is a logical response to the situation of candidates and parties becoming more manipulative.

The voters' policy of open options has also begun to produce an extreme volatility in "trial heat" polls of the electorate. Ticket-splitters may change their minds several times during a campaign, so that in many areas of the country polls are almost worthless. As this trend continues, Presidential and state elections are beginning to look like nonpartisan mayoralty contests. And under these conditions the whole idea of a lasting coalition or an electoral mandate begins to fade, especially when shifts in approval occur after the election as well.

Strategic politics inevitably produces a mutual contempt between political leaders and their constituencies. The strategic politician views the voters cynically because, according to decision theory, they are objectives to be manipulated. The electorate also views the politician cynically since he seems to be playing games with the voters and with other politicians. The two attitudes feed upon each other. As the voter looks on the politician with contempt, his voting behavior becomes more erratic. As this happens, the politician's strategies becomes more short-term, thus incurring more contempt. Both responses are understandable, yet they reinforce each other in a pattern that leads to a degeneration of representative politics. For as the process continues, it sets up impossible counterdemands for a pure ideal of virtue that is as empty as the strategists' pure ideal of power.

The seeds of this degeneracy in our thinking about politics have been widely sown. Almost everyone who rises to the commanding heights of American law, business, advertising, publishing, foundations, and universities has been reinforced in the habits of strategic thinking, by both formal training and informal practice. Men of the generation that came out of World War II, including Richard Nixon and John Kennedy, were educated by concrete experience to view strategy as synonymous with tough-mindedness. They were reacting against the excessive moralism of the American intellectual tradition as well as countering hyperstrategic thinking by the disciples of Hitler, Lenin, and Mao Tse-tung.

More importantly, however, strategic specialties met a sociological need. A major, unremarked achievement of the postwar era has been the broadening of the national elite. Instead of a relatively small, white, Eastern-oriented, Anglo-Saxon, Protestant leadership class, a much larger, multiregional and multitribal meritocracy now rules America.

In the formation of this new class, strategic specialties have been an indispensable recruiting device. They can be taught rather easily in universities, and they are rooted in a mathematical and anticipatory logic that can be tested with far more precision than literary or moral judgment. Since they borrow terms and methods from the natural sciences they seem to be objective. They seem to separate the hard facts of the "real" world from the soft and shifting values of any given moral or political tradition. This apparent value-neutrality has been crucial to their role as a melting pot for the new elite. The doctrine of value-neutrality though now recognized to be untenable even within the exact sciences, has a moral force that has made it impervious to mere philosophical refutation. For it has given Americans the excuse the country badly needed to ignore the social background of aspiring decision-makers, to ignore everything from the color of their skins to the color of their accents. This left the society with an obvious problem; a man's meritocratic rating gives no indication of his character or judgment. To deal with this problem, large organizations have developed a jerry-built system of spot interviews, security checks, psychological testing, telephone tapping, and file raiding.

The laudable attempt to open positions of power to everybody helps explain why strategic thinking now permeates America's vocabulary of leadership. And it accounts, too, for the confidence many of us put in strategic concepts, while we dismiss as naive, archaic, or fuzzy-minded objections to them in the name of trust, loyalty, restraint, integrity, or moral judgment. Yet these concepts are not only more human, they are also more workable, for they alone provide a language in which the new meritocracy can speak to the American people.

So long as political and moral reasoning are seen as less cogent than the logic of conflict, we shall get increasingly strategized perceptions not only of politics but of marriage, education, and all human relationships. The only alternatives our culture seems to offer to this demoralization are the solace of orthodox religion, the embracing of new cults, the escape into drugs and drink, or an ill-defined yet passionate reaction against intellect, expertise, and logical thought per se. Most policy professionals are unable to deal with the rhythms and moral aspirations of everyday life save as abstract values to be plugged in after a strategic calculus is completed. This is a serious cultural failing that will be difficult to correct, without a reappraisal of the role of the new sciences of decision-making.

It does, however, explain two intellectual habits of the American professionals and managers: Their vacillation between extremes of moralism and expertise, and their contempt for party politics. They draw such a rigid distinction between facts and values that they are unable to accept the integrity of an activity in which facts and values interpenetrate. But politics exists in a sphere where values create facts and these facts are then the basis of further values. For example, generations of preaching and reform by those who believe in certain transcendent values have created the fact that Americans will not elect as President an overtly racist demagogue. The very existence of the United States as a nation derives not so much from natural facts of race, migrations, and geography as from shared values and a political tradition forged from them.

THE GRAY AREA

The politician, then, operates almost entirely in the gray area between the neat categories of the moralist and technocrat. His concern is not to impose values upon objective facts but to decide what shall be taken as the relevant fact or value. Those with a specifically political sensibility (and they are by no means confined to elected officials) acquire a habit of seeing things the other person's way, even when they reject it. They see that a value that is very important from one point of view may be trivial from another. They are thus able to occasionally mediate conflict by finding rewards suited to the different parties. The "loser" in a decision may be satisfied with compensation that seems meaningless to the "winner." At his best, the politician acquires a sense of trade-offs between interests that cannot be measured on the same scale, a knack of persuading people to take other perspectives into account. That is why even when he is free of pride and venality, he will always have to descend to the use of flattery and pork-barreling and to judge which will suit whom. Also, there may be occasions when civic accommodation is impossible and force must be used. The political life amply teaches the uses of coercion.

Political sensibility does not come merely from dealing with many different kinds of people—a physician or accountant does this—but from having no specialist's expertise to impose on them. By contrast, the college-educated professional or business executive is trained to make disinterested decisions in accordance with "objective" criteria. He is trained to look at the "cold facts" and is happiest when he can find a single scale or a general principle against which to judge them. Hence he is comfortable with quantitative standards in matters of expertise (profit, GNP, crime rates, income levels, kill ratios) or, alternatively, transcendent principles in the world of values (justice, equality, peace). He is repelled by the use of flexible political standards, and he is contemptuous of the politicians's invocation of the lowest common denominator as the best guideline for decision. Furthermore, his entire training as a professional reinforces a mugwump disdain for political parties, whose main function is to reconcile diverse interests. He views party loyalty as mindless, which in a literal sense it is, since, like loyalty to friends or family, it requires obligations to those who may hotly disagree with him. Therefore he votes for the man rather than the party and prefers ideological movements to avowedly partisan ones.

In sum, he puts impossible and inconsistent demands on the political system. He insists on moral leadership, yet is revolted by the very reconciling of interests that is the basis of politics. He demands of the politician the very highest talent, yet wants to deprive the political sector of the resources that attract such talent to profit-making and tax-exempt activities.[2] He laments that "better people" do not hold office, yet insists on a recruiting system so stringent that no one but a sharp lawyer would dare jump in, for fear that a trivial infraction of some campaign-contribution law will land him in court. He wants special interests to take a lesser role in politics, yet multiplies the regulatory policies that make their heavy investment in influencing government officials inevitable. He deplores the red tape and impersonality of bureaucracy, yet holds himself aloof from the face-to-face politics that is the major alternative to bureaucracy. By polarizing all questions as those of objective facts or transcendent values, he is often unable to see the contingent facts and to mediate values the balancing of which is the very rationale of the political process.

None of these well-meaning but misguided attitudes is new, but until recently people of such views remained on the periphery of politics, or entered the arena slowly, usually to become the "ideological" wing of their party. The main political force of our time, however, is the movement into politics of an energetic class of young professional and business people in a massive way that does not permit a gradual initiation into traditional political processes. The new rules of strategic politics have arisen to manipulate this elite class, and at the same time to create niches for its members by cowing and dislodging party loyalists.

It is wrong to blame the news media for the success of strategic techniques. Rather, game-plan manipulations with respect to partisan politics feed on the gullibility of most educated Americans. Nevertheless, the dominant ethos of American journalism does tend to exacerbate matters. The literary training of many journalists makes them alert to drama, and what could be more dramatic than the striving for power, the intrigues of courtiers, and the birth and death of kings? And, by contrast, what could be more excruciatingly dull than the representative politician on his lowly rounds, wheedling the public works department or being buddy-buddy with the Rotarians? Struggle makes good copy. And the strategist gratifies this appetite of popular journalism by fabricating conflicts, such as Muskie's flawed performance in front of the *Manchester Union-Leader* in the 1972 New Hampshire primary, or Nixon's trumped-up confrontation with anti-war activists in San Jose in 1970. The journalist who sees politics through the prism of *West Side Story,* or his philosophical cousin, the literary intellectual, who sees it through Shakespeare's *Richard II,* is as much the enemy of representative politics as the hyperstrategist and the ideologue. To all of these bedfellows, political parties are irrelevant and representation is defined out of existence.

THE NEED FOR PARTIES

Some will argue that the political parties deserve their demise and that our representative politics was never very representative to begin with. But consider the alternatives. If parties cannot survive, what institutions can be held accountable for the governance of the country? The only real alternatives to parties are bureaucracies, police forces, and courts. All are "above politics." But for this very reason they are unsuited to the mediation of conflict. Courts work best in win-or-lose situations between two adversaries. Bureaucracies can arbitrate among many parties but they lack legitimacy and are notoriously apt to lose touch with public opinion. Police forces currently rate higher in public opinion than our political institutions but countries where the police or the military rule aren't much admired in America.

Some put great hope in public-interest groups like Common Cause or the tax-exempt network of Nader organizations. But these lobby groups have sprung up only because the parties are stagnant and the press unenterprising. They cannot replace face-to-face politics, nor can they recruit and support legitimate leaders.

Some are impatient with a partisan system because it is too crude and banal. Partisan rhetoric does not make the fine distinctions of academia or adhere to the hard quantitative standards of business. But the fact is that the most basic questions of democracy will always be crude and qualitative. They boil down to simple questions of the speed of change, the degree of centralization, the distribution of the tax burden, and the priority of broad national purposes. These questions can be subjected to very sophisticated analyses but ultimately they involve brute choices of a kind that a party system can make. And when things go wrong, isn't it better to throw out one partisan team and replace it with another than to throw out one constitution and replace it with another?

However anomalous it may sound, the proper response to the abuses revealed by Watergate is not less politics but more: spending more money, not less, on recruiting and supporting aspirants for elective office; expanding, not limiting, the already small number of political appointees to bureaucratic posts; not overregulating election campaigns but making entry into them as simple as possible; encouraging journalists not to pant over the war games of a few national figures but to pay more attention to the performance of goverment; not bewailing the corruption of the state legislatures but investing in them the attention and resources that will attract better people; not assuming that politics involves inferior mental processes but making mastery of these processes a condition for entry into positions of authority.

The full agenda of political reeducation cannot be complete without attention to small details of institutional design. The parties, which reflect most purely the political aspects of our political life, are most in need of renewal. The existing two-party system, which developed under Jackson as a response to mass suffrage, has served to mediate regional conflict and to assimilate several generations of new and undereducated participants into the political process. When it has failed, America has resorted to repression of workers, Southerners, immigrants, and blacks. The new task of the parties is, without forfeiting their old role, to initiate a vigorous class of overeducated participants into the realities of representative politics. The new class is mobile, and its political interests cannot always be served by geographically defined units. In accordance with a classical patrician notion of politics, it sees its interests as fulfilled through principles and programs rather than direct patronage. Its demands on politics will require a reconstitution of the representative ideal, both within the established parties and in new kinds of partisan organization.

If there is any comfort in our current situation, it is that the country has recovered from similar problems before.[3] The representative ideal must, it appears, be rescued periodically from some new power cult. Moreover, the Watergate trials provide a natural pause in which to think about the direction of American politics. But the initial reaction has been an armchair outrage that will only make matters worse. The current troubles have produced cynicism rather than activism, a hankering for an independent and forceful leader—a demagogue—rather than a commitment to the concerted action that alone can make such a leader accountable to a constituency. Among the strategic politicians themselves the lesson of Watergate has been not to rededicate themselves to constitutional principles but to be more long-range in their calculations and to avoid the "counterproductive." The fluid voters typically congratulate themselves on their disdain for politics. Their view of themselves as the passive victims of the "politicians" is itself a sign that they don't believe in self-government.

The remedy to all this will not be found in any new law or new institution or new candidate. . . . The remedy will come, if it comes, only from a deep recognition of the true basis of America's greatness. America has no thousand-year-old cathedrals, no foreign conquests of which we are proud, no poetic consciousness of a common blood. Even the continent on which we live has been exploited as a commercial resource rather than loved as a natural home.

The greatness of America lies in its spirit, and its spirit is expressed in a unique form of politics. It settles in a public way questions that are locked in file cabinets in most countries that call themselves free. Its newspapers are able to publish material that would be cause for government seizure in Britain or France. It carries out elections and due process not only in every state and county but in every high school and garden club. These civic practices are not quaint throwbacks to the eighteenth century. They are the tacit basis of our written Constitution. They are the acting out of the deepest ideals of the West.

If we are now betraying those ideals, the responsibility does not lie with a few sinister White House staffers, or even with politicians as a group. It lies with our activist intellectuals, our journalists, our managers, our businessmen, our philanthropists—and it lies with you.

NOTES

1. The most public example we have is a recent press conference in which the President unabashedly said that he had, of course, discussed all his "options" with respect to paying hush money to the Watergate defenders.

2. No proposed reform for honesty in politics would have a better effect than discarding the generally spurious tax collector's distinction between partisan and nonpartisan political activity.

3. For evidence we need only reread Washington's Farewell Address. Its warnings against factional excess, its insistence on constitutional restraint, its appreciation of the importance to politics of religion and education, and its warnings against inflationary debt, foreign intrigue, and large standing military establishments speak directly to us.

4 | The Shame of the Republic

Henry Steele Commager

Casting a wider historical net than Auspitz and Brown, Commager suggests changes in American national character over the last quarter century as the root cause of Watergate. Commager dismisses arguments focusing primary responsibility on Richard Nixon because the American people were well aware of his public career and the things for which he stood. The author notes that the voters have tolerated corruption and dishonesty in government for years and concludes that we get the kind of government we really want and deserve despite our indignation over Watergate. Although references to the works are minimal, this essay reviews three books: The Politics of Lying: Government Deception, Secrecy and Power *by David Wise;* The Crippled Giant: American Foreign Policy and Its Domestic Consequences *by J. William Fulbright; and* Political Prisoners in America *by Charles Goodell.*

I

Watergate and all those attendant usurpations, subversions, and corruptions for which the word has become both a symbol and a short cut, is neither a "deplorable incident"—to use Mr. Nixon's revealing phrase—nor a historical sport. It is a major crisis, constitutional, political, and moral, one that challenges our governmental system. Public attention is, and will long remain, focused on what happened, but already the interest of publicists and scholars is shifting to the more troublesome question of why it happened. That is really the subject of these three books—all of them written before the Watergate scandal

Reprinted with permission from *The New York Review of Books*. Copyright © 1973 Nyrev. Inc. The article appeared in the issue of August 19, 1973, pp. 10-17.

Henry Steele Commager is Professor of American History, Amherst College. He is author of many books including *The American Mind* and *The Search for a Usable Past.*

broke, but all in a sense anticipating the psychological and moral problems that Watergate has raised.

The roots of our current malaise go back to the paranoia about communism—first Soviet, then Chinese—that obsessed Americans after 1947. So deep and pervasive was this paranoia that—like the Southern commitment to slavery before the Civil War, and to white supremacy after the war—in time it came to dominate our lives and our thoughts, to color our views of politics, economy, education, science, and morality. As in the words of Kafka and Orwell, it justified adopting the tactics of the enemy in order to defeat him—just what the Nixon Administration has been doing for the past [several] years, just what that half-baked "Jeffersonian liberal" Mr. Thomas Huston achieved when he sold Mr. Nixon a vast scheme of repression in order to avert repression. In both the McCarthy and Watergate eras it has justified undermining the Constitution and the Bill of Rights in order, presumably, to save them.

Inevitably Watergate (perhaps we should find a different name, like Nixonism) conjures up and reflects McCarthyism. But something new has been added; indeed much has been added that makes it more dangerous, more corrupt, and more subversive than that earlier foray against sanity and decency. For war has been added—a ten-years' war which benumbed the American consicence and blunted the American political intelligence.

The cold war itself was largely a product of deductive and *a priori* reasoning, and therefore a self-delusion, and so, too, in added measure, was the ten-year war against Vietnam. The doctrinaire state of mind lends itself eagerly to paranoia, for real dangers are nothing compared to those our imagination can conjure up. It was almost inevitable that the psychology which imagined the domino theory and envisioned a million Chinese landing (after a good healthy swim) on the shores of California should see in every student demonstration, every sit-down at an airport or a napalm factory, every revelation of government chicanery or of overruns in naval contracts a threat to the survival of the republic. For if the threat of communism is so importunate as to justify the longest war in which we have ever been engaged, the satanic arsenal of weapons used against friends and enemies indiscriminately, the use of napalm, the My Lai and other massacres, the violations of international law and of the laws of war, the destruction of a whole nation, then surely it justifies such minor peccadilloes as wiretapping, or the use of provocative agents, or breaking into safes, or the corruption of elections, or Watergate.

Basic to an understanding of the usurpations, duplicities, and irresponsibilities of the Nixon era is paranoia, which has a life of its own, and which still lingers on—even after the "end" of the war and the rapproachment with China—polluting the moral and intellectual atmosphere of the country. Certainly there is little evidence that Mr. Nixon or his underlings think the new relationship with the Soviet Union and China justifies the mitigation of their own paranoia about "national security," or their conviction that any attack upon official policy is itself a potential threat to security. How else explain the vindictiveness of the prosecution of Daniel Ellsberg and the readiness to subvert justice in that prosecution; how else explain the political skulduggery that persisted long after the 1972 election, the persistent use of the FBI and the CIA for political purposes, the readiness to employ provocative agents, the contumacious boasts at the POW dinner that reliance on secrecy, even useless secrecy, would go on and on; how else explain the determination to bomb Cambodia back to the Stone Age?

Successive presidents have tried to wash their hands of personal responsibility for the lawlessness and corruption so pervasive in our government in the last decade or so. But whoever planned and launched the Bay of Pigs, whoever engineered the Tonkin Bay fraud, deceived the nation about the danger of communism in Santo Domingo, directed the secret war in Laos, authorized the use of napalm and of fire-free zones, acquiesced in the torture and murder of prisoners; whoever concocted Watergate, rifled the safes, installed the bugging devices, planted the agents, accepted and paid bribes, doctored the polls and the cables—for all these ultimate responsibility lodges in the White House. It is the president who sets the moral tone, who selects the assistants he wishes to work with him—above all the attorneys general—and it is the president who profits from such success as the chicaneries of his associates and subordinates may produce. It is the president therefore who must be assigned responsibility not only for failures—as with the Bay of Pigs—or for violations of international law—as with Santo Domingo—but for debasing the political standards and polluting the moral atmosphere of the nation.

II

But it is insufficient, it is almost trivial, to assign full responsibility for our current sickness to particular presidents. After all it is the American people who elected them—in the case of Mr. Nixon by the largest majority in our history. Two competing explanations, or at least illuminations, require consideration. One is that we are confronted not merely with personal offenses and particular failures, but with a major breakdown in our constitutional and political mechanisms. The second is that our government and politics, with all their knaveries, vulgarities, and dishonesties, more or less reflect American society, and even the American character, and that we are, in fact, getting the kind of government that we want. The fault, in short, is in ourselves.

The first of these explanations lends itself more readily to analysis than the second. Put most simply it argues that a Constitution designed for the modest needs of a society of four million people, whose business was mostly farming, and whose political needs were adequately served by local and state governments, and based on the principle that government, like dress, was the badge of lost innocence and that wherever possible the authority of government should be limited rather than enlarged, is no longer adequate to the importunate needs of a nation of 200 million, for effective controls over the economy and technology, for the operation of traditional democracy, or for the requirements of world power and of modern war. Thus those famous constitutional principles established in England and America in the seventeenth and eighteenth centuries—separation and balance of powers, limitations on government inscribed in bills of rights, restrictions on executive authority, especially in the realm of making war, legislative control of the purse, due process of law and the impartial rule of law—are dangerously put out of date.

Equally out of date, so President Nixon proclaims by his conduct if not by his words, are those assumptions about the relations of men to government so fundamental that they were either taken for granted or left to the rhetoric of preambles and bills of rights rather than put into the body of the Constitution. Thus, with respect to the assumption that public servants are precisely that, the Virginia Bill of Rights puts it that "all power is vested in and derived from the people; that magistrates are their trustees and servants, and at all times amenable to them." "Amenable" is not the word that pops into our minds when we contemplate Mr. Nixon, nor does he think of himself and of the Praetorian Guard with which he surrounds himself as servants. He regards the American people as essentially children; he treats their elected representatives with contempt; he says, in effect, that the people have no inherent right of privacy, no inherent right to differ or dissent on great issues of policy, no inherent right even to a free, open, and honest ballot.

No less important, in the eyes of the Founding Fathers, was the assumption of candor and openness in government—the assumption, that is, that the people have the right to know. This was the reason for those provisions in almost every constitution for freedom of the press; this was the logic behind Jefferson's famous statement that given a choice between a government without newspapers and newspapers without a government, he would choose the latter; this was the philosophy that animated that passion for education expressed by most of the constitution makers: that without enlightenment about politics, and information about government, democracy simply would not work.

It is sometimes argued that the Constitution itself was drawn up in secret session. So it was. It was also debated in twelve state conventions during a period of a year, and by almost everyone who had participated in its making. Not only in the *Federalist Papers* but in scores of books and pamphlets every line and word of the document was subjected to the most searching scrutiny. No other political document of our history was more thoroughly—or more publicly—analyzed and explored. And on the whole since Washington, presidents have faithfully continued this early tradition, though there are exceptions. The oft-cited case of Washington's "refusal" to make available to the Congress the papers bearing on the Jay Treaty is of course not an exception. Washington gave the Senate everything it asked for, and the House everything that bore on its constitutional authority to make appropriations. Just as Nixon's is the first administration in our history to attempt prior censorship of the press—the *New York Times* and *Washington Post*—and the first systematically to withhold from the Congress information it requires to fulfill its constitutional obligations, so it is the first to adopt wiretapping as an almost official political instrument, and to condone that habitual politics of lying which is the subject of David Wise's enthralling and sobering book.

All of this—so runs the argument—is rooted nevertheless not in the inadequacy or corruption of the men who happen to be in office at any moment, but in the inadequacy and corruption of the anachronistic mechanisms with which we are saddled when we undertake to deal with the complex problems of modern economy, technology, and war.

This brings us back to the central question: can we run a Leviathan state with an eighteenth-century Constitution?

Perhaps the obvious answer is also the right one: so far we have. Needless to say the Constitution is not merely the original document of 1787; it is also the score and more of amendments, some of them fundamental. It is the gloss of four hundred volumes of Supreme Court opinions. It is that organic growth presided over by President and Congress and not unacceptable to the Court. That growth has been extensive, even prodigious. In the case of the Civil War amendments, it has been revolutionary. But both the organic growth and the revolutions were constitutional. So, too, were such political revolutions as produced, over the years, judicial review, the transformation of the federal system, and the evolution of the welfare state.

Is the crisis of the present so imperative that it requires an unconstitutional revolution—requires, that is, abandoning the separation of powers, discarding limitations on the executive authority, weakening legislative control of the purse, subverting the traditional rule of law, and covering with a fog of secrecy the operations of government? Clearly Mr. Nixon and a good many of his followers think that it is— and now we are back with the phobia about communism and paranoia about national security.

Each generation tends to think—it is of course one of the many forms of vanity—that the crisis which it happens to confront is the gravest in history. Nothing that we face today compares in gravity with the crisis of the Civil War—when it seemed that the nation might be rent asunder and slavery prosper—or the crisis of the great depressions of the 1890s and the 1930s. All three of these were attended by political and constitutional revolution—the Civil War crisis by a very disorderly revolution, but constitutional nevertheless. It might well be questioned whether we even face a crisis today other than the crises we have masochistically brought upon ourselves—the crisis of the cold war, the crisis of our paranoia about China, the crisis of the reckless betrayal of our fiduciary obligation to posterity through the destruction of natural resources, the crisis of confidence in republican government brought about by unconstitutional war and unconstitutional domestic policies, the crisis of morals. It is of course all familiar enough: you create a real crisis by moving convulsively against an imaginary one.

There is indeed no reason to suppose that the problems which confront us cannot be solved by regular political and constitutional means. While it is no doubt true that this administration would be unable to function as it has functioned . . . if it were required to observe the strict limits of the Constitution, the conclusion is not that we should therefore acquiesce in the relaxation of constitutional restrictions but that the administration should abide by them. For in every instance of administrative challenge to the Constitution and the Bill of Rights, it was the challenge that proved disastrous, not the constitutional limitation.

Would we be worse off if Nixon had confined himself to the constitutional limitations of his office? Would we be worse off if he had been unable to wage war in Laos, invade and bomb Cambodia, mine Haiphong Harbor; spread a pall of secrecy over not only military but domestic operations that had any connection with "national security";

establish censorship in many areas of governmental operations; use the CIA not only to subvert foreign governments but in domestic politics, and violate the constitutional obligation to "make a regular Statement of all . . . Expenditures of all public Money" with respect to the five or six billion dollars which the CIA annually spends; destroy domestic programs that the Congress had voted by impounding appropriations; authorize wire taps on foreign embassies, congressmen, the National Security Council, newsmen, and others; invoke executive privilege, and spread the mantle of executive immunity over his henchmen, use *agents provocateurs* to smoke out "antiwar radicals," and subvert the processes of justice by turning the Justice Department into a political agency? What Mr. Nixon complains of being unable to do under a strict interpretation of the Constitution is precisely what those who wrote the Constitution intended he should not do and should be unable to do.

Yet we cannot ignore the fact that one part of the Constitution has always given us trouble, and that is precisely the provision for the executive and for executive power. In no other area has the Constitution had to be so patched up—four amendments no less, all dealing with the executive branch—this compared to one dealing with the judiciary (and that speedily nullified), and one—popular election of senators—dealing with the legislative. Not surprising; after all the office was new and, with the possible exception of some American states, unprecedented; after all, everyone took for granted that Washington would be the first president, and there he sat, presiding over the Convention, the very symbol of rectitude; after all there were as yet no national parties to take charge of elections and even of administrations.

The framers were confronted by an almost insoluble dilemma: fear that power always corrupts and awareness that the man who presided over their deliberations and would be the first president was incorruptible; conviction that the executive power, especially in the area of making war, was highly dangerous, and awareness that Washington had already demonstrated that with a man of honor there was no danger. Nor could they devise any method which would ensure a Washington—or an Adams, a Jefferson, a Madison—in the presidential chair.

They took refuge therefore in studied ambiguity, and ambiguity has presided over the executive power from that day to this. Consider, for example, the problem of the executive power in foreign relations. It is, said Woodrow Wilson a century or so later, "very absolute"; clearly Mr. Nixon thinks so too. But it rests on very uncertain constitutional authority, for that document says merely that the President shall be commander-in-chief (which does not necessarily concern the conduct of foreign relations), that he shall, with the advice and consent of the Senate, appoint ambassadors and make treaties, and that he shall receive ambassadors. That is the whole of it, and what a superstructure has been reared on that foundation!

The dilemma persists. To allow the president to take us to war, as he did on two recent occasions, is to invite disaster; to tie his hands in emergencies is also to invite disaster. Experience, to be sure, has so far justified only the first, not the second, of these dangers. Perhaps such a bill as the Javits-Stennis War Powers Act may at least mitigate the problem, but it is improbable that any legislation can deal adequately with the many-sided facade of executive power as well as with complex problems of tenure, removal, impeachment, succession, and so forth. Perhaps in this respect the only ultimate reassurance can come in a courageous and revitalized Congress, a truly independent judiciary, and that eternal vigilance which the Founding Fathers took for granted.

III

Watergate then cannot be explained merely as the consequence of incompetence or knavery of men in high office: these terms can be applied to the Grant and Harding administrations as well, when not only the republic but the presidency survived and flourished. Nor can the American people so easily shift responsibility onto Mr. Nixon. After all he had not led a precisely private life, and 42 million Americans who should or could have been familiar with his public career after 1946 voted for him. Surely we must conclude that they got not only what they deserved but what they wanted, and that in a democracy the people have a right to get what they want as long as they do so according to law.

Nor can Watergate be explained as the result of intolerable stresses and strains on our constitutional and political mechanisms; these have held up under far greater strains during the Depression and the Great War, and indeed it is not the Constitution and laws that have failed us, but persistent resort to lawlessness.

A third possible explanation is that implied in different ways by Senators Fulbright and Goodell, and by Mr. Wise, namely that responsibility for our crisis is rooted in changes in the American character, the American mind, American habits or traits—use what term you will—over the past quarter century, changes reflected in

Mr. Nixon and his associates and in the current style of American politics.

Much here is in the realm of conjecture, for to fix national traits is like fixing quicksilver, and to go on from there to trace cause and effect is almost to indulge in mysticism. Yet, at some moments of history anyway, national styles do seem to be reflected in politics: the style of the Old South, for example, in the politics of slavery; the style of Bismarck's Germany in the war and diplomacy of the last half of the nineteenth century—how different from the almost music-box Germany of early romanticism; the style of the Japan that launched the great Pacific war. Styles change, and have in the South, in Germany, and in Japan. If Jefferson is a representative figure of the American Enlightenment, faithfully reflecting its virutes, its optimisms, its faith, its limitations, so perhaps Mr. Nixon is a representative figure of contemporary America, reflecting its arrogance, its violence, its passion for manipulation, its commercialism, but not reflecting its generosity or idealism or intellectual ferment.

Consider first something very large, the shift in the concept of America's role in history, and of the American "mission." To Jefferson's generation that role was clear — to provide a model and a moral example to the peoples of the world. The American empire was, in the almost hackneyed phrase of the Founding Fathers, an Empire of Reason. Mr. Nixon too believes in an American mission. That mission is to be achieved, however, not by reason but by power— force at home to whip recalcitrants into line, force abroad to whip lesser breeds into line — force in little things like breaking into safes, force in big things like building the greatest arsenal in the history of the world.

The corruption of the Jeffersonian view of mission emerges wherever we look: for moral mission, the military; for a unique vision of self-government, hostility throughout the globe to the forces of popular insurgency; for a welcome to radicals and dissenters who had fled the tyranny of the Old World, a refusal to grant visas to those whose ideas might be thought radical by the Daughters of the American Revolution; for faith in the wisdom of the people, a conviction that the people are children whose judgment is not to be trusted; for what Jefferson called "the illimitable freedom of the human mind," a deep distrust of freedom as something inescapably tarnished by subversion; for passion for peace and disarmament, an exaltation of the military and a readiness to rely on it without mercy or compassion.

Our search for peace is rooted in the assumption that we are— far more than other great nations—selfless, idealistic, and peace loving. If this is indeed so, then it follows logically that the wars we fight must be an expression of those qualities. When we develop the most elaborate weapons system in the world, it is for peace; when we maintain 2,000 military establishments overseas, it is for peace; when we authorize the CIA to operate secretly in sixty countries and subvert those governments we do not approve of, it is for peace. We changed the government of Guatemala for peace, we invaded Cuba for peace, we landed marines in Santo Domingo for peace, we support the Generals in Brazil and the Colonels in Greece and the colonialists in Portugal for peace; we came to the aid of Diem and Thieu for peace. Now that the war in Vietnam is over, we are bombing Cambodia every day as a kind of peace mission. What is most frightening about all this is that from Mr. Nixon on down the American people can swallow this wonderland logic without gagging.

Nowhere is our changing sense of history more pronounced than in the changing attitude of most Americans toward posterity. The generation whose bicentennial achievements we are about to celebrate was deeply and pervasively posterity-minded: the conviction that everything must be done for the benefit of future generations animated almost everyone of the Founding Fathers. That attitude profoundly influenced the American concept of history, too—that though Old World nations were the prisoners of history, America was not, that though in the Old World history is retrospective, in America it was prospective. Both these attitudes pretty well faded out in the past half century or so and now they are but a memory: who now believes that America is the model for the world, or that the new nations of India and Africa look to us for moral and spiritual guidance? . . .

The growing habit of taking refuge in such terms as "national commitments," "national security," "obligations of power," "peace with honor," along with that jargon which burgeoned so luxuriantly during the Vietnam war — the "free-fire zones," the "protective aerial reaction," the "surgical strikes," and "incontinent ordinance"—all this bespeaks a steady drift away from the world of realism to the world of self-delusion, from the inductive, the functional, the pragmatic in American thought to an indulgence in the abstract, the deductive, and the doctrinaire.

The rationalization of the cold war, and of the Vietnam war, was rooted in this kind of abstraction. We conjured up a world conspiracy, a monolithic communism, a domino theory—what did we not conjure up?—without feeling any need to provide supporting evidence for our fears. President Nixon reduced the whole thing to a kind of obscene absurdity when he announced that the most powerful nation in the world would be a "helpless, crippled giant" if it could not invade Cambodia! It is the implications of that concept, the cost of that kind of thinking, that Senator Fulbright has explored with his customary lucidity, cogency, and judiciousness, but with passion too. "This kind of thinking," he writes, "robs a nation's policy makers of objectivity and drives them to irresponsible behavior. The perpetuation of the Vietnam war is the most terrible and fateful manifestation of the determination to prove that we are 'Number One.' " And he adds that Assistant Secretary of Defense McNaughton's conclusion that "to avoid a humiliating United States defeat" accounted for some 70 percent of the logic of our war in Southeast Asia, "suggests a nation in thrall." We sometimes forget that thrall means slavery.

The two other books under review reveal how we transferred this same phychology—and tactics—from the foreign to the domestic arena. In the realm of the law—the Dennis case is the most notorious example—we conjured up "conspiracy," searched out not dangerous acts but dangerous "tendencies," and created crimes almost as remote from reality as that of "imagining the death of the King." We took refuge in public manifestations of patriotism like compulsory flag salutes, loyalty oaths, and the antics of the state and congressional un-American activities committees whose business was to provide such activities if they could not discover them, and who did.

Senator Goodell's account of the politicizing of our justice—or resort to wiretapping, the use of provocative agents, the misuse of the grand jury, the readiness to prosecute as a kind of political punishment even when evidence of a crime was lacking—and sometimes to provide the evidence itself—all this is chilling but convincing. He was himself, he recalls, a victim of harassment: "When I was in the Senate, speaking out against administration policies, I learned that my official telephone was tapped and that Military Intelligence agents were following me around the country, building a dossier on my public remarks." He learned more about these techniques when he was counsel for Ellsberg in the Pentagon Papers case—the only criminal prosecution, he reminds us, in more than 4,000 instances of the violation of government regulations concerning classified materials; his book was written before the revelations of breaking into the office files of Ellsberg's psychiatrist.

Perhaps even more sobering are two statements which he quotes from men who occupied positions of great power. The first is from William Rehnquist, now sitting on the Supreme Court, who, when assistant attorney general, told the Senate Subcommittee on Constitutional Rights that the Constitution "empowers the President to prevent violation of law by maintaining surveillance of those who *in his opinion, might violate it*" (italics mine). As no one over five can safely be excluded from this category we shall all have to engage in surveillance over each other. The quotation comes from the now happily retired Attorney General Kleindienst, who, in 1971, assured us that it would be unnecessary to suspend the Constitution in order to cope with political unrest because:

> There is enough play at the joints of our criminal law — enough flexibility—so that if we really felt that we had to pick up the leaders of a violent uprising we could. We would find some things to charge them with, and we would be able to hold them that way for a while.

Mr. Nixon and his attorneys-general have indulged in the same kind of thinking, and used the same weapons; if the current *cri de coeur* is no longer simple communism or international conspiracy but "protecting the national interest," the animus is the same, and the logic. The current phrase is potentially even more dangerous than its predecessors; it is broad enough, as Mr. Wise's book shows, to embrace supporting Pakistan against India, asking for prior censorship on the Pentagon Papers, resorting to wholesale wiretaps, authorizing mass arrests without warrants, the corruption of the election process, secret agreements that imply, if they do not require, military commitments with Spain and Portugal—the list could go on and on, and in Mr. Wise's horrifying book it does. But as Governor Reagan has sagely observed, those guilty of misdeeds are not criminals for they meant well. So, no doubt, did Benedict Arnold.

With growth, complexity, and technological impersonality has come, almost inevitably, a weakening of individualism and of that "contrary-minded" quality which used to be so pronounced in the American character. This has meant a readiness to "follow" the president on the ground that he must know best, to accept official handouts at face value, and to resent criticism of the government as something faintly unpatriotic. It has meant, too, a ready acquiescence in regimentation, manipulation, and secrecy.

This attitude is not of course confined to military matters; it is more ostentatious in the readiness to accept the erosion of individual personality and the invasion of privacy in the world dominated by the computer. We are, statistically, far better educated than we were a century ago, but our education takes the form of thinking for ourselves rather less than it did a century ago. Whether because television has shortened our attention span, or the war benumbed our capacity for moral response, we do not appear seriously shocked by My Lai or wire taps, or even by Watergate until it appeared to be connected with the White House. Many Americans see nothing wrong in political threats against newspapers and the television networks; indeed there is a kind of curious counteremotion that the newspapers are being unfair to the president.

We look with indifference, too, at the growth of what would once have been regarded as royal attributes in our rulers—the numerous luxurious residences they require, the special jet planes, the fleets of limousines, the vast entourage which accompanies them wherever they go. How odd to remember that when Thomas Jefferson walked back to his boarding house after giving his inaugural address, he could not find a seat available for him at the dinner table, or that a quarter century later President John Quincy Adams should have the same experience on a ship sailing from Baltimore to New York.

Now government policies and tests screen out strong-minded individualists. It is improbable that any one of our greatest diplomats—Albert Gallatin, John Quincy Adams, Charles Francis Adams—could even get into the Foreign Service today. The world of business, finance, the military, even the world of the great universities, testifies to the same preference for the impersonal chairman of a board rather than a powerful but abrasive personality who will set his stamp on an institution; perhaps it is only in the films, sports, art, music, and literature that Americans still have a cult of individualism.

One of the most pronounced shifts in the American character appears to be a function of this decline in individualism. I mean the growth of a habit of mind that responds uncritically to manipulation. Advertising and "public relations" are the most familiar symbols—and instruments—of manipulation. No previous administration has been so "public relations" minded or has relied so heavily on the manipulation of the public as Nixon's. Everything, so Mr. Nixon and his "team" seem to believe, can be manipulated: elections, justice, the economy, science, great issues of war and peace, the Constitution and the courts; it all depends on the "game plan," on your control of the media, and on your cunning.

Mr. Nixon thought that the Democratic party nomination could be manipulated—and perhaps he was right; that the election could be manipulated—and perhaps it was. Newspapers were not to be won over by sound policies and sound arguments but by petty pressures like excluding reporters from social functions, and by powerful measures like denying them access to information. Congress is to be won over not by arguments but by force or cunning; the courts by playing games with appointments—remember the Nixon caper of the six possible nominees to the Supreme Court. Justice is to be achieved by using provocative agents or rifling files; public opinion polls are made by flooding the White House with phony telegrams; history by doctoring cables; the economy is directed by Alice in Wonderland statistics that never mean what they seem to mean. The president himself is to win the support of the people not through the force of his personality but by some "image" that is created for him.

Wars can be manipulated, too, both for our side and for the enemy —thus the monthly assurance that the war was really over, thus the lies about the Vietnam invasion in 1964 and about Tonkin Gulf; thus the glowing picture of thousands of Asians from Korea to Australia fighting on our side, almost all of whom turned out to be mercenaries (we didn't use to like mercenaries, but that has changed); thus the famous body counts which made clear that there were really no North Vietnamese males left to fight.

Supreme Court decisions, such as those on wiretapping and busing, can be manipulated to mean something different from what they seem to mean. The Constitution itself can be manipulated to prove the opposite of what the Founding Fathers had written. None of this would work if the American people had not been corrupted for more than a generation by the kind of advertising which floods all media day and night, and whose essential principle is manipulation and seduction. A society trained to accept the preposterous claims, the deceptions, and the vulgarities of American advertising can perhaps be manipulated into accepting anything.

An administration which relies so largely on images and packaging and manipulation has neither respect nor capacity for larger ideas or views. In the end it may not be corruption but intellectual aridity that is the distinguishing feature of this administration.

IV

These reflections raise more questions than they answer. We are confronted with the spectacle of our corruption, a corruption not only moral and social but psychological and intellectual, confronted with a threat not only to the constitutional and political system, but to constitutional and political thought. Where is the center of gravity? Is it in the White House; is it in the Praetorian Guard that has infested the White House; is it in the apparatus of secrecy we associate not only with the FBI and the CIA and with the Pentagon; but with the whole of the administration? Or is there perhaps no center of gravity at all, no center of corruption even; do we have the sociological equivalent of Hannah Arendt's "banality of evil"?

Those guilty of what is moral treason to the Constitution, and of subverting the political system, are not evil conspirators, consciously bent upon destroying the America we have known. They are, at the top, the proud products of the American system of Private Enterprise, the very vindication of the American success story; those down the line are for the most part clean-limbed, clear-eyed, upstanding young men, the kind who figure in all our most stylish advertisements, the kind who are commonly voted "most likely to succeed" by their admiring classmates. These are not the makers and shakers of O'Shaughnessy's poem; they are the squares and the jocks of the post-college generation. What kind of society is it that produces and cherishes men of these intellectual and moral standards? If your own conduct was scrupulous, if our own standards were honorable, would we really have permitted the Mitchells and Magruders and Deans and Haldemans and Kleindiensts to have imposed their moral standards upon us? Are we sure we have not imposed our moral standards upon them?

Our indignation and our outrage are both a bit shame-faced. After all there is nothing new about the illegalities and immoralities of the Vietnam War; but we still tolerate the Cambodian war. After all there is nothing new about the iniquities of the CIA; that has been going on now for almost twenty years with scarcely a murmur of protest. After all there is nothing new about the warnings of secrecy in government—that goes back 180 years to the principles of the Founding Fathers. After all there is nothing new about the danger of the arrogance of power and the impropriety of using men and societies for our advantage; that goes back to Kant's great categorical imperative. After all there is nothing new about the moral that power corrupts— you can read that in Plutarch, if you ever bother to read Plutarch— or about warnings against imposing your will on weaker peoples—you can read that in Thucydides, if you bother to read Thucydides.

The Founding Fathers did read Plutarch and Thucydides. They knew that power tended to corrupt and set up a system of checks and balances which they thought would protect the Commonwealth against that corruption. This administration has tried to paralyze those checks and balances and who has protested? Who but a handful of journalists, senators, and scholars?

The Founding Fathers knew instinctively what Montesquieu proclaimed in his *Spirit of the Laws,* that virtue is the animating principle of a republic. And to the Commonwealth they served—almost always at great personal sacrifice—they paid the tribute of virtue. But this administration which gibbers about "peace with honor" does not exalt virtue, and does not practice it.

But do we?

5 | Political Values and Public Opinion

Patrick J. McGeever

The results of the public opinion survey about Watergate reported here give us some idea of the political values of the American citizenry. In fall, 1973, McGeever found that many persons who believed the President to be guilty of wrongdoing in the cover-up were still opposed to his removal from office. Subsequent opinion studies showed similar patterns in attitudes. Even after the public release of the June, 1972, tapes definitely incriminating the President in the cover-up, a Field telephone poll in August, 1974, found only 66 percent of Californians favoring conviction of Mr. Nixon by the Senate. McGeever provides a socio-economic profile of those who opposed removal of the President. He concludes that his findings reveal widespread cynicism about politicians, fear of the impeachment process, and a willingness by many to subordinate rule of law to partisan concerns.

In late September and early October of 1973, over 1000 individuals in a major midwestern metropolitan area were asked a series of questions about their attitudes on the Watergate affair. The purpose was not so much the ostensible one of determining (again!) what people believed about the break-in and cover-up, but to explore a seeming inconsistency that kept cropping up in the national opinion polls: apparently, the great majority of Americans believed President Nixon to be guilty of knowing about or participating in the break-in; but the great majority of Americans did not want President Nixon to resign or to be impeached. We found, in a nutshell, that a significant portion (not a majority, however) of those interviewed did not want their

Reprinted with permission from the *Political Science Quarterly*, 89 (June 1974), 289-299, where it initially appeared as "Guilty, Yes: Impeachment, No: Some Empirical Findings." Copyright © 1974.

Patrick J. McGeever is Assistant Professor of Political Science, Indiana University-Purdue University, Indianapolis.

president to be punished—even when they believed him guilty of major derelictions—for reasons connected with partisanship, class, and (in perhaps a surprising manner) age. This finding in turn raised some fundamental questions about citizen attitudes in the United States: Do we, as a nation, wish our political leaders to be subject to the rule of law in the same way as presumably are other citizens, or do we feel implicitly that these leaders should somehow be above the law?

THE QUESTIONNAIRE

The questionnaire, a brief one, was divided into three parts. The first series of questions attempted to ascertain the degree of guilt the respondents attributed to President Nixon in the Watergate matter, the second series to discover the action (if any) the respondents felt should be taken against him, and the remainder dealt with other, mostly independent, variables which we would attempt to relate to the above responses.

Degree of Guilt

The first variable, degree of guilt, was measured by a series of three questions: (1) "Do you believe President Nixon knew in advance about plans to break into the Democratic headquarters at Watergate?" (2) "Do you believe he later participated knowingly in a cover-up?" (3) "Do you believe he was too lax in supervising the reelection campaign?" The interviewers were instructed to proceed from the first to the second or from the second to the third question only upon receiving a negative or noncommittal response. As soon as any positive response was received, this line of questioning was terminated. The rationale was that if the respondent attributed to the president a larger degree of culpability (e.g., knowing in advance about the planned break-in), then it was immaterial whether he or she believed the president to be guilty of a lesser offense (e.g., participating in the cover-up).

Degree of Punishment

A parallel set of three questions was asked next: (1) "Do you feel that President Nixon should be impeached and removed from office?" (2) "Do you feel he should resign voluntarily?" (3) "Do you feel he should be censured by a vote of Congress?" Again the interviewers were instructed to terminate the line of questioning with the first positive response, in order to ascertain only the most severe punishment the respondent would advocate.

Other Variables

The remaining questions inquired about the respondent's rating of President Nixon's job performance, whether and how the respondent had voted in the 1972 presidential election, and how the respondent would vote if that election were to be held today. In addition, the interviewer recorded the respondent's sex, approximate age (within three broad ranges: their twenties; thirties or forties; and fifties or older), and the apparent economic level of the respondent's neighborhood (poor, middle class, or affluent).

Due to limitations on time and other resources, it was not possible to draw a random sample of the metropolitan area, but the door-to-door interviews were to an extent stratified with respect to income, with 82 interviews (7.3 percent) conducted in poor neighborhoods, 738 (65.9 percent) in middle-class ones, and 107 (9.6 percent) in wealthier neighborhoods—and with an additional 193 (17.2 percent) interviews or questionnaire administrations coming from university students.

It was the large number of interviews (1120) more than the basis of the sample selection which led us to believe that our results would be comparable to those of the professional national polling organizations—an assumption which, as will be seen, proved correct.

Of the respondents, 61.3 percent were female—a preponderance probably due to the considerable amount of daytime interviewing which was done. As to age, 39.4 percent were estimated to be in their twenties, 35.7 percent were in their thirties or forties, and 24.9 percent were in their fifties or older.

FINDINGS

We found that 40.4 percent of the respondents believed that the president knew in advance about the Watergate break-in, and an additional 28.2 percent believed that he participated knowingly in a cover-up. We found that 18.4 percent believed that President Nixon's only failure along these lines was a lax supervision of the reelection campaign (a charge to which he had himself pleaded guilty), and 13.0 percent did not believe him guilty on any of these counts. The first two findings are quite comparable to those of the Gallup Poll in early September—when 39 percent believed Nixon planned or knew about the bugging, and 33 percent felt that he tried to cover it up.[1]

When questioned about the appropriate punishment (if any), 20.9 percent of the respondents said he should be impeached, 15.7 percent believed he should resign voluntarily, 18.7 percent advocated censure by Congress,[2] and a large minority of 44.7 percent opposed all of the above measures. These results are again similar to findings of the national surveys in September—prior, as were Gallup's, to the firing of Special Prosecutor Cox and to the announcement of the missing tapes and erasure.

Thus we found what other surveys had found—that two-thirds and more of those interviewed believed the president to be seriously culpable in the Watergate affair, but that only about one-third of the entire sample wanted him punished in a way that would interrupt his tenure in office.

TABLE 1

Cross-tabulation: Degree of Guilt Imputed to President,
and Degree of Punishment Advocated
(Number of respondents in parentheses)

Degree of Punishment	Degree of Guilt									
	Knew in Advance		Participated in Cover-up		Lax Supervision		None		Total	
Impeachment	16.9%	(189)	3.5%	(39)	0.1%	(2)	0.3%	(4)	20.9%	(234)
Resignation	9.8	(110)	5.4	(60)	0.4	(5)	0.1	(1)	15.7	(176)
Censure	5.9	(66)	7.9	(88)	4.2	(47)	0.6	(7)	18.7	(208)
None	7.8	(87)	11.5	(129)	13.6	(152)	12.0	(134)	44.7	(502)
TOTAL	40.4	(452)	28.2	(316)	18.4	(206)	13.0	(146)	100	(1,120)

To study this interesting relationship between guilt imputed to the president, the punishment advocated, we can turn to a cross-tabulation of the two variables (see Table 1). It may be an aid to analysis at this point if we further aggregate the guilt variable responses into *serious guilt,* including the responses "knew in advance" and "participated in cover-up"; and *light or none,* including the responses "lax supervision" and "none." And we can similarly chunk the punishment variable into *severe,* including "impeachment" and "resignation"; and *light or none* including "censure" and "none" (see Table 2).[3]

TABLE 2

Modified Cross-tabulation: Degree of Guilt with Degree of Punishment
(Number of respondents in parentheses)

Degree of Punishment	Degree of Guilt					
	Serious		Light or None		Total	
Severe	35.5%	(398)	1.1%	(12)	36.6%	(410)
Light or None	33.0	(370)	30.4	(340)	63.4	(710)
TOTAL	68.6	(768)	31.4	(352)	100	(1,120)

The interaction of the two variables will now be clear. Aside from the 1 percent who found Mr. Nixon relatively blameless in Watergate, but still impeachable—presumably on other grounds—the respondents are divided into three approximately equal categories: 35.5 percent believed Mr. Nixon was seriously guilty and should be severely punished; 30.4 percent thought he was not seriously guilty and thus should not be severely punished; and 33.0 percent—almost exactly one-third —believed Mr. Nixon was indeed guilty but did not want to see him seriously punished.

It is this final group which made possible the finding last September (in the major polls) that a great majority of Americans found their president guilty of serious involvement in Watergate, but that a great majority also did not want that president to leave office. And it is this group which was a principal focus of our study. Why did this very sizable group of people—not a majority, but a significant minority— wish their president to go virtually unpunished for those offenses of which they considered him guilty? Why, in other words, would they allow him to be above the law?

POSSIBLE INTERPRETATIONS

There are, of course, many reasons why Americans might be opposed to President Nixon's departure from office, and we heard some of them in the course of the interviews, such as: "He's innocent of serious involvement," or "The evidence isn't conclusive." But the respondents in the final category did not argue in either of these ways; they had concluded that he was indeed guilty of serious involvement. Another line of reasoning ran: "He's guilty in *my* opinion, but a case can't stand up in court." This might (or might not) preclude impeachment and conviction, but would not bar resignation—which these respondents also failed to advocate. Still another group argued that: "He's guilty, but all politicians are crooks," or "He's done a good job in general," or "Anything to keep the McGovernites out," or, conversely, "Why let the GOP off so easily?" While such lines of argument were clearly suasive for some, it is to be noted that their common denominator is cynicism, or the willingness to subordinate, in one way or another, the rule of law to partisan consideration. Finally, some argued along only slightly different lines: "Impeachment is too frightening; Americans aren't ready for it," or "The whole system might fall apart." These apparent *raisons d'état,* however accurate in describing the individual respondent's view, are, when projected upon the nation as a whole, either another and perhaps deeper form of cynicism, or an expression of fear and insecurity.

We were not able to interview respondents in depth about their reasoning (or rationalizations). But we were able, by comparing their responses with other items recorded, to rule out some possibilities and to come up with some perhaps less obvious clues as to why many were willing to retain in office a president whom they considered seriously guilty.

Our method was first to divide respondents into three categories: (1) those who considered Mr. Nixon seriously guilty, and who wanted him to leave office ("Guilty-Yes/Remove-Yes"); (2) those who considered him innocent of serious wrongdoing, and who wanted him to remain in office ("Guilty-No/Remove-No"); and (3) those who considered him seriously guilty, but still wanted him to remain in office ("Guilty-Yes/Remove No"). We excluded from further consideration the 1 percent who wanted him to leave office, although believing him innocent of Watergate-related misconduct. Then we cross-tabulated these three categories with the remaining variables to see what significant patterns would emerge.

Job Rating

The total sample rated Mr. Nixon's performance of his overall job as follows: excellent, 9 percent; good, 30 percent; fair, 36 percent; poor, 25 percent (see Table 3). These findings again are comparable

TABLE 3

Guilt/Removal Cross-tabulation with Presidential Job Rating
(Number of respondents in parentheses)

Job Rating	Guilt/Removal							
	Guilty-Yes/ Remove-Yes		Guilty-No/ Remove-No		Guilty-Yes/ Remove-No		Total	
Excellent	1%	(2)	24%	(80)	5%	(18)	9%	(100)
Good	4	(17)	53	(181)	34	(127)	30	(325)
Fair	41	(163)	19	(65)	47	(173)	36	(401)
Poor	54	(216)	4	(13)	14	(50)	25	(279)
TOTAL	100	(398)	100	(339)	100	(368)	100	(1,105)

$$x^2 = 451.53$$
$$\text{signif.} = .001$$

to those of Gallup in September (with 35 percent approving and 55 percent disapproving).[4] But it will be clear that the most unfavorable evaluation comes from those respondents who want Mr. Nixon to leave office (95 percent disapproval), while the only high approval comes from those who believe Mr. Nixon not guilty (77 percent approval). And the "Guilty-Yes/Remove-No" group is in between, with 39 percent approving and 61 percent disapproving—statistics exactly paralleling the overall sample figures (although only 5 percent of this group rate his performance as "excellent," as against 9 percent overall). Thus it would appear that while one's assessment of Mr. Nixon's total performance does correlate with one's opinion about his guilt and removal from office, the willingness of the "Guilty-Yes/Remove-No" group to overlook the guilt they attribute to Mr. Nixon is *not* based upon an especially favorable evaluation of his performance in office. Among only those who believe him guilty, however, the less favorable their evaluation of his performance, the more likely they are to call for removal.

The 1972 Vote

In 1972 the voters in the overall sample had cast their ballots for Richard Nixon by a margin of two-to-one (see Table 4). Among those

TABLE 4

Guilt/Removal Cross-tabulated with 1972 Presidential Vote*
(Number of respondents in parentheses)

1972 Vote	Guilt/Removal						
	Guilty-Yes/ Remove-Yes		Guilty-No/ Remove-No		Guilty-Yes/ Remove-No		Total
Nixon	35%	(106)	92%	(254)	73%	(207)	66% (567)
Other	65	(194)	8	(22)	27	(75)	34 (291)
TOTAL	100	(300)	100	(276)	100	(282)	100 (858)

*Nonvoters excluded. $x^2 = 216.23$
                        signif. $= .001$

who now wish Mr. Nixon to leave the presidency, this ratio was almost exactly reversed. The ranks of those who find him innocent of serious wrongdoing are drawn almost exclusively (92 percent) from among those who had voted for him—only twenty-two in the entire sample voted for another candidate in 1972 and now consider Mr. Nixon innocent. Finally, the "Guilty-Yes/Remove-No" respondents had voted for the incumbent by a three-to-one margin as compared to the ten-to-one of the "Guilty-No/Remove-No" and the almost two-to-one against Nixon of the "Guilty-Yes/Remove-Yes." Apparently, then, the way the respondents had voted in 1972 is a better clue to their present opinion than is their assessment of the president's performance since 1972.

The 1973 Vote

It may be of general interest to note that if the election had been held in 1973 rather than in 1972, despite their general belief that Richard Nixon was guilty in Watergate, our respondents would have returned him to office (albeit without a majority) over George McGovern or any other suggested candidate (see Table 5).

Again, the correlation of partisanship with one's beliefs about Watergate and impeachment is clear—although it is impossible in this case even to begin to separate cause from effect. Those who want Mr. Nixon

TABLE 5

Guilt/Removal Cross-tabulated with Presidential Vote If Held Today
(Number of respondents in parentheses)

1973 Vote	Guilt/Removal						
	Guilty-Yes/ Remove-Yes		Guilty-No/ Remove-No		Guilty-Yes/ Remove-No		Total	
Nixon	5%	(18)	82%	(237)	43%	(137)	40%	(392)
McGovern	42	(158)	5	(14)	23	(74)	25	(246)
Other	53	(203)	13	(37)	34	(111)	35	(351)
TOTAL	100	(379)	100	(288)	100	(322)	100	(989)

$$x^2 = 415.76$$
signif. = .001

to be impeached or to resign would contribute strongly to both the McGovern vote (64 percent) and the vote for other candidate(s) (58 percent)—with a larger number, interestingly, preferring another candidate. Those who consider Mr. Nixon innocent give him a huge majority (82 percent) of their vote. And those who find Mr. Nixon guilty, but want him to stay on the job, give Nixon a plurality, although still quite short of a majority of their total votes.

Sex and Age

Sex proved not to be a significant variable. Approximately one-third of each category was male and two-thirds female, in line with the makeup of our total sample.

The age variable in some cases caused a surprising result (see Table 6). Those who want the president to be removed from office are drawn

TABLE 6

Guilt/Removal Cross-tabulated with Age

(Number of respondents in parentheses)

Guilt-Remove	Age			
	Younger (20s or under)	Middle-Aged (30s, 40s)	Older (50s, over)	Total
Guilty-Yes/Remove-Yes	43% (176)	33% (124)	25% (65)	35% (365)
Guilty-No/Remove-No	18 (74)	35 (129)	50 (128)	32 (331)
Guilty-Yes/Remove-No	39 (160)	32 (119)	25 (65)	33 (344)
TOTAL	100 (410)	100 (372)	100 (258)	100 (1,040)

$$x^2 = 74.25$$
$$\text{signif.} = .001$$

disproportionately from the young (43 percent of the young vs. 33 percent of the middle-aged and 25 percent of the older respondents). This is not surprising, as younger citizens are known to be unfriendly to the Nixon administration and thought to be more insistent on high standards of public probity in their officialdom. But among those who believe the president guilty, the size of the "Guilty-Yes/Remove-No" category is not significantly larger among the young than among the other age groups, making something of a hash of the accepted wisdom about youth's high moral standards. Put another way, of those young people who find Mr. Nixon guilty, only a slight majority (176 to 160) wish him to leave office. A similarly close majority of the middle-aged group would concur (124 to 119) while the older respondents who perceived Mr. Nixon guilty would split evenly (65 to 65) on the matter of his removal. The significant finding about the older respondents, however, is that they do *not,* except by the barest majority, find Mr. Nixon guilty—50 percent of them show up in the "Guilty-No/Remove-No" group, far out of proportion to that group's share of the total. The middle-aged respondents, by way of contrast, contribute to each of the three groups in close harmony with the totals.

Economic Status

When we took into account the economic level of the neighborhood in which the respondent was interviewed, it proved that each of the three economic levels had a distinctive response pattern (see Table 7). The poorer neighborhoods' respondents fell overwhelmingly (82 percent) into the "Guilty-Yes/Remove-Yes" bracket; those from wealthier neighborhoods went quite strongly (60 percent) into the "Guilty-No/

TABLE 7

Guilt/Removal Cross-tabulated with Economic Status of Neighborhood
(Number of respondents in parentheses)

	Economic Status						
Guilt-Removal	Poorer		Middle Class		Wealthier		Total
Guilty-Yes/Remove-Yes	82%	(65)	34%	(250)	20%	(21)	37% (336)
Guilty-No/Remove-No	1	(1)	33	(239)	60	(61)	33 (301)
Guilty-Yes/Remove-No	17	(13)	33	(245)	20	(21)	30 (279)
TOTAL	100	(79)	100	(734)	100	(103)	100 (916)

$$x^2 = 110.05$$
$$signif. = .001$$

Remove-No" category; and the large number of respondents from middle-class neighborhoods were divided almost equally among the three categories.

SUMMARY AND CONCLUSIONS

Returning to our original question, then, of why a president perceived by most of his constituents as guilty of serious misconduct also had broad popular support for staying in office, we can now list the following clues: (1) It is not because he is thought by those surveyed to have a good overall record in office; only that minority which considers him innocent gives him a favorable job rating. (2) The partisanship of 1972 plays a role; very few of those who voted for him in 1972 now want him removed. (3) This partisanship of 1972 would have been reaffirmed (if less convincingly) in the fall of 1973, more than a year after Watergate: again, only those who want Mr. Nixon to leave office would fail to give him at least a plurality of votes. (4) Many older people refuse to see Mr. Nixon as culpable; the vast majority of younger people take the opposite view, but split almost evenly on his removal from office. (5) The more affluent find him innocent; the poor want him out of office; and the broad middle class, while far from unified in its opinions, shows a noticeable willingness to retain in office a president it perceives as guilty.

Perhaps the clearest conclusion to emerge from the survey is that the process of public-opinion formation on Watergate and Mr. Nixon's role therein has been highly political. Perceptions and judgments on his guilt or innocence, removal from or retention in office, depend largely on one's partisanship, age, and economic circumstance. Public opinion on Watergate is not operating as a dispassionate judge or jury, but as a sounding board for a myriad of hopes, fears, and grievances which frequently have little or nothing to do with the facts of the case.

A second conclusion is that it was a significant minority—about one-third of those questioned—who believed the president was guilty, but still wished him to remain in office. This particular group, aside from being disproportionately young or middle-aged and a bit disproportionately middle class, seems undistinguishable from other respondents with more consistent viewpoints. Since the time of our interviews there has, it is true, been a drift in public sentiment in the directions of attribution of guilt and advocacy of impeachment. But the differential between the percentage who think Mr. Nixon guilty of impeachable offenses and the percentage who advocate impeachment or resignation still consists of approximately one-third of those interviewed in the national polls. Gallup reported in March 1974 that a total of 74 percent of respondents considered Mr. Nixon guilty of planning the Watergate break-in (11 percent), knowing about it in advance (28 percent), or covering it up (34 percent). He also reported that a total of 43 percent of all respondents favored either impeachment or resignation.[5]

Finally, it seems to this observer that the survey data point to a new, or at least newly formalized cynicism or fearfulness in the American body politic. It is, to be sure, part of popular political wisdom in this country that politicians are crooks, and that they rank near used-car salesmen in trustworthiness. But beneath this sometimes jocular understanding there was a conviction that the *system* somehow worked, somehow rose above the venalities and stupidities of the politicians who staffed it. In the wake of Watergate, it is this latter belief which seems to have vanished, or at least to have fallen on hard times. Many who think Mr. Nixon guilty of what the writers of the Constitution might have called "high crimes and misdemeanors," also find the sole constitutional remedy of impeachment inapplicable because it would not improve things, or undesirable because it is too frightening. The system, they seem to be saying, cannot work as designed in our present situation— or they might say that whether it would "work" or not is quite irrelevant. . . .

NOTES

1. *New York Times,* September 23, 1973.

2. There may have been a tendency for respondents to avoid advocating this, simply because they were unfamiliar with the word "censure." Interviewers were instructed to explain that the term implied Congress would express disapproval of the president's actions, without removing him from office.

3. It is, of course, not meant to imply that congressional censure is a mild measure — only that it is much less serious than impeachment.

4. *New York Times,* September 23, 1973.

5. *Gallup Opinion Index,* No. 105, March 1974, pp. 4-5.

Part Two

The State of the Presidency
as an Institution

6 The Imperial Presidency

"R" of Encounter Magazine

During the presidency of John F. Kennedy many Americans liked the sense of style and regal elegance which the Kennedys brought to the White House. In light of the behavior of later presidents who often acted more like kings than elected public servants, some observers are having second thoughts about the rhetoric and manner of the New Frontier. They see in it the origins of an imperial presidency that treats the White House as a court, the citizenry as subjects, and the world as an empire. In this essay (which first appeared in a British journal) the author explores the ideas of Henry Fairlie who wrote in The Kennedy Promise *that Kennedy rhetoric put too much emphasis on moral leadership that would have been better left to religious institutions. Historian Arthur Schlesinger, Jr., has called Watergate a culmination rather than an aberration. The essays in this section elaborate on that theme.*

The question, I think, which Americans, and others who, despite Watergate, continue to believe that the United States still represents the last, best hope of mankind, should ask themselves is: how was it possible for Watergate to have occurred at all? For the answer, I think, should show that Watergate is a consequence, not of President Nixon's personal weaknesses, though these are considerable, nor of those of his staff, nor of anything peculiar to the Republican party or a Republican administration, nor even the taint of corruption which, if we are to believe President Nixon, clings to American politics as a whole.

Anyone looking for an answer to that question could not do better than to turn to Henry Fairlie's book, *The Kennedy Promise: The Politics of Expectation* (New York, Doubleday; London, Eyre Methuen). It has not had a very good press in this country [England] but it has been much praised in the United States; and it throws more light,

Reprinted with permission from *Encounter,* July, 1973, pp. 44-46, where it appeared as "Column." Copyright © 1973.

"R" is the author of "Column," a frequent feature in *Encounter.*

I think, on some of the implications of Watergate than anything else which is available at the present time (unless perhaps we return once again to Tocquevile and Lord Bryce—do foreigners sometimes see things about the United States which Americans, who take them for granted, fail to notice?).

Mr. Fairlie's thesis, which he expounds with great elegance and persuasiveness, is that President John F. Kennedy introduced into the United States an essentially personal style of government which has been imitated and continued by his successors, whether Democratic or Republican. It was a style which rested on three propositions which, taken together, form a theory of government which is not easy to reconcile with the constitution of the United States as it has been traditionally interpreted.

The first proposition is that the President is authorized, and indeed has the duty, to use all the powers which are not specifically denied him by the Constitution, and indeed, it would appear, some that are, like the power to make war and peace. One does not have to be a "strict constructionist" of the Constitution to believe that so sweeping a claim, even though it has deep roots in the Democratic Party, is at variance if not with the letter at least with the spirit of the Constitution.

The second claim was that, by the fact of his election, the President became the direct and personal representative of the hopes and aspirations of all the people of the United States. This was true even if, as in the case of President Kennedy, he was elected by only a minuscule majority of the popular vote. Presidential election confers a mystical authority comparable to that which was conveyed by the ceremonial oil traditionally poured on the head of a Holy Roman Emperor . The President represents the People in a way which no other element of the constitution does and as such his powers are literally inexhaustible.

But the third claim was even wider and more universal. The President of the United States is not merely the electorally anointed head of the American people; as the leader of the "free world" he also represents all those people throughout the world who are denied the right to life, liberty, and the pursuit of happiness which is guaranteed by the American constitution, of which the President is the personal embodiment in every quarter of the globe.

It would not be difficult, and Mr. Fairlie does not find it difficult, to discover in the speeches of President Kennedy repeated assertions of all three of these claims. They constituted the background against which he exercised his own highly personal style of political leadership, and the fact that he did this with considerable charm and panache should not blind one to their dubious legitimacy. By what right, for instance, did President Kennedy proclaim, at the Berlin Wall, *Ich bin ein Berliner!* I am a Berliner! No one was ever less like a Berliner, he was not a native of Berlin, however high his momentary popularity may have been. In fact, as President of the United States he had elected himself to be the personal representative of the great, sad and divided Prussian city on the Spree and he implicitly claimed the right to do the same in any area of the world where democracy might be thought to be in danger, in particular in Viet Nam.

No more universal claim has been made by any emperor, Roman, Byzantine, or Russian. By comparison, the claims of a British King-Emperor (or Queen-Empress) who in fact, though only through responsible ministers, exercised effective dominion over a quarter of the globe, seem almost absurdly modest. There are passages in some speeches of the last three American Presidents which have reminiscences of old promises of world domination:

> *Heute gehort uns Deutschland,*
> *Und morgen die ganze Welt.*
> (Today Germany, Tomorrow the world.)

Sometimes one wonders why President Kennedy did not proclaim Washington the Fourth Rome. Indeed, he came very near to doing so —and a New Athens as well.

A new Rome in fact is what Washington has become. The imperial theme has been repeatedly annouced, and it was impossible not to notice that President Nixon, in his television address to the American nation, even as he apologized, and asumed responsibility for, the most squalid of political manoeuvres, still had the self-confidence to claim that, as leader of the "free world" and in view of the crushing responsibility he bore in that capacity, he should be excused for his failure to notice what was going on in his own back-yard. Imperial power, however, has sad consequences for those who exercise it, and those on whom it is exercised. Emperors need lackeys and eunuchs, kings need courtiers. The essential quality of such servitors is that they exercise power for no other reason than the grace and favour of their master, represent no one and nothing except the will of the reining monarch, and have no fount of authority or legitimacy except the man whom they serve.

It is with such men that President Nixon surrounded himself, but the striking decline that has taken place in certain qualities of the President's advisers since the days of Mr. Kennedy should not conceal the fact that there has been no essential difference in the function they have been asked to perform under any of the last three Presidents, which was to serve the wishes of the President rather than the needs of the nation. In each case, they were drawn from men who had no independent political position, represented no independent political interest, and enjoyed no political authority except through the trust and confidence of the President. Even now, Mr. Nixon seems half-inclined to forgive his subordinates, whatever their misdeeds, because, after all, they were primarily motivated by loyalty to him and Mr. Nixon equates this with loyalty to the nation. It is a mistake which many monarchs have made about many indispensable favorites, and in Washington the result has been the same as at many other courts: the sacrifice of the favourite when it is necessary to preserve the monarch.

CHANGES SINCE ROOSEVELT

In his effort to explain what he believes to be the profound change which has taken place in the character of the American Presidency in recent years, Henry Fairlie very effectively contrasts the way in which the last three presidents have conducted themselves in office with the demeanour of the most formidable of all modern presidents, Franklin Roosevelt. No one could ever have accused Mr. Roosevelt of being a strict constructionist in his view of the constitution of the United States; and, on occasion, he played fast and loose with it and got into serious trouble as a result. Yet, while always believing that the constitution gave the President every power he could require in order to safeguard the wealth, health, and happiness of the United States he also had a very strong sense of the real as well as the formal limitations of the powers of the President. He took care to surround himself with men who, either because of the political interests they represented, or because of their own personal merits and abilities, were able, in serving him, to exercise genuinely independent judgment. As a result he received much conflicting advice, and indeed he seemed positively to enjoy, and to exacerbate, the disagreements which sometimes arose both between individual members of his staff and between his staff and himself. Moreover, he followed the same highly idiosyncratic procedure in his appointments to his cabinet and to the great departments of state. He liked to appoint stubborn and opinionated men who were willing and able to defend established and entrenched positions and were not willing to give them up without good and compelling interests. Consensus was the last thing which he aimed at, whereas consensus, however achieved, has become an almost obsessive interest of more recent presidents.

The results of the continuous process of discussion and debate did not always favour efficiency in government. Sometimes Roosevelt's successive administrations seemed to relapse into a state of open civil war, and there was always something of the atmosphere, not always good-natured, of a bear garden about them. Under Mr. Roosevelt, indeed, consensus was as often lacking as not. Yet his methods of government, confused and bewildering as they often were, ensured that Presidential decisions were made in full awareness of all the long-term, as well as the short-term, interests and opinions which were involved; and they were so far successful that, under Mr. Roosevelt, the United States survived the two greatest crises, in peace and in war, which it has ever faced. A part at least of this success was due to Mr. Roosevelt's gift in choosing colleagues and collaborators who did not find a difficulty in reconciling loyalty to a President with loyalty to the United States as a whole.

Mr. Fairlie quotes an exclamation by Louis Howe, than whom no President ever had a more loyal and devoted servant, on receiving a note from the President: "Tell the President to go to Hell." One somehow doubts that anyone ever thought of talking like that to President Kennedy or President Johnson or President Nixon, and one has the feeling that if they did, they would not have lasted for long. One can talk to Presidents like that, but not to monarchs, hedged round as they are by divinity.

There can be no greater contrast than that between the accounts we have of Mr. Roosevelt's methods of government, which at times created a positive Bedlam of conflicting judgments, and the image of President Nixon, withdrawn and aloof in the White House, access to him rigidly controlled by his staff, and almost entirely insulated from hostile criticism, even when that is meant to assist him. It is the difference between a president and a king; it is also the difference between a situation in which Watergate would have been an impossibility and one in which it, or something like it, is inevitable.

It may well be that, as one might hope, in the end the results of Watergate will not be wholly for the bad. If they are not, it will be because Watergate will have directed men's minds, not so much to the squalid details of the affair and to the personalities involved, as to the dangers inherent in the immense growth of presidential power in the United States in recent years and, even more perhaps, to the particular form it has assumed and the evils which must necessarily accompany it.

7 | The Swelling of the Presidency

Thomas E. Cronin

Focusing on substance rather than style, Cronin sees the problem of the presidency as physical growth in the presidential establishment. The White House staff has increased along with White House powers, and Cronin explains what consequences this has had on the operations of the government. He suggests that these phenomena have multiple causes, including the emergencies stemming from the Depression of the 1930s, World War II, and the Cold War; the greater number of interdepartmental programs needing coordination; and the willingness of Congress to tolerate expansion of the presidential domain. The author finishes with some suggestions about how to make the presidency more manageable.

The presidency has, in fact, grown a full 20 per cent [since 1969] in terms of the number of people who are employed directly under the President. It has swelled to the point where it is now only a little short of the State Department's sprawling domestic bureaucracy in size.

This burgeoning growth of the presidency has, in the process, made the traditional civics textbook picture of the excutive branch of our government nearly obsolete. According to this view, the executive branch is more or less neatly divided into Cabinet departments and their secretaries, agencies and their heads, and the President. A more contemporary view takes note of a few prominent presidential aides and refers to them as the "White House staff." But neither view adequately recognizes the large and growing coterie that surrounds the President and is made up of dozens of assistants, hundreds of presidential advisers, and thousands of members of an institutional amalgam

Reprinted with permission of the author from *Saturday Review of The Society,* February, 1973, pp. 30-36. Copyright © 1973.

Thomas E. Cronin is author of *The State of the Presidency* and co-author of *The Presidency Reappraised.* His most recent affiliations have been with the Aspen Institute for Humanistic Studies and the Center for the Study of Democratic Institutions.

called the Executive Office of the President. While the men and women in these categories all fall directly under the President in the organizational charts, there is no generally used term for their common terrain. But it has swelled so much in size and scope in recent years, and has become such an important part of the federal government, that it deserves its own designation. Most apt perhaps is the Presidential Establishment.

The Presidential Establishment today embraces more than twenty support staffs (the White House Office, National Security Council, and Office of Management and Budget, etc.) and advisory offices (Council of Economic Advisers . . .) It has spawned a vast proliferation of ranks and titles to go with its proliferation of functions (Counsel to the President, Assistant to the President, Special Counselor, Special Assistant, Special Consultant, Director, Staff Director, etc.). "The White House now has enough people with fancy titles to populate a Gilbert and Sullivan comic opera," Congressman Morris Udall has reasonably enough observed.

There are no official figures on the size of the Presidential Establishment, and standard body counts vary widely depending on who is and who is not included in the count, but by one frequently used reckoning, between five and six thousand people work for the President of the United States. Payroll and maintenance costs for this staff run between $100 million and $150 million a year. . . .

LONG HISTORY OF GROWTH

The expansion of the Presidential Establishment, it should be emphasized, is by no means only a phenomenon of the Nixon years. The number of employees under the President has been growing steadily since the early 1900s, when only a few dozen people served in the White House entourage, at a cost of less than a few hundred thousand dollars annually. Congress's research arm, the Congressional Research Service, has compiled a count that underlines in particular the accelerated increase in the last two decades. This compilation shows that between 1954 and 1971 the number of presidential advisers has grown from 25 to 45, the White House staff from 266 to 600, and the Executive Office staff from 1,175 to 5,395.

But if the growth of the Presidential Establishment antedates the current administration, it is curious at least that one of the largest expansions ever, in both relative and absolute terms, has taken place during the first term of a conservative, management-minded President who has often voiced his objection to any expansion of the federal government and its bureaucracy.

Under President Nixon, in fact, there has been an almost systematic bureaucratization of the Presidential Establishment, in which more new councils and offices have been established, more specialization and division of labor and layers of staffing have been added, than at any time except during World War II. Among the major Nixonian additions are the Council on Environmental Quality, Council on International Economic Policy, Domestic Council, and Office of Consumer Affairs. . . .

. . . Perhaps the most disturbing aspect of the expansion of the Presidential Establishment is that it has become a powerful inner sanctum of government, isolated from traditional, constitutional checks and balances. It is common practice today for anonymous, unelected, unratified aides to negotiate sensitive international commitments by means of executive agreements that are free from congressional oversight. Other aides in the Presidential Establishment wield fiscal authority over billions of dollars in funds that Congress has appropriated, yet the President refuses to spend, or that Congress has assigned to one purpose and the administration routinely redirects to another—all with no semblance of public scrutiny. Such exercises of power pose an important, perhaps vital, question of governmental philosophy: Should a political system that has made a virtue of periodic electoral accountability accord an ever-increasing policy-making role to White House counselors who neither are confirmed by the U.S. Senate nor, because of the doctrine of "executive privilege," are subject to questioning by Congress?

Another disquieting aspect of the growth of the Presidential Establishment is that the increase of its powers has been largely at the expense of the traditional sources of executive power and policy-making —the Cabinet members and their departments. When I asked a former Kennedy-Johnson Cabinet member a while ago what he would like to do if he ever returned to government, he said he would rather be a presidential assistant than a Cabinet member. And this is an increasingly familiar assessment of the relative influence of the two levels of the executive branch. The Presidential Establishment has become, in effect, a whole layer of government between the President and the Cabinet, and it often stands above the Cabinet in terms of influence with the President. In spite of the exalted position that Cabinet members hold in textbooks and protocol, a number of Cabinet members in recent administrations have complained that they could not even get the President's ear except through an assistant. In his book *Who Owns America?,* former Secretary of the Interior Walter Hickel recounts his combat with a dozen different presidential functionaries and tells how he needed clearance from them before he could get to talk to the

President, or how he frequently had to deal with the assistants themselves because the President was "too busy." During an earlier administration, President Eisenhower's chief assistant, Sherman Adams, was said to have told two Cabinet members who could not resolve a matter of mutual concern: "Either make up your mind or else tell me and I will do it. We must not bother the President with this. He is trying to keep the world from war." Several of President Kennedy's Cabinet members regularly battled with White House aides who blocked them from seeing the President. And McGeorge Bundy, as Kennedy's chief assistant for national security affairs, simply sidestepped the State Department in one major area of department communications. He had all important incoming State Department cables transmitted simultaneously to his office in the White House, part of an absorption of traditional State Department functions that visibly continues to this day. . . .

LOWERING OF CABINET STATUS

In a speech in 1971, Senator Ernest Hollings of South Carolina plaintively noted the lowering of Cabinet status. "It used to be," he said, "that if I had a problem with food stamps, I went to see the Secretary of Agriculture, whose department had jurisdiction over that problem. Not anymore. Now, if I want to learn the policy, I must go to the White House to consult John Price [a special assistant]. If I want the latest on textiles, I won't get it from the Secretary of Commerce, who has the authority and responsibility. No, I am forced to go to the White House and see Mr. Peter Flanigan. I shouldn't feel too badly. Secretary Stans [Maurice Stans, then Secretary of Commerce] has to do the same thing."

If Cabinet members individually have been downgraded in influence, the Cabinet itself as a council of government has become somewhat of a relic, replaced by more specialized comminglings that as often as not are presided over by the White House staffers. The Cabinet's decline has taken place over several administrations. John Kennedy started out his term declaring his intentions of using the Cabinet as a major policy-making body, but his change of mind was swift, as his Postmaster General, J. Edward Day, has noted. "After the first two or three meetings," Day has written, "one had the distinct impression that the President felt that decisions on major matters were not made— or even influenced—at Cabinet sessions, and that discussion there was a waste of time. . . . When members spoke up to suggest or to discuss major administration policy, the President would listen with thinly disguised impatience and then postpone or otherwise bypass the question."

Lyndon Johnson was equally disenchanted with the Cabinet as a body and characteristically held Cabinet sessions only when articles appeared in the press talking about how the Cabinet was withering away. Under Nixon, the Cabinet is almost never convened at all.

Not only has the Presidential Establishment taken over many policy-making functions from the Cabinet and its members, it has also absorbed some of the operational functions. White House aides often feel they should handle any matters that they regard as ineptly administered, and they tend to intervene in internal departmental operations at lower and lower levels. They often feel underemployed, too, and so are inclined to reach out into the departments to find work and exercise authority for themselves.

The result is a continuous undercutting of Cabinet departments— and the cost is heavy. These intrusions can cripple the capacity of Cabinet officials to present policy alternatives, and they diminish self-confidence, morale, and initiative within the departments. George Ball, a former undersecretary of state, noted the effects on the State Department: "Able men, with proper pride in their professional skills, will not long tolerate such votes of no-confidence, so it should be no surprise that they are leaving the career service, and making way for mediocrity with the result that, as time goes on it may be hopelessly difficult to restore the Department. . . ."

The irony of this accretion of numbers and functions to the Presidential Establishment is that the presidency is finding itself increasingly afflicted with the very ills of the traditional departments that the expansions were often intended to remedy. The presidency has become a large, complex bureaucracy itself, rapidly acquiring many dubious characteristics of large bureaucracies in the process: layering, over-specialization, communication gaps, interoffice rivalries, inadequate coordination, and an impulse to become consumed with short-term, urgent operational concerns at the expense of thinking systematically about the consequences of varying sets of policies and priorities and about important long-range problems. It takes so much of the President's time to deal with the members of his own bureaucracy that it is little wonder he has little time to hear counsel from Cabinet officials.

Another toll of the burgeoning Presidential Establishment is that White House aides, in assuming more and more responsibility for the management of government programs, inevitably lose the detachment and objectivity that is so essential for evaluating new ideas. Can a lieutenant vigorously engaged in implementing the presidential will admit the possibility that what the President wants is wrong or not working? Yet a President is increasingly dependent on the judgment of these same staff members, since he seldom sees his Cabinet members.

CAUSES OF SWELLING PRESIDENCY

Why has the presidency grown bigger and bigger? There is no single villain or systematically organized conspiracy promoting this expansion. A variety of factors is at work. The most significant is the expansion of the role of the presidency itself—an expansion that for the most part has taken place during national emergencies. The reason for this is that the public and Congress in recent decades have both tended to look to the President for the decisive responses that were needed in those emergencies. The Great Depression and World War II in particular brought sizable increases in presidential staffs. And once in place, many stayed on, even after the emergencies that brought them had faded. Smaller national crises have occasioned expansion in the White House entourage, too. After the Russians successfully orbited *Sputnik* in 1957, President Eisenhower added several science advisers. After the Bay of Pigs, President Kennedy enlarged his national security staff.

Considerable growth in the Presidential Establishment, especially in the post-World War II years, stems directly from the belief that critical societal problems require that wise men be assigned to the White House to alert the President to appropriate solutions and to serve as the agents for implementings these solutions. Congress has frequently acted on the basis of this belief, legislating the creation of the National Security Council, the Council of Economic Advisers, and the Council on Environmental Quality, among others. Congress has also increased the chores of the presidency by making it a statutory responsibility for the President to prepare more and more reports associated with what are regarded as critical social areas—annual economic and manpower reports, a biennial report on national growth, etc.

Most recently, President Nixon responded to a number of troublesome problems that defy easy relegation to any one department—problems like international trade and drug abuse—by setting up special offices in the Executive Office with sweeping authority and sizable staffs. Once established, these units rarely get dislodged. And an era of permanent crisis, ensures a continuing accumulation of such bodies.

Another reason for the growth of the Presidential Establishment is that occupants of the White House frequently distrust members of the permanent government. Nixon aides, for example, have viewed most civil servants not only as Democratic but as wholly unsympathetic to such objectives of the Nixon administration as decentralization, revenue sharing, and the curtailment of several Great Society programs. Departmental bureaucracies are viewed from the White House as independent, unresponsive, unfamiliar, and inaccessible. They are suspected again and again of placing their own, congressional, or special-interest priorities ahead of those communicated to them from the White House. Even the President's own Cabinet members soon become viewed in the same light; one of the strengths of Cabinet members, namely their capacity to make a compelling case for their programs, has proved to be their chief liability with Presidents.

Presidents may want this type of advocacy initially, but they soon grow weary and wary of it. Not long ago, one White House aide accused a former Labor Secretary of trying to "out-Meany Meany." Efforts by former Interior Secretary Hickel to advance certain environmental programs and by departing Housing and Urban Development Secretary George Romney to promote innovative housing construction methods not only were unwelcome but after a while were viewed with considerable displeasure and suspicion at the White House.

Hickel writes poignantly of coming to this recognition during his final meeting with President Nixon, in the course of which the President frequently referred to him as an "adversary." "Initially," writes Hickel, "I considered that a compliment because, to me, an adversary is a valuable asset. It was only after the President had used the term many times and with a disapproving inflection that I realized he considered an adversary an enemy. I could not understand why he would consider me an enemy."

Not only have recent Presidents been suspicious about the depth of the loyalty of those in their Cabinets, but they also invariably become concerned about the possibility that sensitive administration secrets may leak out through the departmental bureaucracies, and this is another reason why Presidents have come to rely more on their own personal groups, such as task forces and advisory commissions.

Still another reason that more and more portfolios have been given to the presidency is that new federal programs frequently concern more than one federal agency, and it seems reasonable that someone at a higher level is required to fashion a consistent policy and to reconcile conflicts. Attempts by Cabinet members themselves to solve sensitive jurisdictional questions frequently result in bitter squabbling. At times, too, Cabinet members themselves have recommended that these multidepartmental issues be settled at the White House. Sometimes new presidential appointees insist that new offices for program coordination be assigned directly under the President. Ironically, such was the plea of George McGovern, for example, when President Kennedy offered him the post of director of the Food-for-Peace program in 1961. McGovern attacked the buildup of the Presidential Establishment in his campaign against Nixon, but back in 1961 he wanted visibility (and no doubt celebrity status) and he successfully argued against his being located outside the White House—either in the State or Agriculture departments. President Kennedy and his then campaign manager Robert Kennedy felt indebted to McGovern because of his efforts in assisting the Kennedy presidential campaign in South Dakota. Accordingly, McGovern was granted not only a berth in the Executive Office of the President but also the much-coveted title of special assistant to the President.

The Presidential Establishment has also been enlarged by the representation of interest groups within its fold. Even a partial listing of staff specializations that have been grafted onto the White House in recent years reveals how interest-group brokerage has become added to the more traditional staff activities of counseling and administration.

These specializations form a veritable index of American society: Budget and management, national security, economics, congressional matters, science and technology, drug abuse prevention, telecommunications, consumers, national goals, intergovernmental relations, environment, domestic policy, international economics, military affairs, civil rights, disarmament, labor relations, District of Columbia, cultural affairs, education, foreign trade and tariffs, past Presidents, the aged, health and nutrition, physical fitness, volunteerism, intellectuals, blacks, youth, women, "the Jewish community," Wall Street, governors, mayors, "ethnics," regulatory agencies and related industry, state party chairmen, Mexican-Americans.

It is as if interest groups and professions no longer settle for lobbying Congress, or having one of their number appointed to departmental advisory boards or sub-Cabinet positions. It now appears essential to "have your own man right there in the White House." Once this foothold is established, of course, interest groups can play upon the potential political backlash that could arise should their representation be discontinued.

One of the more disturbing elements in the growth of the Presidential Establishment is the development, particularly under the current administration, of a huge public-relations apparatus. More than 100 presidential aides are now engaged in various forms of press-agentry or public relations, busily selling and reselling the President. This activity is devoted to the particular occupant of the White House, but inevitably it affects the presidency itself, by projecting or reinforcing images of the presidency that are almost imperial in their suggestions of omnipotence and omniscience. Thus the public-relations apparatus not only has directly enlarged the presidential workforce but has expanded public expectations about the presidency at the same time.

Last, but by no means least, Congress, which has grown increasingly critical of the burgeoning power of the presidency, must take some blame itself for the expansion of the White House. Divided within itself and ill-equipped, or simply disinclined to make some of the nation's toughest political decisions in recent decades, Congress has abdicated more and more authority to the presidency. The fact that the recent massive bombing of North Vietnam was ordered by the President without even a pretense of consultation with Congress buried what little was left of the semblance of that body's war-making power. Another recent instance of Congress's tendency to surrender authority to the presidency, an extraordinary instance, was the passage by the House (though not the Senate) of a grant to the President that would give him the right to determine which programs are to be cut whenever the budget goes beyond a $250 billion ceiling limit—a bill which, in effect, would hand over to the President some of Congress's long-cherished "power of the purse."

What can be done to bring the Presidential Establishment back down to size? What can be done to bring it to a size that both lightens the heavy accumulation of functions that it has absorbed and allows the Presidential Establishment to perform its most important functions more effectively and wisely?

First, Congress should curb its own impulse to establish new presidential agencies and to ask for yet additional reports and studies from the President. In the past Congress has been a too willing partner in the enlargement of the presidency. If Congress genuinely wants a leaner presidency, it should ask more of itself. For instance, it could well make better use of its own General Accounting Office and Congressional Research Service for chores that are now often assigned to the President.

Congress should also establish in each of its houses special committees on Executive Office operations. Most congressional committees are organized to deal with areas such as labor, agriculture, armed services, or education, paralleling the organization of the Cabinet. What we need now are committees designed explicitly to oversee the White House. No longer can the task of overseeing presidential operations be dispersed among dozens of committees and subcommittees, each of which can look at only small segments of the Presidential Establishment. Some will complain that adding yet another committee to the already over-burdened congressional system is just like adding another council to the over-stuffed Presidential Establishment. But the central importance of what the presidency does (and does not do) must rank among the most critical tasks of the contemporary Congress. As things are organized now, the presidency escapes with grievously inadequate scrutiny. Equally important, Congress needs these committees to help protect itself from its own tendency to relinquish to the presidency its diminishing resources and prerogatives. Since Truman, Presidents have had staffs to oversee Congress; it is time Congress reciprocated.

Similar efforts to let the salutary light of public attention shine more brightly on the presidency should be inaugurated by the serious journals and newspapers of the nation. For too long, publishers and editors have believed that covering the presidency means assigning a reporter to the White House press corps. Unfortunately, however, those who follow the President around on his travels are rarely in a position to do investigative reporting on what is going on inside the Presidential Establishment. Covering the Executive Office of the President requires more than a President watcher; it needs a specialist who understands the arcane language and highly complex practices that have grown up in the Presidential Establishment.

Finally, it is time to reverse the down-grading of the Cabinet. President Nixon ostensibly moved in this direction with his designation . . . of three Cabinet heads—HEW's Caspar W. Weinberger, Agriculture's Earl L. Butz, and HUD's James T. Lynn—as, in effect, super-secretaries of "human resources," "natural resources," and "community development" respectively. The move was expressly made in the name of Cabinet consolidation, plans for which Mr. Nixon put forward in 1971 but which Congress has so-far spurned. . . .

Reducing the present number of departments would strengthen the hand of Cabinet members vis-à-vis special interests, and might enable them to serve as advisers, as well as advocates, to the President. Cabinet consolidation would also have another very desirable effect: it would be a move toward reducing the accumulation of power within the Presidential Establishment. For much of the power of budget directors and other senior White House aides comes from their roles as penultimate referees of interdepartmental jurisdictional disputes. Under consolidated departments, a small number of strengthened Cabinet officers with closer ties to the President would resolve these conflicts instead. With fewer but broader Cabinet departments, there would be less need for many of the interest-group brokers and special councils that now constitute so much of the excessive baggage in the overburdened presidency.

Meantime, the presidency remains sorely overburdened—with both functions and functionaries—and needs very much to be cut back in both. Certainly, the number of presidential workers can and should be reduced. Harry Truman put it best, perhaps, when he said with characteristic succinctness: "I do not like this present trend toward a huge White House staff . . . . Mostly these aides get in each other's way." But while the number of functionaries is the most tangible and dramatic measure of the White House's expansion, its increasing absorption of governmental functions is more profoundly disturbing. The current White House occupant may regard cutting down (or transferring) a number of his staff members as a way of mollifying critics who charge that the American presidency has grown too big and bloated, but it is yet another thing to reduce the President's authority or his accumulated prerogatives. As the nation's number-one critic of the swelling of government, [the President] will, it is hoped, move—or will continue to move if he has truly already started—to substantially deflate this swelling in one of the areas where it most needs to be deflated—at home, in the White House.

8 | The Isolation of the President

George E. Reedy

Two frequent Watergate-related criticisms of Richard Nixon as Presi-
dent were his isolation in the White House and his tendency to surround
himself with aides who did not challenge his views. Reedy feels these
are general problems facing all presidents because of the deference
shown our chief executives. His analysis is considered prophetic because
it was largely based on experience prior to the Nixon administration.
Reedy does not find the origins of these difficulties in the style of
Kennedy or the growth of modern government, but instead in the
Founding Fathers' decision to combine in the presidency the roles of
head of government and head of state. This created, he argues, an
office of such great status in the present day that people in politics
inevitably treat the president like a king and refuse to bring him
bad news.

The factor that I have missed in most of the works on the presidency
I have read is the impact of the institution on individuals. The literature on the subject seems to assume that the White House somehow
molds the man and his assistants into finer forms and that the major
problem of government is to assure channels through which these forms
will have full expression. It is virtually taken for granted that the
proper objective of a study of our chief executive is to identify those
inhibiting factors which frustrate his efforts to resolve national problems
and to devise mechanisms which will remove those frustrations. This
is a type of study which should be continued on a priority basis. The
frustrations are many and could be catastrophic.

But the analysis is inadequate. It ignores the fundamental reality
of society, which is that institutions are manned by individual human

Reprinted with permission of The New American Library, Inc. from *The Twi-*
light of the Presidency, Mentor edition, pp. x-xiii, 17-19, 20-27, 100, 115-116.
Copyright © 1970 by George E. Reedy.

George E. Reedy was Special Assistant to President Lyndon B. Johnson and also
served for a time as his press secretary. He is currently Dean, School of Journalism, Marquette University.

beings and that government—regardless of the managerial flow charts produced by the behavioral scientists—is still a question of decisions that are made by people. The basic question is not whether we have devised structures with inadequate authority for the decision-making process. The question is whether the structures have created an environment in which men cannot function in any kind of a decent and humane relationship to the people whom they are supposed to lead. I am afraid—and on this point I am a pessimist—that we have devised that kind of a system.

To explain this, I must start with a highly personal reaction. The trouble with the White House—for anyone who is a part of it—is that when he picks up a telephone and tells people to do something, they usually do it. They may sabotage the project, after they have hung up the phone. They may stall, hoping that "the old son of a bitch" will forget about it. They may respond with an avalanche of statistics and briefing papers in which the original purpose will be lost and life will continue as before. But the heel click at the other end of the wire will be audible and the response—however invalid—will be prompt. There will be no delay in assurance, however protracted may be performance.

This is an unhealthy environment for men and women whose essential business is to deal with people in large numbers. It is soothing to the ego, but it fosters illusions about humanity. It comforts the weary assistant who may have gone round the clock in his search for a solution to an insoluble problem, but it paves the way for massive disillusionment. And for the very young, the process is demoralizing. It creates a picture of the world which is ill adapted to that which they will face once the days of glory come to an end. There should be a flat rule that no one be permitted to enter the gates of the White House until he is at least forty and has suffered major disappointments in life.

My own heart is back in the Senate, where I spent so many years of my adult life either as a newspaperman or a staff assistant. This is not because the people at the other end of Pennsylvania Avenue are any better in terms of character, wisdom, or goals. It is simply that their egos must face daily clashes with similarly strong egos who stand on a par and who do not feel any sense of subordination. In the Senate, no course stands the remotest chance of adoption unless a minimum of fifty-one egotistical men are persuaded of its wisdom, and in some cases the minimum is sixty-seven. These are pre-conditions under which even the most neurotic of personalities must make some obeisance to reality. . . .

The White House does not provide an atmosphere in which idealism and devotion can flourish. Below the president is a mass of intrigue, posturing, strutting, cringing, and pious "commitment" to irrelevant windbaggery. It is designed as a perfect setting for the conspiracy of mediocrity—that all too frequently successful collection of the untalented, the unpassionate, and the insincere seeking to convince the public that it is brilliant, compassionate, and dedicated.

There are, of course, men who seethe inwardly over this affront to human dignity—most of whom either go smash or leave quietly, their muscles set rigidly to contain an indescribable agony. There are, of course, the warm and relaxed permanent White House staff members, secure in their mastery of the essential housekeeping machinery of the Mansion and watching with wry amusement and some sympathy the frenetic efforts to shine forth boldly of those who have only four years out of all eternity to grab the brass ring. But the men of outrage are few and for some reason avoid each other after they slip out the side door. There are experiences which should not be shared. A reunion would lead only to a collective shriek.

It is not that the people who compose the ménage are any worse than any other collection of human beings. It is rather that the White House is an ideal cloak for intrigue, pomposity, and ambition. No nation of free men should ever permit itself to be governed from a hallowed shrine where the meanest lust for power can be sanctified and the dullest wit greeted with reverential awe. Government should be vulgar, sweaty, plebeian, operating in an environment where a fool can be called a fool and the motivations of ideological pimpery duly observed and noted. In a democracy, meanness, dullness, and corruption are entitled to representation because they are part of the human spirit; they are not entitled to protection from the harsh and rude challenges that such qualities must face in the real world.

It is not enough to say that the White House need not be like this if it is occupied by another set of personalities. It is not enough to point out that I may subconsciously be exaggerating the conditions which I describe in overreacting to the reverence that has characterized most studies of the presidency. The fact remains that the institution provides camouflage for all that is petty and nasty in human beings, and enables a clown or a knave to pose as Galahad and be treated with deference.

Is my reaction purely personal disappointment or shaped by service in a specific White House in a specific administration? Obviously, no man can be truly objective about an experience so central to his life and so vital to all his goals and his aspirations. All I can say is that I am fully aware of the treacherous nature of one's sensory mechanisms in surveying the immediately surrounding universe. I have taken this factor into account and tried to allow for it in every possible way—, which is why this [writing] has been so long delayed. I believe that what I am saying is more than the conclusion of one man in a unique set of circumstances. . . .

MAINTAINING CONTACT WITH REALITY

A president cannot have problems which are personal to him alone. His troubles are the troubles of the nation and if they become disastrous, the nation is in peril. It is vital, consequently, to identify those aspects of his position which are most likely to bring him to grief. And the most important, and least examined, problem of the presidency is that of maintaining contact with reality. Unless a president starts giving thought to this question—and on the available evidence, very few do—immediately following the fine flush of his election victory celebration, he is headed inevitably for trouble.

There are very few warnings to the president-elect that this problem will be encountered. No one has placed over the White House door the admonition *"facile decensus Averni."*[1] No one comes rushing to him with somber warnings and Dutch-uncle talk. The state of euphoria induced by political success is upon him at the very moment that caution, introspection, and humility are most needed. The process of erosion by which reality gradually fades begins the moment someone says, "Congratulations, Mr. President."

There is built into the presidency a series of devices that tend to remove the occupant of the Oval Room from all of the forces which require most men to rub up against the hard facts of life on a daily basis. The life of the White House is the life of a court. It is a structure designed for one purpose and one purpose only—to serve the material needs and the desires of a single man. It is felt that this man is grappling with problems of such tremendous consequence that every effort must be made to relieve him of the irritations that vex the average citizen. His mind, it is held, must be absolutely free of petty annoyances so that he can concentrate his faculties upon the "great issues" of the day.

To achieve this end, every conceivable facility is made available, from the very latest and most luxurious jet aircraft to a masseur constantly in attendance to soothe raw presidential nerves. Even more important, however, he is treated with all of the reverence due a monarch. No one interrupts presidential contemplation for anything less than a major catastrophe somewhere on the globe. No one speaks to him unless spoken to first. No one ever invites him to "go soak your head" when his demands become petulant and unreasonable.

In theory, privilege is accorded to, and accepted by, a man in accordance with his responsibilities. It is a supposed compensation for heavier burdens than those carried by lesser mortals. In practice, privilege is a status that feeds upon itself—with every new perquisite automatically becoming a normal condition of life. Any president upon entering office is startled—and a little abashed—at the privileges that are available to him. But it is only a matter of months until they become part of an environment which he necessarily regards as his just and due entitlement—not because of the office but because of his mere existence.

It is doubtful whether even Harry S Truman—the most democratic of contemporary presidents—wore the same size hat when he left the White House as he did the day he entered.

This status was built into the American government by the Constitution itself. The founding fathers had rejected the concept of the divine right of monarchy. But when they sat down to write a constitution that would assure freedom, they were incapable of thinking of government in any terms other than monarchy. Someone, they reasoned, must reign and rule. Someone must give orders that could not be questioned. Someone must have ultimate and final authority. Therefore, their conclusion, although not stated in these terms, was a solution which placed in office a monarch but limited the scope of the monarch's activities. . . .

EFFECTS OF CONSTITUTIONAL DECISIONS

The framers of the Constitution had no way of foreseeing the effects of their most important decision—to give the presidency the functions of both chief of state and chief of government. It is doubtful whether they were aware at the time that the functions could exist separately. They knew that there had to be someone who spoke for all the government. They also knew that there had to be someone to manage the affairs of the country. The concept that these functions could be separated was alien to their experience, even though the origins of separation were already apparent in the relationship between the king of England and the English prime minister.

They lived in a universe dominated by the concept of ownership and in which management independent of ownership was unknown. The parallel to government seemed obvious in their minds. Furthermore, they were confronted with an immediate and apparent problem which far overshadowed what could then only be abstract ideas of the distinction between reigning and ruling. They had a nation which was being pulled apart by the centrifugal forces of state pride. Their task was to devise some method by which thirteen quite independent political units could be merged into a collective whole. Their problem was to find some counterweight that would balance forces of disunity and induce Americans to think of themselves as citizens of the United States rather than as citizens of Connecticut, New York, Virginia, or Georgia.

The most practical method of unifying people is to give them a symbol with which all can identify. If the symbol is human, its efficacy is enhanced enormously. The obvious symbol was the president—the man who held the role of commander-in-chief of the armed forces; the man to whom all could pay respects as the first citizen. In short, the founding fathers established the presidency as a position of reverence and, as they were truly wise and sophisticated men, their efforts were as effective as human wisdom could make them.

The consequences of this decision were ultimately inescapable although not immediately discernible. In the simple society of the eighteenth-century United States, it was not easy to conceive of the Federal government in terms of grandeur. An Abigail Adams could hang her washing in the East Room; a Dolly Madison could act as a porter, running to safety with important works of art in advance of British occupation; an Andrew Jackson could invite all his frontier friends into the White House for a rollicking party where they could trample the official furniture with muddy boots and pass out dead drunk on the plush carpets of the Oval Room. But even in a nation as close to the realities of the frontier as the United States, a position established to inspire awe and reverence would inevitably pick up the trappings of reverence. And the trappings could not fail to have an effect upon the man whom they served as a buffer against the rest of the world.

Among the fundamental characteristics of monarchy is untouchability. Contact with the king is forbidden except to an extremely few people or as a rare privilege to be exercised on great occasions. The king's body is sanctified and not subject to violation by lesser mortals unless he himself so wishes. He is not to be jostled in crowds; he is not to be clapped on the back; he is not to be placed in danger of life or limb or even put to the annoyance of petty physical discomfort. Nor can he be compelled to account for his actions upon demand.

By the twentieth century, the presidency had taken on all the regalia of monarchy except robes, a scepter and a crown. The president was not to be jostled by a crowd—unless he elected to subject himself to do so during those moments when he shed his role as chief of state and mounted the hustings as a candidate for reelection. The ritual of shaking hands with the president took on more and more the coloration of the medieval "king's touch" as a specific scrofula. The president was not to be called to account by any other body (after the doctrine of executive privilege was established). In time, another kingly habit began to

appear and presidents referred to themselves more and more as "we"—
the ultimate hallmark of imperial majesty.

These are the conditions under which a president-elect enters office
in the modern era. In fact, the aura of majesty begins to envelop him
the moment it becomes apparent that the electorate has decided upon
its next president. Trusted assistants who have been calling him by his
first name for many years switch immediately to the deferential "Mr.
President." The Secret Service agents who have been protecting him
during the campaign are suddenly joined by their chiefs who, up to
that point, have stayed away from him and the other candidates in
order to emphasize their neutrality. Members of the Army Signal
Corps almost silently appear with communications equipment such as
he has never seen before. All these developments take place as he
bathes in the universal congratulations that always come to the successful candidate, even from his bitterest opponents. The agents that
corrupt the democratic soul creep into his life in the guise of enthusi-
astic supporters, tactful policemen, self-effacing telephone linemen, and
well-trained house servants. Even the members of the press, for a few
months at least, regard him with some awe. The apotheosis has begun.

During the early days of a president's incumbency, the atmosphere
of reverence which surrounds him acquires validity in his own eyes
because of the ease with which he can get results. Congress is eager
to approve his nominees and pass his bills. Business is anxious to provide him with "friends" and assistants. Labor is ready to oblige him
with a climate of industrial peace. Foreign ambassadors scurry to locate
suitable approaches.

It is a wonderful and heady feeling to be a president—at least for
the first few months.

The environment of deference, approaching sycophancy, helps to
foster another insidious factor. It is a belief that the president and a
few of his most trusted advisers are possessed of a special knowledge
which must be closely held within a small group lest the plans and
the designs of the United States be anticipated and frustrated by
enemies. It is a knowledge which is thought to be endangered in geo-
metrical proportion to the number of other men to whom it is passed.
Therefore, the most vital national projects can be worked out only
within a select coterie, or there will be a "leak" which will disadvantage
the country's security.

Obviously, there *is* information which a nation must keep to itself
if it is to survive in the present world climate. This means that the
number of minds which can be brought to bear on any given problem
is often in inverse proportion to the importance of the problem.

The steps that led to the bombing of North Vietnam were all discussed by a small group of men. They were intelligent men—men of keen perception and finely honed judgment. It is doubtful whether any higher degree of intelligence could have been brought to bear on the problem. But no matter how fine the intelligence or how thoroughgoing the information available, the fact remained that none of these men was put to the test of defending his position in public debate. And it is amazing what even the best of minds will discover when forced to answer critical questions. Unfortunately, in this as in many other instances, the need to comment publicly came after, and not before, irreversible commitment.

Of course, within these councils there was always at least one "devil's advocate." But an official dissenter always starts with half his battle lost. It is assumed that he is bringing up arguments solely because arguing is his official role. It is well understood that he is not going to press his points harshly or stridently. Therefore, his objections and cautions are discounted before they are delivered. They are actually welcomed because they prove for the record that decision was preceded by controversy.

As a general rule, the quality of judgment usually varies directly with the number of minds that are brought to bear upon an issue. No man is so wise as to play his own "devil's advocate," and workable wisdom is the distillation of many different viewpoints which have clashed heatedly and directly in an exchange of opinion. To maintain the necessary balance between assurances of security and assurances that enough factors have been taken into consideration is perhaps the most pressing problem of statecraft. The atmosphere of the White House, in which the president is treated constantly as an infallible and reverential object, is not the best in which to resolve this problem.

PRESIDENTIAL BLUNDERS

In restrospect, it seems little short of amazing that President Kennedy would ever have embarked upon the ill-fated Bay of Pigs venture. It was poorly conceived, poorly planned, poorly executed, and undertaken with grossly inadequate knowledge. But anyone who has ever sat in on a White House council can easily deduce what happened without knowing any facts other than those which appeared in the public press. White House councils are not debating matches in which ideas emerge from the heated exchanges of participants. The council centers around the president himself, to whom everyone addresses his observations.

The first strong observations to attract the favor of the president become subconsciously the thoughts of everyone in the room. The focus of attention shifts from a testing of all concepts to a groping for means of overcoming the difficulties. A thesis which could not survive an undergraduate seminar in a liberal arts college becomes accepted doctrine, and the only question is not *whether* it should be done but *how* it should be done. A forceful public airing of the Bay of Pigs plan would have endangered the whole project, of course. But it might have prevented disaster.

On a different level can be cited the far less serious setback suffered by President Lyndon B. Johnson when he attempted to merge the Commerce and the Labor departments into one agency. Out of a desire for a "surprise" headline, this proposal was held in the utmost secrecy between the president and his speech writers until a few moments before his State of the Union message was scheduled for delivery. Quick calls were made to the secretaries of labor and commerce, who were pressed for a quick response and who reacted as any government official reacts to such a call from the White House. They said, "Yes."

In a matter of days, it was apparent that the project had as much chance of getting off the ground as a kiwi. To organized labor, still headed by men with long memories, the Labor Department was a sacrosanct institution for which they had fought and bled in their youth. They had no intention of acquiescing to the removal from the cabinet of what they regarded as "our spokesman." Business, while far less emotional, made it quite clear that industrialists did not relish the prospect of "our agency" being merged with what they regarded as the opposition. The president quietly buried the whole idea.

The truly baffling question, however, is how a man with the political sensitivity of Lyndon B. Johnson would ever embark on such a futile enterprise. The basis of his success as the Senate Democratic leader had been his insistence upon touching every base before launching a project. He was famous throughout the political community for "taking the temperature" of every affected group in advance and laying careful plans to meet any objections they might have before the objections were even raised. And yet here was an instance where even a perfunctory conversation with a few of his friends would have made clear that humiliation was the only conceivable outcome of his proposal.

The only conclusion that an observer can draw is that the atmosphere of the White House—the combination of sycophancy and a belief in the efficacy of closely held knowledge—had done its work. The man regarded as the outstanding politician of the mid-twentieth century had stepped into a buzzsaw which could have been foreseen by a wardheeler in any major city of America.

A reader of history will find innumerable and startling examples of political bloopers committed by men with a record of political sagacity. How is one to explain President Truman's inept handling of the Communist spy scare of the late 1940s—a mistake which opened up the era of Joe McCarthy? How is one to explain Franklin D. Roosevelt's futile effort to "pack" the Supreme Court? How is one to explain Woodrow Wilson's clumsy treatment of the Senate, which led directly to its refusal to permit United States participation in the League of Nations? None of these men had shown themselves politically inept on such a grand scale at any previous moment of their lives. It is only an inference but an inescapable one that the White House is an institution which dulls the sensitivity of political men and ultimately reduces them to bungling amateurs in their basic craft—the art of politics.

The real question every president must ask himself is what he can do to resist the temptations of a process compounded of idolatry and lofty patriotic respect for a national symbol. By all the standards of past performance, he should be well equipped to face it. As a general rule, he has fought his way up through the political ranks. He has flattered and been flattered—and the mere fact that he has survived to the threshold of the White House should indicate a psychological capacity to keep flattery in perspective. He has dealt with rich people, wise men, fools, patriots, knaves, scoundrels, and wardheelers. Had he not maintained his perspective on human beings generally, it is doubtful that he would ever have received his party's nomination.

But the atmosphere of the White House is a heady one. It is designed to bring to its occupant privileges that are commensurate in scope with the responsibilities that he must bear. A privilege is, by definition, a boon not accorded to other people. And to the extent that a man exercises his privileges, he removes himself from the company of lesser breeds who must stand in line and wait their turn on a share-and-share-alike basis for the comforts of life. To a president, all other humans are "lesser breeds."

Furthermore, a president would have to be a dull clod indeed to regard himself without a feeling of awe. The atmosphere of the White House is calculated to instill in any man a sense of destiny. He literally walks in the footsteps of hallowed figures—of Jefferson, of Jackson, of Lincoln. The almost sanctified relics of a distant, semimythical past surround him as ordinary household objects to be used by his family. From the moment he enters the halls he is made aware that he has become enshrined in a pantheon of semidivine mortals who have shaken the world, and that he has taken from their hands the heritage of American dreams and aspirations. . . .

THE PRESS AS FORCE TOWARD REALITY

Of the few social institutions which tend to keep a president in touch with reality, the most effective—and the most resented by the chief beneficiary—is the press. It is the only force to enter the White House from the outside world with a direct impact upon the man in the Oval Room which cannot be softened by intermediary interpreters or deflected by sympathetic attendants.

This state of affairs does not arise out of any special integrity on the part of the press which, after all, is an institution manned by human beings subject to the same forces that govern conduct generally. Neither does it spring from any unusual defenses or counterforces working against manipulation on the part of the president. It is simply a matter of the press function, which is to inform the public of the president's actions. No matter how sympathetically that function is performed, a foolish act will appear foolish, an unpoular act will arouse antagonism, and an act in conflict with previous actions will appear contradictory. . . .

Since the press as a whole cannot be "won over" by tactics which political leaders regard as legitimate, it is inevitable that newspapermen eventually become the "enemy." In addition, they also become the personification of all the frustrating forces that make the life of a president so difficult. Therefore, over a period of time, it is certain that the political leader will vent his spleen against the press, never realizing that what he is really doing is venting his spleen against the whole intractable environment that surrounds him. It is a very easy matter to find legitimate grounds for criticizing the press. It is a less easy matter to realize that all these grounds apply to the world generally.

Every president has his collection of inaccuracies in press coverage and is willing to regale his listeners by recounting them for hours. Seen in perspective, these inaccuracies are usually trivial and reflect merely the fact that reporters are human beings who are bound to make errors under the constant pressure of reporting world-shaking events almost as soon as they happen. An objective evaluation would be that the degree of accuracy with which the news is reported is astounding when it is contrasted with the conditions under which it is gathered. But a politician smarting under the lash of public criticism is not very likely to be objective.

Every president has his horror stories of press arrogance. But press arrogance is merely a reflection of public arrogance. Almost every American feels qualified to give the president advice on the most complicated and subtle questions of economics, law, and international relations. It would be surprising if newspapermen were exempt from this universal temptation.

Every president can recite valid examples of press bias and is entitled legitimately to some sympathy for the manner in which he is treated by opposition newspapers. But the assumption that bias is a journalistic characteristic rather than a condition of humanity is a distorted view of the universe. When a man enters politics, he undertakes to deal with *all* human characteristics and it is not an acceptable alibi to cite some of them as overwhelming. If press bias were an absolute bar to political success, this nation would never have had an Abraham Lincoln, and Franklin D. Roosevelt and Harry S Truman would have been denied second terms.

In reality the problem of a president in dealing with the press is precisely the same as his problem in dealing with the public at large. But no president can find it within his ego to concede that he has failed in any degree with the public. It is far more satisfying to blame his failures on the press because his problems then can be attributed to a conspiracy. He can blame the "Eastern press," the "Republican press," or the "liberal press." He then does not stand indicted within his own consciousness (the most terrible court of all) as having failed. He was merely the victim of vindictiveness on the part of a selfish group and his failure can be attributed to the meanness of others rather than to his own inadequacies. . . .

NOTES

1. ["the descent to Hell is easy."]

9 | The Constraining of the President

Richard E. Neustadt

Neustadt finds certain structural changes in American politics to be more important causes of the increase in presidential power than any formal expansion in presidential functions. He points out how the informal checks and balances provided by the party system have declined as the strength of political parties has dwindled. This in turn has had adverse consequences on the ability of the Congress and the Cabinet to constrain the President. The author also contrasts the internal checks and balances of recent presidents that stem from their temperaments and philosophies. He concludes on a note of partial optimism, suggesting that Watergate may temporarily restore the effectiveness of informal constraints on the presidency.

The White House was once—and will be again—a great place for a young man to work. I did it myself and have never been sorry. Fate was kind and my age was right: It was Harry Truman's White House, and I worked for Charlie Murphy—Charles S. Murphy, to give him his due. He was the President's Special Counsel, successor to Clark Clifford in that post and one of Truman's senior aides. Working for Murphy and with him for the President was a fine experience, as unlike Egil Krogh's or Gordon Strachan's as day from night. A story illustrates what made it so, and the story is a starting point for looking at the Presidency now, by light of Watergate.

In December, 1950, at the wrenching turn of the Korean war, amidst Chinese attack, American retreat, renewed inflation, fears of World War III, Truman met at the White House with the Congressional

Richard E. Neustadt is Professor of Government, Harvard University. He is the author of *Presidential Power: The Politics of Leadership* and *Alliance Politics*.

leaders of both parties. Their meeting in the Cabinet room was largely symbolic, underlining events; it was an occasion for briefings, not actions. Soon after it broke up, a White House usher came to Murphy's office with a memorandum found under the Cabinet table. This was a document of several pages addressed by the staff of the Senate Minority Policy Committee to Senators Robert A. Taft and Kenneth S. Wherry, the Republican leaders. Some of his assistants were with Murphy at the time, and we fell upon it with whoops of joy. As I recall, one of us read it aloud. It dealt with the contingency (which had not arisen) that the President might use that meeting to seek pledges of bipartisan support for the administration's future conduct of the war. This, the memorandum argued, ought to be resisted at all costs. By Easter recess the war could have taken such a turn that Republicans might wish to accuse Truman of treason, and they should be free to do so. The term "treason" fired in me and my associates an outrage we wanted the world to share. With the loyalty of subalterns, more royalist than the king, we cried, "Get it copied . . . show it to the President . . . leak it to the press!" Murphy smiled at us, took the memorandum from us, sealed it in an envelope, summoned a mes-senger and sent it by hand to Senator Taft. End of story.

Murphy's conduct showed propriety—indeed, for me defines it— so that much recent White House staff behavior simply shocks me. His conduct also showed prudence. He worked in a White House where seniors had constant incentive to contain themselves and restrain the young.

The Presidency as we know it now took shape in Franklin Roosevelt's time, the product of Depression, war, the radio and Presidential per-sonality. Truman inherited and consolidated. In terms of personnel, both military and civilian, the Federal Government during his later years was roughly the same size as it is now. (The great growth of civilian public service since has been at state and local levels.) In con-stitutional and statutory terms, the Presidency's formal powers then were much what they are now. Like President Nixon, Truman fought undeclared war, imposed price controls, presided over a great turn in foreign policy, sought changes in domestic policy and championed "executive privilege." But if, in these respects and others, Presidential powers are substantially unchanged, what has changed is a set of inhibitions on their use.

Formal powers stay about the same, but their conversion into actual power—into making something happen—takes place with less restraint than formerly. If the Nixon regime felt itself under siege in 1971, so did Truman's in 1951. Yet there were no do-it-yourself White House horrors. Had propriety not barred them, prudence would have done so.

Almost surely, Watergate's effect upon the Presidency will be to prop up old incentives, for restraint, restoring White House prudence to something like its former state. Such a prop is artificial and cannot last forever, but it should hold good for years to come. Score one for Watergate! In that perspective it is not a tragedy—far from it.

So the modern Presidency's past and prospects are bound up with the questions: What was prudence made of? What became of those ingredients? And on what terms does Watergate restore them?

A generation ago, our system's formal checks and balances were strongly reinforced by an array of informal constraints on White House conduct. Some were external, imposed on the White House, equally affecting President and staff. Others were internal, products of his operating style, affecting the staff more than him. External constraints reflected his dependence upon men whom he could not control for work he wanted done. Such men were found in many places, but let me single out three: the Congress, the party and the Cabinet. As for internal constraints I shall single out another three: his schedule, press conferences, and the staff system.

THE CONGRESS

Those men on whom the President depended were his "colleagues" in the quite specific sense that while he needed them, their power did not stem wholly from his. To need is to heed, or at least to listen. Truman had one such set of colleagues on Capitol Hill: the Speaker of the House, the House and Senate floor leaders and the committee chairmen. As the modern Presidency emerged before and during World War II, it was assumed that those posts would go to men of the same party as the President. So it had been for all but four years since the turn of the century. So it remained in Truman's time for six years out of eight. Under F.D.R. and Truman this assumption was built into Governmental practice, not least at the White House where it moderated tones of voice, promoted consultation and preserved respect, at least for working purposes. Speaker Sam Rayburn and the floor leaders met Truman every week. They were colleagues together: At Rayburn's wish they met alone, no staff—and no recordings.

While all the posts of power on the Hill were manned by men who shared the President's party label, Truman could not do what he did in 1948 and in effect run against Congress, lambasting it for a "do-nothing" record he himself had forced on it by seeking bills he lacked the votes to pass. But that was the 80th Congress, elected two years earlier with Republican majorities in both Houses. Truman could not turn as sharply on an institution led by Rayburn. Nor would he have wanted to. Nor could his staff. Family quarrels were of a different quality than conflict with the rival clan.

And even as he rose to the attack in 1948, Truman carefully walled off from party battle what he took to be the cardinal field of foreign relations, including European policy, and especially the Marshall Plan. Under the aegis of Senator Arthur H. Vandenberg, the Congressional Republicans did likewise. For limited purposes, the Truman-Vandenberg connection linked the White House to Republican leaders as closely as ever to Democrats.

In 1954, Truman's successor General Eisenhower faced the reverse situation when the Democrats regained control of both houses of Congress. He then faced it continuously for six years. Eisenhower was a national hero, consciously so, and only lately become a Republican. He joined Rayburn and the latter's protégé, the new Senate Leader Lyndon Johnson, in a loose but comfortable connection. Over a wide range of issues this served much as Truman's with Vandenberg.

What Truman had for two years and Eisenhower for six, Nixon now has had for more than four, with no prospect of change: Congress organized by the other party. But Nixon, despite intermittent caution in his first term, seems not to have wanted special connections of the sort his predecessors threw across the party breach between themselves and Congress. And after his triumphant re-election, he immediately tried a reverse twist on Truman's warfare with the 80th Congress. Truman had made demands that Congress would not meet, and cried "do-nothing"; now Nixon made budget cuts that Congress would oppose, and readied taunts of "fiscal irresponsibility." In such a game the negative makes for even less retraint than the affirmative. Truman wanted the program he requested but lacked votes and did not get it. Nixon no doubt wants to keep the cuts he made, and wields the veto. Until scandal overtook him I think he was winning hands down . . . .

THE PARTY

Twenty years ago, both parties were what they had been since Andrew Jackson's time: confederal associations of state parties grouped together for the sake of Presidential nominations and campaigns. The state parties, in turn, consisted of some relatively standard parts: city machines, court-house gangs, interest-group leaders, elective office-holders, big contributors. Stitching them all together nationally every fourth year was a task for party regulars assembled in convention. Barons strongly based in interest groups or regions or machines collectively had power to decide, or at least veto, and their number at a given time was never very large. Perhaps 50 or 100 men—buttressed, of course, by aides and friends and clients—were crucial to each party's nomination and campaign, crucial in convention and in canvassing and funding. And they were a known circle, shifting over time but usually quite easy to identify at any moment.

As with Congress, Truman was linked in stable fashion to the party leaders by a common interest: the Presidential succession. Such a relationship constrains one politician's staff in dealing with another politician, and even more so when, as was usually the case with Truman, he needed more help than he could give. Gallup Poll approval of his conduct fell to 32 per cent in 1946 and then as low as 23 per cent in 1951, eight points below Nixon's low last August. Not coincidentally, in 1946 Truman was requested by the Democratic National Committee *not* to campaign for Congress. In 1948 the railroads withdrew credit and his famous whistle-stop tour almost stopped for lack of funds. In 1952 Governor Adlai Stevenson of Illinois persistently evaded his embrace, insisted on a draft, refused a White House build-up. The party barons out in states and cities may have liked the President and felt some kinship for him, but few if any were prepared to die for him, and none, so far as I know, were content to work through staff in lieu of him. Like Rayburn, they preferred to deal, and to be known to deal, and to be known to deal directly. In Truman's situation their preferences mattered a lot.

As organizations our two national parties have never been twins. But insofar as both shared features of the sort I have described, both are now changed almost beyond recognition. TV and jet aircraft, primaries and ticket-splitting join with education, affluence and population shifts to outmode old customs and weaken old fiedoms. We have left the age of barons and entered the age of candidates. Its hallmarks are management by private firms, exposure through the tube, funding by direct-mail drives as well as fat-cats and canvassing by zealous volunteers.

For the Republican party nationally, 1964 exposed the passing of the old regime; for Democrats the year was 1972. Nixon in a sense is our first President to deal with party ties wholly in terms of the new conditions. Watergate sheds light on how his White House dealt. What it shows is an inordinate concern for raising money, coupled with a campaign organization run by White House aides. The Committee for the Re-election of the President was wholly independent of the Republican National Committee; it remained in existence after the campaign. Perhaps coincidentally, the White House planned that after the election those aides and others should fan out all over town, taking up sub-Cabinet posts or civil service supergrades in every major agency. Much of this actually happened last winter; it was the most determined such effort by any Administration in memory.

Why grab so much money? Why carry on C.R.P.? Why scatter subalterns all over the place? Likelier than not the answer lies in sheer momentum, in doing what comes naturally (and to excess, as was typical of the Nixon staff). But possibly they are related. It is conceivable these three developments were part of a scheme for dominating not only the Administration, but also the Republican succession. In an age of candidates, could White-House controlled bank accounts combined with White-House controlled agencies provide a substitute for defunct party baronies? As hopefuls crowded the primaries in 1976, could these assets have given the power of decision or veto to the White House staff? In any event, the setting does not make for much constraint!

THE CABINET

Truman's Cabinet officers were his appointees, for the most part, but rarely his creatures. Some of them (not many) had party standing of their own, linked to a faction of those old-style barons. Some bureau chiefs (a lot) had the equivalent in links to leading Congressmen and vital interest-groups. Everyone, regardless of his standing, owed a duty to the statutory programs he administered, and so to the Congressional committees that controlled their life blood: laws and funds. Since the "Compromise of 1789"—when Congress took the power to create department, leaving the Presidents the discretion to dismiss department heads—it had been recognized in practice, if not always in words, that "executive" agencies of all sorts were subordinate at once to President *and* Congress, a triangular relationship that left them with two masters who could frequently be played off against each other. J. Edgar Hoover's practice of this art in 1971 seems newsworthy today but would have seemed the norm for any self-respecting bureau chief in 1951 or earlier, the period when Hoover perfected his technique.

So it was in Truman's time, and so with variations it appears to have remained. But the variations are important. They suggest that Nixon's White House up to now has rarely felt the full constraint shared mastership used to impose. That Nixon's aides thought otherwise— as their extraordinary memoranda show—hints at either ignorance or paranoia.

Viewed from a distance, two changes stand out. As of, say, 1970 compared with 1950, most Cabinet officers seem less important to the

President, while bureau chiefs appear less certain of Congressional support against the President, or anyway less likely to invoke it. The latter change reflects what may have been a passing phase—much of Washington heeds the dictum "never hit a man unless he's down," and Nixon, like Truman before him, has become vulnerable. Or maybe it reflects a downward shift of levels for Congressional support deep into program management, and well below the bureau chiefs, almost out of sight. And possibly the change is greater than it would be if party ties helped connect committees to agencies. But if this change is hard to pin down, the Cabinet change is not.

The low estate of most contemporary Cabinet posts reflects reduced White House dependence on departments as well as increased dependence of departments on each other. Twenty years ago the President relied on Cabinet members for a great deal of the staff work now performed inside the White House. President Eisenhower was the first to pull into the White House the detailed work of lobbying with Congress for Administration bills; Truman had mostly kept it out. And the hiring and firing of agency officials below Cabinet rank is now centralized as never before. Whatever its purpose—partisan or managerial or both—the fanning out of Nixon aides last winter into agencies reflects unprecedented White House planning and initiative in lower level appointments. Initiative once rested mostly with department heads; they usually won their contests with the White House staff. (It has been only a dozen years since Kennedy's Defense Secretary rejected out of hand a White House proposal for Secretary of the Navy, none other than Franklin Delano Roosevelt Jr.)

In Truman's years, moreover, a department head could look down at his bureaus, out to their clients and up to subcommittees on the Hill without having to think hourly about other departments. A bailiwick was still a bailiwick. For many department heads this is no longer true. I once worked closely with the head of the housing agency that preceded HUD. I do not recall that he gave a thought to the Federal Security Agency, the forerunner of HEW. But there was then no Model Cities Program.

Since President Johnson got his chance to put through Congress a whole generation's worth of Democratic programs—many stemming from Truman proposals stalled since the nineteen-forties—new endeavors have entangled departmental jurisdictions in such a web of overlapping statutes, funding, staffs and clientele that no one moves without involving others, often painfully. I gather it is even hard to stand still on one's own. In dealing with the consequences, bureaus are important, and so are Presidential staffs; the bureaus can operate, albeit on a narrow front, while the staffs can coordinate, at least in terms of budgets. Department heads are often poorly placed to do either. Their positions often are at once too lofty and too low.

Johnson once wanted super-managers to rationalize his programs as they built them up. Nixon called for super-managers to rationalize those programs down, and build up revenue-sharing. From either standpoint, Cabinet posts seemed cramped in White House eyes. In addition, the incumbents were cramped for time. New programs conferred on most departments new relationships with more Congressional committees than before. These Cabinet members still were in position to testify. So they did, over and over. It took a lot of time. But it added little to their weight at the White House. And Ehrlichman condescended.

Down the drain went still another set of Presidential colleagues—and constraints.

THE SCHEDULE

As for internal constraints on Truman's Presidency, the first derived from his operating style. He was accessible beyond contemporary belief. Following Roosevelt's peacetime practice and a long Presidential tradition, H.S.T. stood ready to see any member of Congress, granting 15 minute interviews to anyone who asked, if possible within 24 hours of the asking. The same rule held for Cabinet and sub-Cabinet officers, heads of lesser agencies and governors of states—these among others. His days were chopped up into 15-minute segments, morning and afternoon. He managed to include not only those who wanted to see him but also those he wished to see. He was available to staff early and late. And he met weekly, in addition, with the legislative leaders, the Cabinet, the National Security Council and the press—all this on top of ceremonies and aside from reading, late into the night.

Those 15-minute interviews, on the callers' business, at their option, took a large amount of time—no mean constraint—and also follow-up, which constrained his staff all the more, as Truman like Roosevelt before him, usually met his callers alone. Inefficiencies resulted, and waste motion. But at the same time, this President was personally exposed, day in and out, to what a lot of people wanted from him; he learned what they cared about, believed, hoped and feared. And constraining or not, I think Truman liked the flow. He found in it large compensations.

Eisenhower, by contrast, chafed under it, found it intolerable, channeled off all he could to his aides. Until his heart attack in 1955, members of Congress complained, and so did Cabinet members and others. Afterwards, acceptance set in. Before President Kennedy took office he was warned (to his discomfort) that he would be pressed to resume Truman's custom. But this did not occur. Washington had accepted the Eisenhower custom. Kennedy and Johnson were as free as has been Nixon to receive or put off whom they chose. Their choices were very different from his. But their freedom to make them eased his choice of relative isolation.

THE PRESS

Twenty years ago, another internal constraint derived from White House press relations, above all from the press conference as a regular weekly undertaking. These were no longer the intimate affairs of Roosevelt's time, with reporters crowded compatibly into the Oval Office; by Truman's second term they had become big-scale affairs in larger quarters, less educative for the correspondents, less fun for the President. But they still served many other functions, communications functions *within* Government, connecting our peculiarly separated branches, as well as informing the public. Regular press conferences gave the White House staff a chance to put the President on record unmistakably with Congressmen or bureaucrats or interest groups or partisans who could not be convinced at second-hand. They gave those others chances to check up on the assertions of the staff. They gave the President himself a chance to reinforce or override the claims made in his name by staff and everybody else. They gave him, finally, opportunities to puncture myths and gossip.

Truman did not always turn these chances to his own account. Sometimes he backed into unintended promises, disclosures or embarrassments. Thus press conferences constrained him. But I think they constrained others more, not the least his staff. At any rate, whatever pain they caused, those regular press conferences offered all concerned, the President included, compensations not obtainable from any other source. This we found out after Johnson impaired them by irregularity, still more after Nixon virtually shut them down. By Johnson's time, of course, press conferences had come to be live television shows. He reacted against the risks to his own image and his programs inherent in exposure through an entertainment medium, where many things besides words are conveyed to many publics viewing as a passive audience. Endowed with different style and temperament, Kennedy had faced those risks with relish. Not Johnson, and not Nixon. Seeking to safeguard their public relations, these Presidents backed out of regular press conferences; in the process—inadvertently perhaps—they impaired their internal communications.

THE STAFF

The last constraint I want to mention arose from Truman's staff system, which as its central feature made him his own chief of staff. He chaired the morning staff meeting; he parceled out assignments; he watched the White House budget; he approved new staff positions. He dealt directly, one by one, with all but junior aides; he allowed few of these, kept an eye on them and made sure that in meetings they saw a lot of him. He was immersed in detail, and it all took time. Thereby he was constrained. His aides, though, were also constrained —by him.

In this and other respects Truman followed rather closely, although not very consciously, the pattern F.D.R. had brought to Presidential staffing in his second term. Roosevelt's pattern had four features; he clung to them consistently, and so did Truman. First, the President, and only the President, was the chief of staff. Second, there was a sharp distinction between "personal" and "institutional" staff. The latter worked in such places as the Budget Bureau, with a mandate to think always of the Presidential office apart from personal politics. The former, the White House staff per se, would think about the President's personal interests, while he could weigh both views and choose between them. Third, personal staff meant only those who helped the President to do what was required of him day by day, manning his schedule, drafting his speeches, guarding his signature, nursing the press corps or, during the war, dealing with Stalin and Churchill. "This is the White House calling" was to mean the President himself or someone reliably in touch with him. Roosevelt cared devoutly for the symbolism of that house. All other aides were "institutional," to be kept out of there and off that phone. He overlapped staff duties, reached out to departments, pored over newspapers, probed his visitors and quizzed his wife. Not only was he chief of his own staff, he also was his own director of intelligence on happenings in his Administration. Except when they embarrassed him, he looked upon press leaks as adding to his sources.

The Rooseveltian pattern has had a curious history over the years. It evolved under Truman and then was abandoned by Eisenhower. The General could not abide it and thought it wrong in principle. Rather than immersion he sought freedom from detail and built a bigger staff than Truman's to relieve him of it. He made someone else his chief of staff, and created a swirl of secretariats to serve committees of Cabinet members. In reaction, Kennedy scrapped most of that and consciously restored the Rooseveltian arrangement, adapting as he went but following all its features. Johnson adapted further, but with less care as he grew more and more immersed in his war. Nixon evolved a different pattern that somewhat resembled Eisenhower's, but with a marked change in its means for tackling policy. Committee secretariats became substantive staffs, with initiative and discretion independent of Cabinet members. A much larger White House staff resulted. Seeking freedom for himself, Nixon left its management to others.

Thus in the more than 30 years since the White House staff became a major feature of our Government, we have alternated between two contrasting patterns for its composition and control. Numbers tell part of the story. In 1952, civilian aides with some substantive part in public business numbered 20. In 1962 the number was the same. In 1972 it seems to have been somewhere between 50 and 75 (depending on how one counts the third-level assistants). Moreover, the alternation follows party lines; the contrasting patterns have almost become matters of party philosophy. At least they are matters of party experience, handed down through the political generations from old cadres to the young. When a Haldeman eloquently testifies on the philosophy of Nixon's system, Democrats scoff. Republicans did likewise at the lack of system in Roosevelt's arrangements, to say nothing of Kennedy's. . . .

A staff system that liberates the President to think frees staff men from his watchful eye. The price he pays for liberty comes in the coin of power. So we have seen with Nixon . . . .

It is a matter of coincidence, I think, that even as the old constraints of prudence slackened, the White House staff fell under the control of senior aides so lacking in propriety as those we saw this summer on our television screens. Men like these are the opposite of Truman's Counsel, Murphy. Not everyone who ever served in the White House met his standard. But few if any ever fell so far below it as those Nixon aides. Men of their extraordinary impropriety have not been found there before, at least not in such numbers. Their like might not have been there under Nixon, or not so many of them, had he won the Presidency eight years earlier, succeeding Eisenhower. Even in 1969 they did not have the place all to themselves, but had to share it for a while with seniors of a different sort, men who were old hands at governing, experienced downtown and tempered by long contact with the Hill. Murphy's sensitivities owed much to the flavor of Congress— especially the Senate (where he himself had been a legislative counsel) and most especially the Senate of the old Southern ascendancy, exemplified by Senator Richard Russell. (In 1951, Russell's masterful performance in the chair of the MacArthur hearings caused the General to fade away, no harm to the Republic, and set a high standard for Senator Ervin.) But in Nixon's White House those most respectful of the Hill's old flavor did not long survive a contest with the masters

of new-style campaigning. Zealous for their chief, the winners packed
the place with second and third-level men of their own mind, magnified
his wishes by their own means and wound up blighting the bright
prospect of his second term.

THE FUTURE

Excess has now bred its own corrective. Watergate puts new life
into old constraints, and more precisely, it assures a set of temporary
substitutes. If the White House is forced into continuous give-and-take,
this after all is what the Constitution intended. If the give-and-take
sometimes degenerates into sheer nastiness, this will reflect the way
it all began, in White House zealousness.

. . . But [Nixon] would have faced some shortfall even if Watergate
had not happened. The failure of Phase Three to keep down prices,
and the failure of bombing in Cambodia to bring "peace," assured that
opposition would revive on the Hill and in the press.

The modern Presidency is a sturdy vehicle. Hardship and untidiness
are frequently its lot. But at worst a President retains his formal powers.
These put him at the center of the legislative process, the administrative
process, national politics, foreign relations; combined they make him
central to the news. Accordingly, so long as he has time ahead, there
will be men in every part of Washington who are mindful of his wishes
because they in their own jobs have need of him in his. Until his last
appointment, his last budget, his last veto, his last summit, he cannot
sink to insignificance in Government; his office will uphold him. As for
changes in the office of the sort now being argued both in Congress
and the courts—limiting impoundment, or his use of force abroad,
or claims to executive privilege—each dents the Presidency at an
outer edge, narrowing discretion, reducing flexibility, but strikes no
vital spot. What is vital to the office is that combination: processes,
politics, peace and the news. Within our Government the combination is unique, and so confers unique advantages. These remain.

(The Nixon proposal for a single six-year Presidential term is in
a different category. It would change the Presidency's central core,
to my mind, for the worse. We now have, in effect, an eight-year term
subject at midpoint to an opposition audit reviewed by the electorate
and then a vote of confidence without which he retires. The required
re-election at midterm is one of the most democratic features of the
office and adds to its legitimacy in a system of popular sovereignty.
Removal of this feature to protect us from its possible corruption is a
frivolous proposal for a President to make, especially when his regime

has been the most corrupt. Nixon, I hope, was not serious.)

The Supreme Court last interfered with Presidential powers in 1952 when Truman was denied authority to seize the nation's steel mills. But the Court managed not to say it never could be done again in any circumstances. On the contrary, the artful spread of concurring opinions left the future relatively open. The Presidency is limited only a little. This is the likeliest outcome again when current issues reach the highest Court. The net result may be to make some future Presidents work harder, under more restrictions, conciliating more, and forcing issues less than Nixon chose to do in his first term—or Truman at the time of the steel seizures. The Presidency won't be flattened by that!

To write of Truman is to recall the trouble and the pain associated with his Presidency: the pain of the Korean war and those interminable truce talks; the pain of domestic reforms deferred, of foreign developments blighted; the pain of MacArthur, and McCarthy; the China charges; the corruption charges; the list goes on and on. But where is that pain now? The young know nothing of it; the old have long since put it out of mind. A few of us would gladly show our scars, but we have no viewers except for historians, and not even many of them. Truman never captivated the campuses. And so I predict it will be with our current trouble. At the same time, though, short-term results have a way of shedding light on problems for the more distant future.

If the value of Watergate is great as a temporary renewer of old constraints, it is not unqualified. We now are in a period of antipolitical politics, with journalists and politicians playing to their own sense of successive, cumulative, public disillusionments. Watergate feeds the mood. When such a period descended on us in the early fifties we got Eisenhower for President, the hero-above-politics. Since we lack heroes nowadays, the next time could be worse. Moreover, the renewed constraints on Nixon cannot last forever. Watergate's effects will wear off over time, perhaps by his successor's second term (taking us no farther than 1984). As this occurs the weakened state of old constraints will be exposed once more: the parties beyond recall, the Congress mortgaged to ticket-splitting, the Cabinet frayed by overlapping jurisdictions, the dependence of all the rest on the President's own style.

But separated powers still define our system, so new colleagues, bringing new constraints, may replace the old, and some of the old may revive. What happens in our parties is especially important. We may face perpetual disarray, a dire prospect. But renewal is by no means inconceivable. For instance, big-state governors, linked to professional managers and money, may revive party baronies in the guise of perpetual candidacies. Reagan and Rockefeller may be precursors. As part of the same vision, or perhaps quite separately, cadres of volunteers funded by direct-mail drives may come into existence state by state to man elective party posts and staff campaigns, substituting, in relatively stable fashion, for old-style machines. "Favorite sons" may come to have renewed significance. The national convention may again become the place for interstate negotiations (especially if the TV networks cut back live coverage). A President, like others, then negotiates again.

If national parties revive, this makes it the more likely that Congress and the White House will some day be run again by men with the same party label. A President then will welcome back old colleagues. As for executive operations, residual price and wage controls—an incomes policy with some sort of club in the closet—may well join revenue sharing and resource regulation as likely long-term features of the Federal scene. White House attention may be focused on them in the future, along with defense and diplomacy. If so, no matter what becomes of traditional Cabinet posts, the President will gain new executive colleagues: corporation officials, union leaders, governors, mayors.

Even the traditional executive positions may again turn more collegial from a President's standpoint than most of them were six months ago. Much depends upon the evolution of relationships with Congress. Senator Walter F. Mondale recently has urged, as one of several new checks on the White House, a televised Senate question-period for Cabinet officers. This is an old proposal, but with the new addition of television, no small matter. Such appearances would distance Cabinet members from the President and so make them more important to him, in the very act of making them perform independently. But television is not without risk. While distancing them, it might also diminish them —and the Senate along with them—especially if viewers were to compare Senate sessions with, say, the press conferences of a J.F.K. The tube is a two-edged sword; thus, so is Mondale's scheme. But it suggests how readily the future may be open to some changes in the status of traditional Cabinet posts.

In short, I think it possible that 20 years from now constraints upon a President will be at least as strong as 20 years ago. While we wait for the emergence of new colleagues or a welcome-back to old, we have little to depend on by way of these informal checks and balances, except constraints of the other sort, those of operating style. Then the man's methods alone define the sense of prudence he may call to the support of his own sense of propriety. All is subjective, turning on him, much as it was until lately with Nixon.

But for a while Watergate supervenes. Nixon's successor, I predict, will not be tarred by it. Indeed he probably will be its beneficiary, winning as a "Mr. Clean." Almost surely he will pledge to make himself accessible and to rein in his staff. So did Nixon five years ago, but the next President will have more need to be serious about it, and more reason, and he may well possess a temperament more suited to the task. Voters, I suspect, will shun secretive types. God willing, they will welcome humor. At worst we should get prudence with a pretense of propriety. At best we will get the genuine article.

10 | Putting the President Back into Politics

Thomas E. Cronin

Public attitudes toward the presidency have significant effects on presidential power. In an important essay, "Superman, Our Textbook President," Cronin pointed out that the American people tend to view their presidents as omnipotent and benevolent, and he showed how these ideas are reflected in political-science textbooks. In the present essay Cronin explores another facet of the public mind—the desire for presidents to be above politics and play the role of statesman. He notes how President Nixon exploited this expectation and what consequences it had for decision-making in the White House. By comparing the worlds of foreign policy and domestic affairs, the author indicates how much more freedom presidents have in their role as world leaders and why they prefer to deal with foreign affairs rather than with the frustrating realm of domestic politics.

The regrettable state of affairs today is that being President means never having to say you're sorry, wrong, and, perhaps more importantly, that you are being political. The perceived shame of politics and the indignities of sounding partisan have had grievous impact on the exercise of national leadership in America. In their most manifest form, they prompt a President to say piously that he is above politics and that he acts solely as President for all the people. As a result, both partisan leadership and controversial domestic policy decision-making are increasingly contracted out or down and, in any event, disassociated from the overt visible (and thus accountable) actions of a President.

Reprinted with permission from *The Washington Monthly.* Copyright © by the Washington Monthly Co., 1028 Connecticut Ave., N.W., Washington, D.C. 20036. This article appeared in the issue of September, 1973, pp. 7-12.

Thomas E. Cronin is author of *The State of the Presidency* (1975) and co-author of *The Presidency Reappraised.* His most recent affiliations have been with the Aspen Institute for Humanistic Studies and the Center for the Study of Democratic Institutions.

A standard diagnosis of what's gone wrong in the White House is that the presidency has become too politicized. The White House "enemies" list adds substance to this impression, as have President Nixon's attempts to use the classic above-politics defense of politicians in trouble. His April 30 [1973] plea to be excused from thinking further about Watergate so that he could return to the "larger duties" of his office had its similarities to Adam Clayton Powell's "let me serve my people" and Teddy Kennedy's anxiety about "getting this [the Chappaquiddick investigation] over, so I can get back to my Senate duties." A Harris poll released on August 6 [1973] shows that the creaking ploy has paid off once again: by a 54 to 38 per cent margin, a majority of the people agreed that "the President was right in saying it is more important for him to spend his time working for the country than to be trying to find out what happened in the Watergate affair."

The very phrasing of this question—implying as it does that the President would be neglecting the country's welfare if he cleaned out the Watergate gang rather than toasting the Shah of Iran—suggests the absurdity of the over-politicization diagnosis. A more helpful approach to the recent failures of the presidency is to realize that Presidents have tried too hard to hold themselves above politics—or at least to give that appearance—rather than engaging in it deeply enough.

Theodore White's book, *The Making of the President 1972,* is an important document for understanding these developments. For while White has written another excellent chronicle of the election process, by far his best since 1960 and perhaps the best of his entire series, one crucial failure in his understanding illuminates a larger failure in the way we judge our Presidents. . . .

INTERVIEWS WITH NIXON

Nowhere is this more evident than in the three interviews with Nixon that White describes in the book. The latest of these took place on March 17, 1973, by which time enough of the Watergate scandal had been aired to raise an unmistakable odor.

"I asked none of those questions [about Watergate] that Saturday afternoon," White writes in preface to his interview. "They did not, at the moment, seem relevant." One wonders what it might have taken to excite his interest. Instead, White and the President sat back and chewed over the "larger duties" of the office, in a rambling discussion that always seemed to find its way back to foreign affairs:

> I wanted to turn the conversation to home affairs; and I said
> that I had once quoted him on the presidency and the nation

in a conversation of 1967, in which he had said, "I've always thought this country could run itself domestically without a President; all you need is a competent Cabinet to run the country at home." . . . Since that remark had been re-quoted and misinterpreted so often, what about it?

He was easy this afternoon, and toyed with the question as if trying to find a shape to the answer. "People don't respond in domestic affairs," he said. "Unless it touches them directly—like busing—they don't give a damn. But when it comes to foreign affairs, everyone wants to be Secretary of State, every columnist, every commentator, every writer." Domestic questions, he felt, just weren't that exciting. Take a question like revenue-sharing—only the specialists wanted to probe that one. . . .

So the domestic field was where Presidents usually ran into trouble. The nation tended to unite behind a President on foreign policy. But on domestic policy, "Presidents are usually losers, because domestic affairs divide." FDR had an emergency at home, the Depression, which united people behind him—but it was sad that so many of our great Presidents had to have a war to unite people behind them. . . .

It was clear where his heart and attention still lay as we came back to talk of foreign affairs. We talked of his visit to China; of his May 8th decision to mine Haiphong and bomb Hanoi. Those were presidential tasks.

Of course, one cannot fault White for failing to produce an exhaustive critique of the Nixon presidency in a book that is supposed to be about the campaign. Yet the ease with which White accepts Nixon's attempts to separate his "presidential tasks" of war- and peace-making from the thankless "loser's" work of running the economy or passing education bills is perhaps the most revealing aspect of the book. In agreeing that the President becomes more "presidential" when he drifts above the compromise and negotiation that make up the political process, White is acquiescing in a general debasement of the value of politics. This is just the feeling that Nixon appeals to with his "larger duties" speeches. The intention is to propel himself above the tawdry concerns of ordinary "politicians" and emerge, isolated and pure, as statesman and national leader.

Even for those who automatically suspect Nixon's motives, part of the appeal works, for we share that same view of the political process as cheap and corrupt. It has been so long since anyone has been able to use terms like "free democracy" or "legislative deliberation" seriously that we find it hard to imagine they represent any actual processes. The contempt expressed in John Ehrlichman's remarks about alcoholism on the Senate floor was unusual only in its bitterness.

Certainly there are dishonest men in politics, but we have come in danger of forgetting that there *is* a clean politics, and that it is the only way a democracy can work. The Ervin committee, even by the most cynical evaluation, has at least demonstrated the willingness to listen that has been so strikingly absent from the White House.

THE USE OF DIPLOMACY

From the President's point of view, there are obvious attractions to having the public define "presidential tasks" on a global scale. As a literal student of White's earlier books, Nixon must have understood the advantage of running as "The President" rather than as candidate Dick Nixon, and of spending his time in foreign capitals rather than shaking hands with county political chairmen. Presidential counsel Leonard Garment explained to White:

> In foreign policy, you get drama, triumph, resolution—crisis and resolution. So that in foreign policy Nixon can give the sense of leadership. But in domestic policy, there you have to deal with the whole jungle of home problems.

It is this same view of politics as a "jungle" that is reflected in the Harris poll and the President's avoidance of domestic politics. To those in the White House, other parts of the political process may also start to look like a jungle: the courts, local political groups, the press, in short, anything that impedes the President's progress between deciding he wants something done and seeing it happen. Since the impediments are minimal in foreign affairs, Presidents turn more of their attention there.

As George Reedy pointed out in *The Twilight of the Presidency,* a political philosophy which respects individuals and institutions only to the extent that they support the President's decisions is the death of reality in the White House. In setting policy there are always differing opinions to take into account, objections to programs, needs that have not been detected. Because the structure of the White House staff makes it unlikely that the President will ever hear these dissenting opinions from his own advisers, it becomes all the more important that he is forced to take part in political negotiation.

The means for bringing him in touch with reality is the process of political bargaining—with the delays it requires, the necessary changes of course, the arguments, and the listening. What makes domestic politics so distasteful to Presidents—that it is full of groups to persuade and committees to inform—is precisely its virtue, for it is the major hope of retaining an open presidency, one neither bound by its own

sources of information nor aloof to the point where it will no longer
listen. But by calling the President more "presidential" whenever he
ignores partisan politics, we encourage him to even greater isolation.

One illustration from the last campaign may help clarify the point.
In deciding to do what most people lauded—keeping himself "above
politics" and miles away from the Republican Party—Nixon was able
to ignore the local politicians and set up his own Committee to Re-elect
the President. From a management point of view it had the same
advantages as secret diplomacy: everything was under control, the
employees followed orders. Yet CREEP ended up committing exploits
which the National Committee could never have accomplished. This
was not so much because of different moral standards in the two groups,
as because of the political theorists' old principles of pluralism and
mutually restricting greed. National Committeemen from all over the
country would have screamed bloody murder at $350,000 going to
some non-candidate named Gordon Liddy while the friends back home
weren't able to pay their printing bills.

FOREIGN AFFAIRS VERSUS DOMESTIC POLITICS

The same phenomenon takes on more disturbing dimensions when
the President's foreign policy decisions—those that add to his stature
as Statesman—are contrasted to what he must actually do to get any
domestic policy enacted. As John Newhouse has illustrated in his
superb new book, *Cold Dawn: The Story of SALT,* in foreign policy
the President may make the most crucial of decisions, take those steps
that literally mean survival or extinction for most of the people on
earth, without consulting anyone more closely in touch with the democratic pulse than Henry Kissinger. More important, the President can
see his decisions carried out without resistance, debate, or the threat of
publicity. While some such autonomy is probably necessary for effective
negotiations, it is also subject to abuse. When Presidents get the idea that
only they know all the facts about the country's safety, then they feel
uniquely qualified to make the decisions about what is justified in the
name of national defense. The "if you knew what I know" explanation,
applied to events as diverse as the Dominican Republic invasion and the
Daniel Ellsberg break-in, is a difficult one to counter, because the public
can never be confident that this time the President isn't finally telling the
truth. Thus, in foreign policy—the area in which the President is seen
by the public to be a superman—his powers most nearly approximate
those of superman. The only people he deals with in the government
are his underlings; they must do what he tells them and keep quiet

about it. Those he deals with outside the government may be most effectively handled with blanket secrecy.

Consider the same President, having spent the morning working on a missile treaty with the Russians and sending a fleet of bombers to Asia, as he summons Gerald Ford and Carl Albert to the Oval Office. All he wants is a minor change in the public works laws, or a new educational program. Suddenly the controlled world of the treaty-makers is replaced by the hurly-burly of people and politics. The chess game of foreign policy has turned into a greased-pig contest.

No longer is the President talking to his own employees, who feel honored by his very presence and who can be relied on to try to please him. The timeless senators and congressmen he must flatter and win have seen him come and will see him go. They have their own pride, their own views, their own groups to represent. None of the congress-men—or the labor leaders or foreign veterans' groups—is individually the equal of the President, but many of them can resist on specific points. The President has no way to enforce the code of *omerta* [silence] on them—and no claim to a monopoly on relevant information.

When the President wants his goals accomplished in domestic legis-lation, he uses the tactics of secrecy and arrogance only at his peril. To obtain even small concessions, the President must practice the art of politics in its finest sense. He must cajole, persuade, compromise, entice—and above all, listen, for otherwise he will not understand how he can persuade. George Reedy explained the techniques necessary for persuasion:

> The master practitioners of the Senate . . . live in an atmo-sphere which will instill some degree of humility into even the most arrogant of men. They walk every day through an adver-sary atmosphere. They have before them constant reminders of the swift penalties for failure to take into account the strong feelings of other men. They not only receive letters and tele-phone calls from their constituents, but run into them in the corridor daily. Reality is never very far away.

It can be small wonder that a man who has seen alliances formed and villages destroyed at his whim will have little patience for the elderly committee chairman who demands a respectful hearing before he will do the Administration a favor. The public attitudes toward the presidency—those mirrored in White's book—encourage the Presi-dent to feel contempt for the congressman.

By turning up our noses at "politics" in the White House and urging the President to get on to his real business of guiding the nation, we set the two important conditions for the secrecy and duplicity with which we have recently become so familiar. First, with all the apparatus for secret statesmanship at hand, it is much easier for the President to ring up the plumbers when something needs fixing than to persuade the public or Congress to his point of view. Second, since the President will look "unpresidential" if he participates in normal party politics, his aides must go through grotesque contortions to prove that their boss never thought about anything except being President of All the People.

The tactic of secrecy, so tempting to those who have it within their grasp, amounts to insulating the President from the normal checks and balances of the political system. It will take new bait to lure Presidents out of this comfortable sanctuary and into the morass of open politics, for now the enticements are small. Theodore White and Richard Nixon didn't invent the notion of the apolitical statesman-President. A deep popular sentiment rouses with indignation at the idea that a President is "playing politics" with an issue, or is neglecting the general welfare for any "partisan" cause. Foreign policy is more fun, and besides, you can win the Nobel Peace Prize; the openness of domestic politics has few compensating advantages.

PREVENTING FUTURE ABUSES

The way to prevent future abuses, as has often been noted, is to make the White House more open. The way to do that, as has not so often been suggested, is to start regarding the President as a politician once more. A President cannot and should not avoid being openly political. A President in a democracy has to act politically in regard to controversial issues if we are to have any semblance of government by the consent of the governed—that is, he must negotiate and mediate between groups, compromise polar differences, and find acceptable alternatives.

We can no more take the politics out of the presidency than we can take the presidency out of politics. It is a very political office, and political and partisan leadership are as much needed as foreign policy statesmanship and symbolic leadership.

Most of the men who have been effective Presidents have also been highly political—in an open, rather than covert, sense of that term. Unlike Nixon, they loved politics, and they understood the multiple purposes for which the powers of the presidency are granted. The best of our Presidents have been those who understood the importance of political parties and who listened to the people, and did not condescendingly view the American common man as childlike and dependent on an omniscient President. As a nation, we must mature to the recognition that Presidents have to be political and they ought to be vigorously partisan leaders as well. And if the presidency is recognized as the highly political office it necessarily is, then we have to strive more rigorously to strengthen rival and alternative political institutions that can keep it accountable, pose alternative programs, offer alternative definitions of the national purpose, and let the sun shine in. Sunlight, they say, is the best of disinfectants, but bringing Presidents to heel will require attitudinal changes, party-building efforts on a grand scale, and harsh rebukes to any President who either unwittingly or deliberately tries to hide behind the disingenuous protective shield of being above politics.

11 | Government and the People

Aaron Wildavsky

Agreeing with Cronin's analysis of the preference of presidents for foreign affairs over domestic politics, Wildavsky argues that this trend is due to a public tendency to make incompatible demands on government, which in turn makes it difficult for presidents to benefit politically from domestic programs. The author mentions a number of developments in presidential politics that he feels are a consequence of these changes in the nature of social pressures on political institutions. They include the decline of party loyalty in voting, the new emphasis by presidents on public relations rather than substance, the bureaucratization of the White House, and to some extent Watergate itself. Wildavsky suggests that the social problems government has tried to solve in the last decade are increasingly difficult, but politicians have continued to administer ineffective programs because of the optimism of American national character.

We shall never learn what needs to be learned about the American political system until we understand not only what the system does to the people, but what the people do to the system. Political institutions are no different from other organizations: to the great question of organizational life—who will bear the costs of change?—the answer, in the public as in the private sphere, is, "someone else, not me." The universal tendency to make life easy for ourselves and to impose difficulties on others applies equally to politicians, and when they find their lives intolerable no one should be surprised that they react by seeking to lay their burdens on the shoulders of others.

Especially during the past decade, almost our whole attention as

Reprinted with permission of the author from *Commentary*, August, 1973, pp. 25-32. Copyright © 1973.

Aaron Wildavsky is Dean of the Graduate School of Public Policy, University of California, Berkeley. He is editor of *The Presidency* and author of *Presidential Elections* (with Nelson Polsby) and several other works.

citizens has been devoted to the ways in which politicians have failed to serve the people. Few have asked how politicians manage to live in the world, because it is assumed that they are doing fine and that the problem is to make them behave decently towards us—almost as if politicians lived somehow apart from American life. Yet it would be strange indeed if our politicians were a special breed, uninfluenced by their milieu, springing full-born like Minerva from the head of Jove in a world they never made, but on which they work their mythical powers.

Polticians are like other animals; indeed their behavior, like our own, can often be analogized to that observed in lower forms of life. Laboratory experiments show that rats who are consistently given contradictory commands become neurotic, if not psychotic. The same phenomenon is readily visible among politicians. Give them incompatible commands, insist that they fulfill contradictory impulses at the same time, and they too will show the classical symptoms—withdrawal, self-mutilation, random activity, and other forms of bizarre behavior unrelated to the ostensible task at hand. An occasional deviant is even known to lash out at his experimenters, or at least at the apparatus in which he is enmeshed, though he remains quite incapable of understanding why he worked so hard to accomplish so little, or why life is so bitter when it should be so sweet.

We are all, in fact, doing better and feeling worse.[1] Every standard of well-being, from housing to health, shows that every sector of the population, however defined, including all racial, religious, and ethnic groupings, has improved its lot in past decades. Even the twin problems of crime and drugs, areas in which we are vividly conscious of recent deterioration, have been considerably reduced in severity, so far as we are able to judge, since the turn of the century. When heroin was legal there were proportionately more addicts in the population; when the nation was younger and poorer there were more criminals, or at least a correspondingly greater degree of crime. Why, then, do so many feel so bad—and why do they continue to feel so bad when, of the two causes reflexively invoked to explain this feeling, the first, the Vietnam war, has come to an end while the second, racial inequity, has clearly and visibly diminished? I cannot pursue this subject in all its ramifications here. Instead I wish to add another element to the puzzle—the manufacture of incompatible policy demands that impose burdens on government which no government can meet.

The fact that the public demands on government in the various areas of policy are contradictory, in the sense that pursuing one policy inevitably means prohibiting the enactment of another, does not mean that an evil genius has been at work programming the political system for a nervous breakdown. Coordination need not require a coordinator;

it can be tacit and informal as well as overt. Men coordinate their activities through adherence to a common body of assumptions or through the sharing of a common world view. Quite the same kinds of contradictions can be created by various people in different places making vocal demands that turn out to be mutually opposed. The lack of central direction, in fact, is an advantage because it adds to the general confusion: politicians are given a hard time but they do not know on whom to vent their own frustration. For our purposes it is not necessary to know whether demands on government are made by those who wish to see it fail, and therefore delight in giving it tasks it cannot manage, or who wish to see it succeed, and take pleasure in asking it to perform feats hitherto unaccomplished. Whether it stems from those who love government too little or from those who love it too much, the results of this pressure are the same: government is asked to perform wonders, but the attainment of one wonder often automatically precludes the possibility of attaining another, or many others.

The incompatibility of policy demands is a manifestation of a more general withdrawal of sovereignty from government in America. The rights of government and of politicians are being systematically whittled down. Public officials and professional politicians can no longer organize their political parties as they please or hold meetings in closed sessions, or keep their papers secret, or successfully sue others for slandering them—even when they can show the allegations to be false —or make the smallest decisions without being hauled into court to convince judge and attorney they have followed standards of due process, considered every conceivable alternative, consulted all who might possibly be injured, or otherwise abandoned virtually every sense of what it used to mean to rule by enforcing binding regulations. We demand more of government but we trust it less. Angered and annoyed by evident failures, our reaction is not to reduce our expectations of what government can accomplish but to decrease its ability to meet them. That is how a society becomes ungovernable. . . .

EFFECTS ON GOVERNMENT

What are the consequences of constructing and defining issues so as to pose incompatible demands on decision-makers? Both the kinds of policies we get from government and the kinds of attention paid to the various realms of policy are affected. Within the executive branch a greater emphasis will naturally come to be placed on foreign than on domestic policy. Because the foreign realm seems less forbidding to

Presidents and even given a random occurrence of events it seems likely that some good can be achieved—for which, moreover, credit may accrue to the President. In domestic policy, on the other hand, Presidents have come to see little for which they will be applauded, and much for which they will be condemned for even attempting. . . .

. . . The critics of social policy have overplayed their hand; they wanted more and better, instead they are getting less and worse. The Nixon administration eventually came to the conclusion that since no visible credit was forthcoming from the presumptively natural supporters of social programs, it might as well gain whatever benefits it could from the conservatives who opposed them. Like any other institution that wishes to remain solvent, governmental bodies must reestablish their credit when their policies begin to earn a deficit of political support.

"Government," Alfred Marshal wrote, "is the most precious of human possessions; and no care can be too great to be spent on enabling it to do its work in the best way: a chief condition to that end is that it should not be set to work for which it is not specially qualified, under the conditions of time and place." Once government is given not just one or two things it cannot do, but a whole host, the effect will be felt throughout the political system. Voters, for instance, have begun to lose their sense of identification with the major political parties, because they, like the government, cannot deliver on their promises. The nature of political campaigns has also changed. In 1972, instead of defending their record, the leaders of government concentrated on the alleged horrors about to be perpetrated by the opposition—or that had been perpetrated by their own party's past. "Elect me," promised Richard Nixon in effect, "and I will save you from that fellow who created a $33 billion deficit. Elect me, and I will protect you from my Justice Department's former position on busing. Elect me, and I will save you from quotas imposed by my Department of Health, Education, and Welfare." The President was running against himself, monopolizing the advantages of incumbency while at the same time pretending he had never been in office. No doubt future challengers will learn the wisdom of being vague, lest their promises, rather than the government's performance, become the focal point of the campaign.

If parties cannot make good on the promises of their candidates for office, what can they make good on? Party structure, for one thing; they can promise to organize themselves in a given way, if only because this is something over which they can exercise control. Thus parties, like politicians, move more strongly into the realm of the expressive and the symbolic rather than of substantive policy. The Democratic party can arrange itself in order to contain certain proportions of this or that ethnic group or gender. It can conduct endless meetings, primaries, conventions, all the while gradually shifting the definition of a party from an instrument seeking to govern the nation to an instrument seeking to govern itself. What parties contribute to the nation, then, is not so much candidates attached to a policy as procedures that meet certain visible but internal norms.

Politicians, too, are shifting emphasis from substantive policy to personal political style. They talk of basic changes in the political process, but move into action only when this consists of a form of opposition. They offer adherence to proclaimed moral principle, where they cannot fail, instead of offering innovation in policy, where they cannot succeed. They are often "against" what is happening but see themselves under no obligation to suggest viable alternatives. A sign of the political times is the growing proportion of Presidential candidates who come from the United States Senate, for that is the office which combines the longest term and the highest national visibility with the least responsibility. When people are angry they may picket mayors and shout down governors, but they rarely advance on the Senate or its occupants. The Senate is the place where a man can say his piece while others worry about the responsibilities of office.

Not only the Senate but the House as well, Congress as a whole, is involved in the dilemma of acting responsibly at a time when substantive achievements are hard to come by. The quandary in which Congressmen find themselves is illustrated in the controversy over impoundment. It is all too easy to blame the conflict entirely on the President; he had ample discretionary powers under the Anti-Deficiency Act of 1951, but he chose instead to throw down the gauntlet by saying that he might refuse to spend money in appropriations bills even after they were passed over his veto. That bit of arrogance deserves what it got. But underneath the surface clash of personalities lies a deepseated unwillingness in Congress to accept responsibility for raising the revenues required to support its own spending desires. It is easier to vote for this or that while laying the burden of reduced expenditures, or of finding new revenues, at the door of the President. The growing practice of Presidential impoundment may be part of a tacit agreement that Congress will get credit for voting the funds while the President takes Congress off the hook by refusing to spend. By allowing impoundment to go on for as long as it did and to cover so extensive a range of policies, Congress demonstrated its apparent willingness to see spending cut if only the blame could be placed elsewhere.

CONNECTIONS TO WATERGATE

Of all our institutions, the Presidency has been the one most deeply affected by government's inability to get credit for domestic policy, because it is the single most visible source of authority and hence the most obvious target of demands. Even the Watergate affair, about which it is plausible to argue that the mentality that produced it is of a singular kind attributable only to President Nixon and his close associates, may be seen to have connections with the fate of the Presidency as an institution in recent years. This is hardly to deny, much less to excuse, the element of personal pathology, or criminality, involved, but even so extreme a series of events as those surrounding the Watergate affair may be clarified by reference to the general issue of the impact of public policy on the Presidency in the past decade.

The climate of opinion that made Watergate and its cover-up possible is part of (and will contribute further to) the delegitimation of government . . . . Although it is convenient now to forget this, from the middle 60's onward, national leaders of government have been subject to a crescendo of attack and even personal abuse. They have been shouted down, mobbed, and vilified in public. It was not possible for men like President Lyndon Johnson and Vice President Hubert Humphrey to speak where they wished in safety, or to travel where they wished without fear. Not merely their conduct as individuals, but the political system of which they were a part, has been condemned as vicious, immoral, and depraved. This, after all, was the justification offered for the stealing of government documents—that the government from which they were taken had no right to be doing what it was doing, that it was not legitimate. The rationale offered by Daniel Ellsberg for taking and publishing government documents was the same as that offered by the Watergate conspirators—national interest, a higher law than that applying to ordinary citizens.

Watergate emerged, in my opinion, out of an environment in which people who identified with government sought to delegitimate the opposition just as they believed the opposition had sought to delegitimate government. Presumably no one, in their view, had a right to beat President Nixon in 1972, so they sought to get Senator Muskie out of the race.[2] They broke into Watergate ostensibly to find evidence that the Democrats were being financed by Cuban (Communist) money, as if to say that their own illegality was permissible because the Democrats were not then a legitimate American political party. The blame, to be sure, is not the same. Ellsberg was not entrusted with the care of government, and the Watergate conspirators were. But they cohere in the same syndrome; the one is a reaction to the other, each party rationalizing its exceptional behavior on the grounds of its enemy's illegitimacy.

Watergate is a curious scandal by American standards, in that it is not concerned with money; nor is it, like a British scandal, concerned with sex. By contrast, it resembles a French scandal, one in which small groups of conspirators make and execute their clandestine plans in the service of ideologies held by no more than 1 or 2 per cent of the population. Watergate may thus represent another step in the "Frenchification" of American political life begun in the mid-1960's, a mode of politics in which apparently inexplicable behavior is found to derive from attachment to ideologies of which the vast bulk of the citizenry knows little and cares less. We may have to accustom ourselves to men on the Left out to save us from Fascism and men on the Right from Communism, men who point to one another's activities as justification for illegal acts.

The French analogy gains strength in light of the entire pattern of President Nixon's conduct before Watergate. Seemingly disparate occurrences fall into place once we understand that Nixon had adopted a plebiscitary view of the Presidency, a view that has echoes in the American past but none in the contemporary Western world except in the Presidency of Charles de Gaulle and his successor in France. From this perspective the position of Nixon's Attorney General on executive privilege, with its suggestion that the Presidency exists wholly apart from other institutions, becomes more explicable. So does Nixon's march on the media. For if the Presidency is not part of a separation of powers with Congress, but of a unity of power with the people, then its survival is critically dependent on direct access to them. His victory at the polls in 1972 seems to have inspired in him the conviction that as the embodiment of the national will he should brook no opposition from Congress. If he said "no" on spending and the legislature said "yes," so much the worse for *it*. Even the Republican party could not share in his triumph—it neither ran his campaign nor got any of its leaders appointed to high positions—lest it become another unwanted intermediary between the President and the people. . . . It was his plebiscitary view of the Presidency that led Nixon to attempt to run a foreign and defense policy without the Senate, a budget policy without the House, and a domestic-security policy without the courts.[3]

CAUSES OF EXECUTIVE BUREAUCRACY

I have momentarily digressed on the subject of Watergate only to suggest that there was more than personal idiosyncrasy at work here, and that there is reason to look upon Nixon's Presidency as the continuation and exemplification of a number of long-term trends in the political system as a whole. In like fashion, the organization of the executive office under Nixon continues an ever-growing trend toward bureaucratization, a reaction in turn to the perceived failure of the Presidential office to influence public policy in ways that will redound to its credit. And just as President Kennedy's and President Johnson's associates sought to lay the blame for bad public policy on the regular bureaucracy, so Nixon's men were following precedent when they sought to debureaucratize the bureaucracy while themselves becoming more bureaucratic. For bureaucratization is a way of seeking shelter from a stormy world.

The Presidential office has, as everybody can now see, become a bureaucracy in the same sense that Max Weber meant by the term: it has grown greatly in size and it is characterized by specialization, division of labor, chain of command, and hierarchy. At the same time it criticizes, castigates, and blames the regular federal bureaucracy and attempts to circumvent it and intervene directly in the political process at lower and lower levels. From the perhaps three secretaries that Franklin Roosevelt inherited, the executive bureaucracy has risen to several thousand. There are (or recently were) two specialized organizations for dealing with the media, one to handle daily press relations and the other concerned with various promotional ventures. There is a specialized bureaucracy for dealing with foreign policy, begun when John F. Kennedy appointed McGeorge Bundy to the White House; Henry Kissinger's shop now boasts a staff of about one hundred. There is a domestic council to deal with policy at home, started by Richard Nixon. And there is also the Congressional liaison machinery instituted by President Eisenhower. Since 1965 the growth of the executive office of the President has been geometric. The largest increases of all occurred in Nixon's first term, but he was merely accelerating a trend, not initiating it.

Because President Nixon, especially at the start of his second term, apparently set out to alienate every national elite—the press, Congress, the Republican National Committee—the fact that he had long been attacking his own federal bureaucracy has escaped notice. Such incidents abound, however. At ceremonies establishing the special Action Office for Drug Abuse Control, for example: ". . . the President told an audience of 150 legislators and officials that 'heads would roll' if 'petty bureaucrats' obstruct the efforts of the office's director, Dr. Jerome H. Jaffe. . . . The President said that above all the law he just signed put into the hands of Dr. Jaffe full authority to 'knock heads together' and prevent 'empire building' by any one of the many agencies concerned" (New York *Times*, March 22, 1972). President Nixon also "informed a group of Western editors in Portland that he had told Secretary Morton 'we should take a look at the whole bureaucracy with regard to the handling of Indian affairs and shake it up good.' The President blamed the bureaucracy for Indian problems, saying that 'the bureaucracy feeds on itself, defends itself, and fights for the status quo. And does very little, in my opinion, for progress in the field' " (New York *Times*, September 29, 1971.).

Here too, Nixon was not so much initiating as continuing a trend. Much the same hospitality to the bureaucracy had been manifested by his immediate predecessors. Accounts of staff men under Johnson and Kennedy frequently reveal a sense of indignation, if not outrage, at the very idea of the separation of powers; federalism is an anathema to agents of the executive branch. Who are all those people out there thwarting us? they ask all but explicitly. Who do they think they are in the Congress and the state capitals? Strongest of all is the condemnation of the bureaucracy. The White House staff has great ideas, marvelous impulses, beautiful feelings, and these are suppressed, oppressed, crushed by the bureaucratic mind.

Why is it that the President on the one hand seeks to bureaucratize his own office, while on the other hand he holds the bureaucracy to blame for all his ills? In the end we return to our beginnings. Presidents have been impelled to attempt stabilization of their own office and destabilization of the regular bureaucracy because of radical changes in public policy demands. The structure of domestic political issues is now such that no government, and hence no President, can get the credit for what is done. Like all the other actors in this drama the President and his men head for cover in the White House stockade and shoot at others more vulnerable than themselves.

It would appear amazing, in retrospect, that we thought about the Presidency as if it were uncaused, as if the things that affected and afflicted us as citizens had no impact on the men who occupy public office. How long did we expect attacks on the man and the institution to go on before there was a response? Nixon's counter-attack, it now appears, may have threatened our liberties. Did the growing popularity of the idea that illegality was permissible for a good cause have no impact on the men surrounding the President? Did this political peril have nothing to do with the demands we make on our Presidents but only with their designs on us? John F. Kennedy struggled mightily with a sense of failure before he was assassinated. Lyndon B. Johnson was forced to deny himself the chance for reelection. . . . Richard Nixon fights for a chance to serve out his term. One or two more experiences like these and someone may think it is more than coincidence.

It might be argued that my portrait of the Presidential office in particular, and of politicians in general, treats public officials as if they were the innocent victims of social pressures rather than active participants in the political process capable of shaping it to their own ends. Politicians, moreover, have faced conflicting demands in the past, and might reasonably be expected to face them successfully in the future. Problems arising from incompatible goals are what leaders are there to help solve. A purpose of leadership, after all, is to clarify what can and cannot be done, to set priorities, and to gain some agreement on a schedule of accomplishment. Is this too much to ask of a politician who wants to make a career out of leadership?

It is not. My thesis, however, is that the problems being allocated to government are not just a random sample of those ordinarily associated with governing, some of which, at least, are eminently soluble, given hard work and good judgment, but that government is increasingly getting a skewed distribution of problems that are insoluble precisely because people demand of government what government cannot do. What remains to be explained is how politicians have become strapped to this particular wheel and why they are so maladroit in getting off it.

AMERICAN POLITICAL IDEOLOGY

Politicians are Americans and they, too, are caught up in American optimism. Just as the Vietnam war was a symptom of the optimistic belief in the boundless possibilities of American intervention abroad, so, too, the War on Poverty was a symptom of an optimistic belief in the boundless possibilities of government intervention at home. By the time public officals began to realize they could not do everything all at once, or even some things at all, they had become committed to a broad new range of social programs. And they did not call a halt to these indecisive engagements because they were liberals, that is, Americans.

America lacks an intellectually respectable conservative tradition. It has always, as Louis Hartz has sought to show, had a liberal tradition. For present purposes this means that equality, no matter how abused or disused, has always been the prevailing American norm; the long tradition of hypocrisy on the issue is itself eloquent testimony to its power. The new social and political programs, whether designed for increased participation in decision-making or a greater share in the good things of life, came into the world bearing the banner of the liberal concept of equality. It was hard to oppose, or even think clearly about opposing, these programs without appearing to be against equality or in favor of inequality. Individual politicians might have doubts, a few deviants might voice them, but there was too much guilt engendered by the rhetoric of equality to make collective action possible.

After the deed comes the rationalization. John Rawl's distinguished book on equality, *A Theory of Justice,* though long in the making, appears now as a gloss on the domestic programs of the 1960's. Its guiding principle is that no inequality is justified unless it helps those who are worst off. Armed with this communitarian thrust to liberal principle, one can defend any sort of policy which proclaims its purpose as that of aiding the worst off but which does not bother to balance smaller benefits to some against larger benefits to others. A few pundits aside, there is not now, if there ever was, a social stratum able to support a conservative ethic against the forces in favor of pushing public policy over the egalitarian precipice. Under the Nixon administration, instead of a social response we got a pitiful outbreak (or break-in) like Watergate.

The American politician, like the American political system, has been attacked at the most vulnerable point. The system is being asked to make good on its most ancient and deeply-held beliefs, and it hovers between an inability to abandon its faith and an inability to make its faith manifest to the believers. This is the American crisis of confidence, evident in professors who do not profess, scientists who call for alternative approaches to science that smack of witchcraft, and politicians who condemn politics.

The expectations created by the body politic (or by a small but influential part of it), the rewards and punishments it administers, go far to shape the successes and failures of public officials. Anyone who writes or speaks or thinks seriously about public policy has a special obligation to consider what his contribution, even when placed in the context of many others, implies for the ability of government to perform adequately. Otherwise, private vices will become public vices as well (to reverse Mandeville), and government, seeing that the game is rigged, will respond once again by secretly attempting to change the rules.

NOTES

1. See my essays, "The Empty-headed Blues: Black Rebellion and White Reaction," *Public Interest,* No. 11, Spring 1968; "The Revolt Against the Masses," *The Revolt Against the Masses and Other Essays on Politics and Public Policy* (Basic Books, 1971); "The Search for the Oppressed," *Freedom at Issue.* No. 16, November-December 1972.

2. I pass over the intriguing question of what lesson the Democratic party might learn when its worst enemies conspire to nominate the candidate it was bent on selecting itself.

3. Nixon did not have these views when he came into office. It was his experience in office that led him to such desperate expedients. No doubt each man comes bringing his own desperation with him. But Nixon was already President. To go so far after four years in office he must have been more frustrated than anyone knew.

Part Three
The Personality in the White House

From Machiavelli to Freud

12

Arthur Woodstone

Woodstone was the first journalist to explore seriously in print the possibility that self-destructive tendencies existed in Richard Nixon's political behavior. His work, Nixon's Head, *is unusual because of its publication before Nixon's handling of the Watergate crisis made such an interpretation popular. To support his argument the author provides evidence of self-defeating behavior by Nixon in several political campaigns, asserting that "when he won the Presidency in 1968, a great many Americans took his victory as irrefutable proof that [the last press conference of 1962] was a solitary systems failure, Nixon's single neurotic aberration." In this selection from the preface, Woodstone comments on the reluctance of members of the press to write about such behavior despite their willingness to talk about it among themselves.*

When President Eisenhower had his first heart attack, for the next several days the Vice-President, next in line of succession, was mentioned in every conceivable context but one. The media dredged up the Hiss case and the campaigns of 1946, 1950, 1952 and 1954; political analysts said that Richard Milhous Nixon was admired (never loved) and hated (never pitied) as a politician (never as a man); the overnight biographers, pulled off city desks to summarize his life, said he was the father of two girls, a Californian of humble origins and a Quaker. But no newspaper, wire service or broadcaster defied the conventions for examining important public figures, as if having achieved prominence entitled Nixon to less probing as a human being rather than more. So when they asked what made Dick Nixon "tick," it was a gesture; the answers were skin-deep. They did write that he had a strong desire to win. However, so do football heroes and

Reprinted with permission of St. Martin's Press from the Preface to *Nixon's Head* by Arthur Woodstone. Copyright © 1972, St. Martin's Press.

Arthur Woodstone is a journalist and political consultant who resides in New York City. Numerous national journals have carried his articles including *Variety* for which he covered the Kennedy-Nixon debates in 1960.

corporation presidents. Nobody asked (in the presence of the public) why the desire in Nixon sometimes seemed so overwhelming.

The next year, 1956, during the period when he was seeking re-election, the Vice-President's eccentric moments so multiplied in number, intensity and even type that to more observant reporters covering the campaign, it seemed the man was begging them to spell it out. Still, correspondents limited what they reported to diffident hints that public figures were not always coldly rational men. For example, a star reporter for *The New York Times* wrote that late one night, when he and others covering the Nixon campaign had nothing better to do, they sat around psychoanalyzing the Vice-President without reaching any conclusions. Of course, he couldn't very well have written of the conclusions they had not reached, but the reporter never even mentioned the facts that prompted these professional journalists to play amateur analysts.

In 1960 and again in 1968, during the Presidential campaigns, some professional skeptics in the press convinced themselves that by stressing Nixon, the shady political animal, they were winning a tough battle against press handouts and other packaged news. But in addition to its familiar ring, such reportage camouflaged the possibility that something besides cold political judgment made candidate Nixon tick. The image of the calculating politician, encouraged by Nixon's boasts of his own cunning, was so strong that it made his "last" press conference in 1962 after the California gubernatorial race seem an isolated emotional aberration.

Once Nixon was President, many White House correspondents felt that his peculiarities should concern no one but the man, his God and—if he had one—his analyst. Evoking "objectivity" as their goal, they limited themselves to taking down Nixon's words. And insofar as they played any personal role in the process, they provided neat language and a logical order to official statements—which made them little more than illustrious stenographers. In fact, these correspondents were often such fine writers that they gave the President a clarity and a logic that, at the moment of observation, he may not have truly possessed.

The better journalists covering Richard Nixon at the start of his term, knowing they were unqualified to sit behind "the couch," felt they had no right to speak in print of the aspects of the President's behavior which often disturbed them most. But more inhibiting than the knowledge of their own deficiencies as clinicians was their fear that once you've probed the quality or stability of a man's mind—especially if you are suspicious of his politics—you have opened the door to thought control and tyranny by the press.

By 1970, however, enough had happened to make it difficult for honest observers of the White House scene to report comforting certainties that frequently did not exist: Many of the President's assaults on his opponents to win votes or legislative programs no longer seemed reasoned or pragmatic—any more so than Lyndon Johnson's scalding treatment of his own aides or his discomfort among northern intellectuals. Urged on by at least two successive Administrations in which expediency and politics often seemed to play smaller roles than ego and emotion, these few journalists stopped nodding incessantly at Machiavelli and began talking more in public of Freud. . . .

13 | Portrait of a Presidency

Peter Jenkins

In this essay Jenkins reviews various theories about the causes of Watergate and concludes that Richard Nixon's personality was the source of the troubles. Examining examples of what he considers Nixon's irrational behavior, Jenkins raises questions about Nixon's emotional stability and concludes that the thirty-seventh President can be labeled at least a psychopath. According to the Comprehensive Dictionary of Psychological and Psychoanalytic Terms, *a psychopath is a person with any mental disorder regardless of its seriousness, although the term also has been used more narrowly to refer to an individual with a specific personality disorder.* The Encyclopedia of Psychology *says that a psychopath (or sociopath) "in attempting to extricate himself from difficulty . . . often produces an intricate and contradictory web of lies and rationalization, coupled with theatrical and sometimes convincing explanations, exclamations of remorse and promises to change."*

"How could it have happened? Who is to blame?" Richard Nixon asked these questions rhetorically on April 30, 1973, when flanked by a bust of Abraham Lincoln and the American flag, he addressed the people for the first time on the subject of Watergate. . . .

A year later to the day, the President released a 1,200-page transcript, edited in the White House, of tape-recorded meetings and telephone conversations covering chiefly the six weeks preceding that first public defense of himself on television . . . the transcripts utterly condemn his Presidency. They present an intimate portrait of a man morally unfit to occupy his high office. They question the previous judgment—of most critics and admirers alike—that Richard Nixon, whatever his deficiencies, is a man of quick mind and firm grasp, a consummate

Reprinted with permission of the author from *New York Magazine*, June 24, 1974, p. 36ff. It first appeared in the Bristish journal *New Statesmen*. Copyright © 1974.

Peter Jenkins is a former Washington correspondent who is now a London columnist for *The Guardian*.

politician. The questions he asked himself about Watergate—"How could it have happened? Who is to blame?"—must now be asked about his Presidency. How did such a man come to occupy the White House?

There are, broadly, four explanations advanced for Watergate, although they need not be mutually exclusive:

1. *Watergate was systemic:* (a) *left-wing version*

On the student Left, even now, impeachment has not caught on as a cause, certainly not one comparable with the antiwar movement. That Nixon should commit crimes was no surprise to the Left—look at the crimes he had committed in Indochina. The emergence of a parallel police state had been in progress for years under the guise of a national security requirement born of the cold war and in large part sustained by American imperialism. Noam Chomsky, arch intellectual critic of the Indochina war from a Marxist-Leninist standpoint, saw Watergate as a botched coup d'etat. It demonstrated "once again how frail are the barriers to some form of fascism in a state capitalist system of crisis." It was a deviation from past practice not so much in scale or principle as in the choice of targets; that is to say, it picked on the wrong people, not on Communists but on fellow members of the Establishment, co-repressors. The crimes complained of were far less serious than the war crimes committed in Asia. "If we try to keep a sense of balance," wrote Chomsky in *The New York Review of Books,* "the exposures of the past several months are analogous to the discovery that the directors of Murder Inc. were also cheating on their income tax. Reprehensible, to be sure, but hardly the main point."

(b) *neo-conservative version*

Watergate was backlash, an extremist reaction against the social engineering of liberals, the protesting of students, permissiveness, the "New Politics," etc. This theory is congenial to apostate liberals, to the Intellectuals for Nixon of 1968 and 1972. Seymour Martin Lipset and Earl Raab, students of right-wing extremism and joint authors of *The Politics of Unreason,* for example, interpret Watergate as "not just the creation of evil men" but as "the symptomatic rumbling of a deep strain in American society of which Richard Nixon has come to seem the almost perfect embodiment." . . .

. . . "The behavior summed up in the name Watergate," wrote Lipset and Raab in *Commentary* [see chapter 1, above], "was typical, at least in form, of American backlash extremism." Yet to the majority of Americans Nixon seemed less extremist in 1972 than McGovern. "If American society is to avoid backlash extremism in the future it will have to find ways of preventing the disenfranchisement of the electorate by ideological factionalists, and of making the politics of pragmatism and democratic restraint prevail once again on the national

scene." In other words, McGovern and the Left were also to blame
for Watergate.

2. *Watergate was endemic in the office of the Presidency.*

There are several variations of this thesis advanced from different
positions in the political spectrum, but essentially it is a thesis of the
moderate Left. Its most distinguished exponent is Arthur Schlesinger Jr.
In his book *The Imperial Presidency* he writes:

> Nixon's Presidency was not an aberration but a culmination.
> It carries to reckless extremes a compulsion towards Presidential
> power rising out of deep-running changes in the foundations
> of society. In a time of the acceleration of history and the
> decay of traditional institutions and values, a strong Presidency
> is both a greater necessity than ever before and a greater risk—
> necessary to hold a spinning and distracted society together,
> necessary to make the separation of powers work, risky because
> of the awful temptation held out to override the separation of
> powers and burst the bonds of the Constitution. The nation
> required both a strong Presidency . . . and the separation of
> powers. . . .

In other words, in Schlesinger's view, the power of the Presidency
has increased, and is increasing, but ought not to be diminished.
Rather, Nixon should be impeached in accordance with the constitutional procedure whose genius "lies in the fact that it can punish the
man without punishing the office." As to the office, it must be checked
not by law but by politics: America must return to Theodore Roosevelt's
conception of a strong Presidency held strictly accountable to what
Schlesinger calls "the discipline of consent."

3. *Watergate was innate in Nixon's personality and politics.*

It was the logical conclusion, wrote Frank Mankiewicz in his
Perfectly Clear: Nixon from Whittier to Watergate, of "the unbroken
series of frauds and deceptions that have marked a quarter of a
century and more of what will now be called 'Nixon politics.' " A man
devoid of ideology or conscience, Nixon in his lust for electoral victory
took advantage of the country's obsession with national security to
advance his own career and seek power unlimited by constitutional
checks or internal self-restraint. Watergate was not the result of excesses
by his subordinates but of their "acting squarely within the approved
limits of the closed Nixon society. . . . For this was not a right-wing
movement, or a Republican movement—it was a *Nixon* movement,
and it had been building its moral standards for 25 years."

4. *Watergate was an aberration.*

The whole thing was a ghastly mistake and blunder, committed by
over-zealous aides in the heat of a campaign and out of misguided

but genuine concern for national security. Essentially this is Nixon's defense, the thesis favored by the diminishing number who hold him not to blame . . . and who explain the cover-up . . . by the President's concern to spare aides who believed themselves to have been acting in the national interest.

OPERATION CANDOR

None of these theories solves the mystery of Nixon the man. We are obliged to consider seriously, the more so in the light of the new evidence of the tapes, whether the root explanation is that the White House in 1969 became occupied by a psychopath, possibly a schizophrenic. Several of the transcripts reveal "P" playing twin roles, one moment Richard Nixon (Mr. Hyde) and another the President of the United States (Dr. Jekyll). According to reports from Washington, the tapes themselves reveal the contrast of tone and voice in which he acts out this split personality. Washington has long been rife with rumor concerning the President's mental health, some of it well authenticated from within the administration. Certaintly his observable behavior has often been strange, to say the least, although paranoia and manic-depression, too easily mistaken for schizophrenia (a rare complaint), are conditions frequently to be found in the wielders of great power.[1]

In the streets of Paris after Pompidou's funeral the President appeared seriously disturbed—"This is a great day for France." He revealed a morbid concern for his health in a speech to members of the White House staff last summer after his discharge from the hospital where he was treated for what was officially diagnosed as viral pneumonia. He pledged himself to disobey the advice of his doctors to ease up:

> I just want you to know what my answer to them was and what my answer to you is. No one in this great office at this time in the world's history can slow down. This office requires a President who will work right up to the hilt all the time. That is what I have been doing. That is what I am going to continue to do. . . . I know many will say, "But then you will risk your health." Well, the health of the man is not nearly as important as the health of the nation and the health of the world.

There is the famous incident at the height of the Cambodian crisis. At 4:55 A.M. on May 9, 1970, Nixon crept out of the White House, accompanied by his valet, Manolo Sanchez, and three Secret Service agents. He headed to the Lincoln Memorial, where he discussed football with a handful of demonstrators. Then he took Sanchez on a personal sunrise tour of the deserted Capital. At the House of Representatives, he was met by H. R. Haldeman, Ron Ziegler, and Dwight

Chapin. The President climbed onto the dais, sat down, and simply stared out at the empty chamber.

For me, the most striking insight into the President's mentality came last year during his short-lived and inevitably doomed Operation Candor. In Memphis, Tennessee, he met behind closed doors with Republican governors who were desperate for reassurance that it was his intention to have out the truth. "Mr. President, are there any more bombshells in the wings?" he was asked. He replied that there were none.

The next day, back in Washington, Judge Sirica was informed that eighteen and a half minutes of a crucial tape recording had been mysteriously obliterated. Later testimony in the court allowed no doubt that the President was aware of this, and aware that it would have to be revealed to the court, when he gave the governors the assurance they asked for in Memphis. This was not the behavior of a politician. A politician, surely, would have said to them: "I know this is going to look bad for me, but I want you to know about it now and to know that it was an accident, and that no one in the White House deliberately erased that tape." A politician would have tried to defuse the bombshell in the wings. Nixon instead behaved like a child denying that a vase has been broken while the pieces are lying on the floor in the next room, bound to be discovered. Either he had become utterly reckless, no longer concerned with his credibility, or he was unable to connect with reality.

How are we to explain the tapes—not their contents but their very existence? They are the central mystery of the man and his Presidency. Richard Nixon will go down as the first of the United States, indeed so far as we know the first leader in the history of the world, to have bugged himself. The system, which would pick up any sounds of conversation in the President's offices, including the lowest tones, was automatically activated by voice. The President retained no manual control over its operation.[2]

Other Presidents had made use of tape recordings, but none, so far as we know, had so violated their own privacy. That Nixon may have wanted to get the goods on his colleagues, friend and foe alike ("Nobody is a friend of ours. Let's face it," he said to John Dean), does not explain why by his choice of system he should entrap himself. All he needed was a button under his desk, as L.B.J. had. Nor does the official explanation that they were installed to record events for posterity, for the Nixon library, wash. Were the tapes to be deposited in the Nixon library with their expletives undeleted? Was posterity to be shown a Nixon totally different from the image projected to the public in his lifetime?

GUARDED WITH FAMILY

The contemporary Nixon insists on coats and ties being worn in the presence of the President. "I hope to restore respect to the Presidency at all levels of my conduct," he told an interviewer. "I believe in keeping my own counsel," he told another, Stewart Alsop. "It's something like wearing clothing—if you let down your hair you feel too naked." According to Garry Wills, whose *Nixon Agonistes* is the best book on the subject, "Nixon, so ill at ease among strangers, remains guarded with intimates, with his very family—hiding grievances from his brother under strict decorum, writing his mother in tones of a geriatric manual." Was posterity to be given the unexpurgated Nixon?

Whatever his intentions concerning the tapes, his assumption presumably was that they would remain firmly with his control, preferably and probably their existence even unknown. Yet this was risky. Haldeman knew; Alexander Butterfield knew; the Secret Service knew. The risk became greater as the Watergate scandal began to break open —yet the reels continued to turn. So were the tapes intended to be the means of last resort for the President's vindication? One problem in reading the transcribed version is to judge to what extent the President (and his men) were speaking for the record. For example, on March 21 in the famous talk with Dean:

> D: You are not involved in it and it is something you shouldn't—
> P: That is true!
> D: I know, sir, I can just tell from our conversation that these are things you have no knowledge of.
> P: You certainly can! Buggings, etc.!

Later in the same transcript, after Haldeman has joined them, Haldeman cuts him short, warning, "Be careful." Yet the conversation is not consistently self-serving. Indeed, it can be construed as a conspiracy to obstruct justice and, specifically, to authorize the payment of hush money to Watergate conspirator Howard Hunt. Nor is it consistent with self-vindication or the entrapment of Dean that when Haldeman enters, the President asks him nothing about what he has just been told, supposedly for the first time, and their conversation continues without recapitulation.[3]

With Dean still in the room and the tape recorder still turning, they got down to discussing what to do. The most potentially incriminating exchange of all then takes place:

> D: They're [the Watergate defendants] going to stonewall it as it now stands. Excepting Hunt. That's why his threat.

P: That's why for your immediate things you have no choice
but to come up with the $120,000, or whatever it is. Right?
D: That's right.
P: Would you agree that that's the prime thing, that you
damn well better get that done?
D: Obviously he ought to be given some signal anyway.
P: (expletive deleted) get it. In a way that—who is going to
talk to him? Colson?[4]

The existence of the tapes, the way in which they were made, poses
an unanswered question concerning the President's mentality, indeed
his rationality. Their contents, even as edited for publication by the
White House, fly in the face of the received view of the President's
political abilities. Not only do they reveal a man devoid of moral
sense but also one severely lacking in common sense. Columnists
Rowland Evans Jr. and Robert Novak, while underlining his limitations,
wrote in their book, *Nixon in the White House,* that "his steel-trap
mind could comprehend difficult concepts and memorize great quanti-
ties of facts." The transcripts provide no evidence of such capacity,
rather the reverse: the President rambles indecisively; he has difficulty
marshaling the facts; he reveals elementary ignorance of the American
legal system.

We feel ourselves in the presence of a thoroughly second-rate mind,
a crude and vulgar intelligence, a man with no command of language,
a man wholly concerned with appearance rather than substance—
with "how it will play," with what he calls "PR." From this authentic
encounter with the private Nixon it is hard any longer to imagine the
public Nixon, or the official Nixon, the foreign policy President with
his encyclopedic knowledge and expert's grasp of foreign affairs, the
ideological conservative, the student of Woodrow Wilson. But what
if, after all, he is a psychopath?

THE BORN LOSER

His entire Presidency, the rise and fall of Richard Nixon, and
Watergate too, its genesis and its meaning, begin to focus if we examine
him not as a success but as a failure. He had failed, although narrowly,
in his bid for the Presidency in 1960; he had failed, humiliatingly,
in his run for the governorship of California in 1962; and in 1968,
when a donkey could have beaten a Democrat, Richard Nixon, born a
loser, nearly managed to snatch defeat from the jaws of victory. It
should have been impossible that year to come near losing. Nixon
had going for him Johnson's withdrawal, Rockefeller's haverings, Bobby
Kennedy's assassination, Humphrey's catastrophe at the Chicago con-

vention. The spirit of that year was caught by Walter Lippmann, who wrote:

> It is better that Mr. Nixon should have full authority if repression should become necessary in order to restore peace and tranquility at home . . . Repression of some sort may be unavoidable. If that is what the country is going to face, it is better that the Republicans should have the clear responsibility for the measures that are taken, and that the Democrats should be out of office and free to play the indispensable role of the opposition party.

The Democrats were in disarray, liberals on the run, old ideologies and old alignments were crumbling; a great vacuum opened up in American politics, and Richard Nixon was the only body available to fill it.

MEN WITHOUT IDEOLOGY

He never for a moment forgot during his first term that he was the "43 per cent President." He lacked legitimacy, felt himself to be a usurper in Washington, that enemy city still in the hands of "H.O.D.'s" (held-over Democrats). His entire first term was a campaign for re-election, and not just for re-election, as he seemed to see it, but for election, for a victory that he could count according to his own strange standard, by which anything short of total victory is defeat. It is not easy to discern in his first term any other purpose. His 1968 campaign was without theme, lacking in serious policy content. It was run by men without ideology. There was not even a "plan" to end the war, although he claimed there was. His strategy for winning rested on the assumption that the Democrats would lose. His early successful campaigns in California, all of them unscrupulous and dirty, had been conducted according to the principle that negative attacks on the incumbent are what win elections. He attributed his defeat in 1960 to the fact that he was on the receiving end of Kennedy's oppositional assault. In 1968, he was back where he belonged and liked to be—on the negative side of the question.

John Mitchell early on told civil-rights activists: "Don't watch what we say, watch what we do," and it was good advice, because the administration, in its perennial search for some conceptual framework for itself, said things which bore little relation to its actions or intentions. The only strand of coherence was in its determination to retain power. This meant, first and foremost, holding together the conservative forces which had produced the hairbreadth victory in 1968. The strategy for 1972, put simply, was 1968 plus Wallace. That made Mitchell's "Southern strategy" the keystone throughout. Everything else was subordinate, appearance, "PR."

Changes in policy were simply new game plans. Policy toward Vietnam was conducted on the assumption that anything which looked like a defeat would alienate the 1968 constituency. "Vietnamization," which turned out to be a popular policy, was at first conducted covertly for fear that it would alienate the Right. In 1970, announcing the Cambodian invasion, Nixon declared: "I would rather be a one-term President . . . than a two-term President at the cost of seeing America become a second-rate power and to see this nation accept the first defeat in its proud 190-year history." But in 1971, following the disastrous midterm campaign, at the time of the Laotian operation, and with things going badly all around, it was decided that Nixon should present himself in 1972 at the peace candidate.

It was the same story on the home front. Patrick Moynihan interested him in Disraeli, so for a time "reform" became the catchword of the administration. But the program for reform lacked coherence. Moynihan's plan for guaranteed family incomes to replace the welfare mess conflicted with the Southern strategy, so a work requirement was added, and the plan eventually collapsed under the weight of its own contradictions, abandoned by a President who had never been committed to it except as a game plan.

"My strong point, if I have a strong point," Nixon told an interviewer, "is performance. I always produce more than I promise." But the performance of his administration was mostly poor, for all its military staff structures and systems-analysis jargon. It was not until 1972, with the visits to Peking and Moscow, that anything began to go right for the Nixon administration.

The fear, the real fear, of losing in 1972 goes a long way toward explaining Watergate, by which we mean not simply the break-in at the Democratic National Committee headquarters but all the other abuses of power—bribery, corruption, sabotage, and espionage—which went on. Because by the time of the actual Watergate break-in in June, 1972, Nixon had his re-election virtually sewn up; and because with McGovern for an opponent he won by a landslide of the votes cast, it is easily forgotten just how vulnerable he was—or felt—at the early, formative stages of the affair. In mid-1971, a White House aide told Haynes Johnson of *The Washington Post:* "The President was walking into a one-term Presidency on almost every issue." The opinion polls showed Ed Muskie, the hero of the mid-term campaign, running ahead of the President, with Kennedy and Humphrey running Nixon neck and neck. By May, Muskie was beating Nixon 47 per cent to 39 per cent!

THE POWER MACHINE

The narrow win in 1968, and the grave uncertainty concerning 1972, had another consequence. Nixon never felt that he possessed adequate power, or adequate power that he could use openly. His conversation with Dean on September 15, 1972, by which time his re-election was certain, is revealing:

> P: We are all in it together. This is a war. We take a few shots and it will be over. We will give them a few shots and it will be over. Don't worry. I wouldn't want to be on the other side right now. Would you?
>
> D: Along that line, one of the things I've tried to do, I have begun to keep notes on a lot of people who are emerging as less than our friends because this will be over some day and we shouldn't forget the way some of them have treated us.
>
> P: I want the most comprehensive notes on all of those who tried to do us in. They didn't have to do it. If we had a very close election and they were playing the other side I would understand this. No—they were doing this quite deliberately, and they are asking for it, and they are going to get it. We have not used the power in this first four years as you know. We have never used it. We have not used the Bureau [F.B.I.], and we have not used the Justice Department, but things are going to change now. And they are either going to do it right or go.

There is no suggestion here that self-restraint has held them back. The suggestion rather is that there were things they didn't dare do, or thinks they couldn't do through insufficient control of the power machine. For example, J. Edgar Hoover had vetoed a plan approved by the President in July, 1970, which would have authorized breaking and entering and other illegal acts by the intelligence gathering and law enforcement agencies. In consequence, a covert parallel network began to be constructed in the White House: in December of 1970 an Intelligence Evaluation Committee to collect domestic intelligence, and in June, 1971, the Plumbers unit, which we may assume was not idle between the Ellsberg burglary in September of that year and the Watergate operations in the early summer of 1972. And we should remember that Nixon's one decisive act after his re-election, before his administration became crippled by Watergate, was the brutal terror bombing of the North Vietnam cities in December, 1972.

The decision-making structure of the Nixon administration reflected the same concern with the lack of effective power. The White House staff grew from 250 to 510. Foreign policy was conducted from the basement of the White House, and Henry Kissinger's National Security

Council apparatus effectively replaced the State Department. The State Department was "bureaucracy," a bad word in the vocabulary of Nixonism. The budget was similarly drawn into the White House. In order to narrow the bases of decision-making (and also to spare the President human contact, which he found so uncongenial), overlordships were created in each major area of government. The wires led back to the White House, where the President could deal with one man per subject. H. R. Haldeman and John Ehrlichman exercised power far greater than any cabinet officers except John Mitchell and John Connally during his brief tenure as Secretary of the Treasury.

CONCENTRATED POWER

The cabinet fell into disuse. In 1972 it met only six times. In that year there were only six bipartisan meetings with the congressional leadership, only twelve with the Republican leadership. There was nothing new in Presidential impoundment of funds voted by Congress, but the Nixon administration's use of that power was novel and ominous. For impoundment was used to remove from the Congress the power of the purse, the power to determine national priorities.

It was the same story with the party. The election campaign was run from the White House through CREEP (the Committee for the Re-election of the President). In 1972 Nixon did not run as a Republican candidate but simply as Richard Nixon. As in the midterm elections, reactionary Democrats in the South were helped in their campaigns against Republican candidates; other Republicans received little help from the President and none of the vast sums of money that had accumulated at CREEP.

Within the White House, too, power was concentrated in fewer and fewer hands. A former campaign staffer, Richard Whalen, one who got out in good-time, has described how Haldeman and Ehrlichman "regarded governing as little more than an extension of campaigning. Campaign politics, regardless of party and candidate, is inherently conspiratorial. Because the only purpose and binding force of the enterprise is victory, almost any means toward that all-important end can be justified with a modest amount of rationalization." Others have since testified of this atmosphere.

Hugh Sloan told the Ervin committee: "There was no independent sense of morality there . . . If you worked for someone, he was God, and whatever the orders were, you did it . . . It was all so narrow, so closed."

Dean: "The White House is another world. Expediency is everything."

Tom Huston (a sponsor of the plan which Hoover vetoed): "No one who had been in the White House could help but feel he was in a state of siege."

Jeb Magruder: "Because of a certain atmosphere that had developed in my working at the White House, I was not as concerned about . . . illegality as I should have been."

The men around Nixon were men without constituency, without commitment; not one of them had ever run for office. They were men from advertising agencies, real-estate men, salesmen and image manipulators: in Whalen's words, "buttoned-down, scurrying aides," who "had the mission of protecting the President from disorder. . . ." Haldeman, who had seen Nixon break down in his 1962 California campaign, had the special task of preventing this from happening again. Haldeman and Ehrlichman controlled the flow of information to him, were intermediaries to his decisions and orders. Ehrlichman once told a cabinet officer that the President had no philosophy, that he did only what was feasible and tactically rewarding. "There is no ideology, no central commitment, no fixed body of thought," said another White House aide proudly. Whalen quotes another as saying, "Haldeman and Ehrlichman shield the President by monopolizing him. One of them is present at every meeting—he sees no one alone. He has made himself their captive. Sometimes the 'Germans' don't carry out Nixon's orders, or they let papers sit on their desks for a while, because they are certain he won't find out. How *can* he find out? All the channels flow back to Haldeman." When the President on April 30, 1973, the night of their resignation, described Haldeman and Ehrlichman as "two of the finest public servants it has been my privilege to know," he meant it. The transcripts show that he could hardly contemplate life without them.

SPLIT PERSONALITY

Nixon was not corrupted by power; he corrupted power. A powerful Presidency doesn't have to produce a crook any more than a strong man has to be a thug. Richard Nixon was not inevitable. Watergate was not decreed by the Vietnam war, nor by the civil war at home: Hubert Humphrey could have been elected President in 1968 and very nearly was. Nixon very nearly won in 1960, and at that time there was no war, no social disorder. McCarthyism rose and fell under Truman and Eisenhower, militarism and obsessive concern with national security grew under subsequent Presidents; but there were no Watergates.

Nixon's Presidency is the projection of his personality. Lacking any firm commitment or ideological belief, he made do with the traditional, fundamentalist values of his Middle American background which he expounded in public. The force of his destructive personality is evil, but happily his exercise of power has been inept and lacking in direction, mistaking appearance for substance, concerned more with petty vendetta than with wide-scale repression. As Haldeman lamented: "We are so (adjective deleted) square that we get caught at everything." A PR man does not have the makings of an effective tyrant. Watergate was entirely characteristic of Nixon's Presidency—dishonest, disgraceful, inept.

"How could it have happened?" It happened because the American people elected Nixon to be President, an unfortunate choice. But how were they to know that he might be a psychopath? "Who is to blame?" Nixon is to blame—Nixon's the one.

NOTES

1. See Hugh L'Etang's "The Pathology of Leadership," on Churchill's cyclothymia; Churchill called his depression "Black Dog."

2. Although he retained no mechanical control over the system he could, of course, at any time order its suspension. We now have reason to believe he sometimes did. This could explain the missing tapes, but it makes even more remarkable the recording of conversations such as that of March 21, 1973, in which the commission of crimes was, at very least, contemplated.

3. On March 21, Dean told Nixon of the "cancer within the Presidency," that the White House was being blackmailed. When Haldeman enters, Nixon doesn't say something like "John here has been telling me one helluva (expletive deleted) story." What he actually says is: 'I was talking to John about this whole situation and he said if we can get away from the bits and pieces that have broken out. He is right in recommending that there be a meeting at the very first possible time. I realize Ehrlichman is still out in California but, what is today? Is tomorrow Thursday?" Nixon consistently maintained that March 21 was the first time he received information that led him to suppose that White House staff were involved in Watergate. In fact on March 13, Dean told him that Haldeman's man, Strachan, knew. "I will be damned," he said. He jumped to the conclusion that probably Haldeman knew. Probably Colson also. Why hadn't he been told? He guessed because there had been "poor pickings." "If they ever got any information they would certainly have told me. . . ."

4. In fact, the money was paid over that night. At a second meeting that same day, March 21, Nixon appears to have learned that the money had been paid, or was being paid.

D: It bothers me to do anything further now, sir, when Hunt is our real unknown.

P: Do you think it is a mistake to talk to him? [They have been discussing whether to talk to Assistant Attorney General Henry Petersen.]

D: Yes, I do.

P: It doesn't solve anything—it's just one more step [i.e., talking to Petersen].

H: The payment to Hunt does.

D: The payment to Hunt does. That is why I say if somebody would assess the criminal liability.

14 | The Tragic Flaw in the Nixon White House: Self-Pity

Max Ways

In agreement with Jenkins that problems of personality were at the heart of Watergate, Ways asserts that paranoia, which is a psychosis, is too strong a term to apply to Nixon or his aides. (According to one dictionary, "Paranoia is characterized by delusions of persecution or grandeur. The paranoid system is relatively isolated and leaves the rest of the personality unaffected as distinguished from paranoid schizophrenia.") Instead, Ways suggests that excessive self-pity is the best description of the emotional patterns which permeated the Nixon White House. He indicates how this flaw adversely affected the White House's relationships with other political institutions and ultimately led to Watergate. Treating Watergate as a case study in management, the author shows how the President violated all the rules of good organizational leadership despite his being the most management-minded president in recent years.

. . . The errant thread that, when pulled, unraveled Nixon's skein of triumph was, of course, Watergate, the weird sequence beginning in the summer of 1971 before the break-in at the psychiatrist's office and running on and on through the slow disintegration of the cover-up in 1973. Watergate will not become, as some of those hurt by it have suggested, a mere footnote to history. For generations ahead, political scientists, lawyers, and moralists will be sorting out this jumble of facts, quasi-facts, confessions, lies, and accusations. Since it involves organized activity, Watergate can also be approached as a study in management.

Reprinted from the November, 1973, number of *Fortune* Magazine by special permission; © 1973 Time Inc. The article begins on page 109 of that issue under the title 'Watergate As A Case Study in Management.''

Max Ways is a staff writer for *Fortune* and a frequent contributor to that magazine.

The prime measure of management is effectiveness—often expressed as a relation of benefit to cost. Although neither benefits nor costs need be monetary, effectiveness is a frankly pragmatic test, separated from larger considerations of legality and morality. Speaking managerially, one gang of assassins may be judged "better" than a rival gang. One monastery may be judged "better" than another although both pursue high ends with equal ardor. A well-run gang of assassins may even be "better"—managerially—than a sloppy monastery.

That kind of statement does not imply that management in real life has nothing to do with morality. Like any other specialized approach, a managerial analysis is incapable of expressing the whole truth about a messy mass of phenomena from which the material under study has been selected. A look at Watergate as management, then, is not meant to evade or supersede judgments made from political or legal or moral viewpoints. On the contrary, a management analysis may throw some peripheral light on larger issues, and vice versa.

AN EXECUTIVE'S NIGHTMARE

Managerially, Watergate is an obvious disaster area. Its participants whoever they may be assumed to be—incurred "costs" so much larger than "benefits" that it would be hard to think of an organized peacetime operation with an effectiveness rating farther on the wrong side of zero. Bad luck will not begin to explain the Watergate calamity. No matter which of many possible assumptions is adopted about how much Nixon knew at what "points in time," Watergate from its start to the present reeks of mismanagement. . . .

. . . Organizational objectives were ill selected and ill defined. Choice of people, that key management function, was poor, not so much in terms of their over-all quality but rather in the casting for the particular roles they played; somewhere a personnel manual must exist that warns against slotting the likes of Liddy, Hunt, and Dean in the operational spots they came to occupy. Coordination was weak. Cooperators, who needed to communicate, didn't. The enterprise was so overcapitalized that money was recklessly sloshed around in a way that facilitated detection. The burglaries were overmanned; nobody can argue with the judgment of the former New York cop, Anthony Ulasewicz, that professionals" would not have walked in with an army." Indeed, analysis of Watergate can be discouraged or misled by the very richness of its pathology. So many people at so many levels in and around the White House made so many different kinds of mistakes that the observer is first tempted to say that this was the stupidest lot of managers ever assembled.

That lazy hypothesis is demolished by the plain fact that neither Richard Nixon nor the men around him are stupid—managerially or otherwise. Nixon is believed by some shrewd observers of government to be the most management-minded of recent Presidents. Those who viewed the parade of witnesses before the Ervin committee knew they were listening to intelligent men. Management analysis of Watergate, then, must turn upon the question of why officials, whose ability ranged from average to very high, made so many mistakes.

Much of the answer must lie in the ambience of the group, the cognitive and emotional patterns that permeated and shaped its organizational style. Such a collective atmosphere is not necessarily the exact sum of the attitudes, ideas, suppositions, desires and values of the individuals who make up the group. Every organization has its own character, its own way of acting and reacting, and this quality powerfully colors what its members feel, think, say, and do within the organization. . . .

THE PREVALENCE OF OGRES

These footless ventures would remain forever incomprehensible unless we turned to the beliefs and emotional patterns of the participants. Their attitudes were shaped in part by the general ambience that enveloped the White House and the Committee to Re-elect the President, and the ambience included a lot of fear, suspicion, and hostility. Although the word "paranoia," used by many people, is too strong, it is correct to say that a high level of self-pity influenced the style of the Nixon White House.

The seeds of this attitude were sown long before Watergate. Self-pity was evident, though excusable, in many of Nixon's periods of adversity, and it had not melted away in the warm sun of ambition fulfilled. The public utterances of President Nixon, and those he encouraged Vice President Agnew to make in the early years of their first terms, often contained a strong theme of complaint against the unfairness of adversaries. The internal atmosphere of the White House was even more marked by this air of hostility and suspicion toward such outside bodies as Congress, the federal bureaucracy, and the press. All Presidents have had adversaries, but no other White House institutionalized its hostility by keeping, as Nixon's did, an "enemies list."

The U.S. organizes its political life, as well as its business life, through competition. Not only do we have competing parties, but government has many separate elements that are simultaneously in cooperation and competition with one another. Among the people themselves we don't expect—and don't want—a placid homogeneity of outlook and aims. In our kind of pluralist politics, a degree of combativeness, an awareness of adversaries, is inevitable and constructive. But there's a line, blurred but real, beyond which a normal self-assertion in the face of opposition can move over into either arrogance or self-pity.

Many business managers have seen in their own sphere examples of the damage that can be done when this blurred line is crossed. It is desirable, for instance, that a sales force be on its toes, alert to spot and to counter moves by its opposition. A given sales force can become too proud of its competitive ability and be made vulnerable by overconfidence. Or it can become demoralized by the pressure of competition. A sensitive executive would worry if his salesmen were constantly telling him and one another about the perfidy of their competitors, dwelling on their dirty tricks, exaggerating their unfairness. In that ambience his own salesmen would have a built-in excuse for poor performance, or they might goad themselves into foolish and imprudent acts.

The nearest business equivalent of the Watergate folly was the great electrical price-fixing conspiracy uncovered in 1962. The question that then ran through the business world was: how could experienced executives in well-run companies do anything so stupid? Much of the answer lay in the ambience of the conspirators. They felt overpressured —by their bosses, by rising costs, by government regulations they considered unfair. One executive in the industry, trying to explain his colleagues' gross misjudgment, told a Fortune reporter at the time that the conspirators did what they did because they were "distressed men."

The distress, of course, was not visible in their objective condition of opulence and success. The distress was in their minds. So, too, powerful men in the White House came to think of themselves as inhabitants of a beleaguered and distressed city, surrounded by enemies whose strength and malice they exaggerated. An intense will to win, coupled with the belief that the situation is desperate, can release a lot of energizing adrenalin. If it goes too far, such a state of mind can also trigger reckless misjudgments. Whom the gods would destroy they first make unduly sorry for themselves.

A SURPLUS OF SINCERITY

Nixon's White House, of course, was not the first to overstress the power and menace of its adversaries. Franklin Roosevelt had depicted himself as standing, along with the weak, against the "economic royalists" who, he implied, were really in charge of the country. This tactic was so brilliantly successful that all subsequent Presidents have flirted with it. But in Roosevelt's underdog posture there was always a saving measure of insincerity. He never really believed his histrionic pretense that the dragons he opposed were all that monstrous. Nor did the men around him, cheerfully manipulating the reins of power, lose themselves in the dramatic myth he had created. Nixon's aides, unfortunately, seem to have let the role of victim capture their hearts and minds.

In a culture that prizes justice, fears power, and roots for underdogs, the temptation to cast oneself as a victim is ever present. The average American, when looking privately at his own situation, resists this temptation rather effectively; he knows—most of the time—that he is not doing too badly. But in any public discourse or in any capacity where he represents others, the contemporary American tends toward donning the victim's robe.

Listening to the speeches of businessmen, with their frequent emphasis on the abuse of government and labor-union power, an observer may worry lest their self-pity blind them to the ever expanding scope of action that beckons to business. Spokesmen for blacks or women can express real grievances in terms so extravagant that their followers will not perceive actual opportunities; the result can be stagnation or angry, self-destructive action. This unhappy pattern even extends to sports. One September night this year in Baltimore the managers of both baseball teams were thrown out of the same game for protesting too raucously against the injustice of the umpires. Passionate complaint is the almost unvarying tone of those man-in-the-street interviews cherished by producers of TV news programs. If Americans ever became, in fact, as sorry for themselves as they sound in public discourse, the country as a whole might begin to act as foolishly as the "distressed" men who blindly stumbled into Watergate.

Nixon early recognized the danger in protest run wild. It was he who laudably set out to "bring us together" and admonished us to "lower our voices." One of the deepest ironies of Watergate is the public demoralization that has occurred because the Nixon White House got carried away by its own agonized indignation toward the "unfairness" of its adversaries. The public in 1973 would never have had occasion to "wallow in Watergate" (as the President expressed it) had not the White House, years before, wallowed in self-pity.

ARISTOTLE WOULD UNDERSTAND

Watergate is often referred to as a "tragedy," as indeed it is in the sense that it blasted lives and caused suffering. But Watergate imitates in many other ways the structure of classic tragedy as Aristotle described it. . . .

In the Watergate case, the flaw obviously was not pride, which scorns to slink about by night in other people's offices. If we think of self-pity as the tragic flaw in Watergate, then all the wild imprudence of the consequent actions . . . becomes less baffling. The literary analogy may illuminate details of a problem in management analysis.

Act I, Scene I occurs in the summer of 1971, in the ruler's room of state. He is giving urgent orders to members of his staff. The precise content of his instruction is not known to us, but its tone and general import are clear. His government is bedeviled by leaks of information to a press deemed hostile. He invokes his highest responsibility, that in respect to the national security, as he tells them he wants his government sealed against leaks.

So far, there is nothing irrational about the ruler's attitude or the gist of his instruction. Leaks are no trivial matter. They can impair national security—and some have done so. More often they are devices employed by a government official to support a policy he favors, to hurt a rival, or advance his own career. Such leaks sow distrust among officials, inhibit frank discussion, and demoralize government. Now, publication of the Pentagon Papers, a veritable Niagara of a leak, requires drastic and immediate remedy.

At first the plumbers' unit interprets its responsibility in a normal and harmless way. Its members start to carry out a staff assignment to needle the chiefs of line departments and the regular investigatory agencies into greater vigilance against leaks. But progress, if any, is too slow. At this point, the tragic flaw in the spiritual ambience of the White House group begins to manifest itself.

In and around the plumbers' unit, deviation from organizational normality takes two forms. The atmosphere of a besieged city over-motivates the staffers involved. They wish so intensely to succeed in their assigned task that restraints of ordinary prudence drop away. The second manifestation of the flaw is more specifically managerial: they transform a staff function into a line operation. They decide that they themselves will gather the evidence that will retard leaks.

Their master, the President, deploys under his hand the largest, most expensive, and most professional array of investigatory agencies this side of the Soviet border. Yet these agencies are bypassed when the plumbers' unit decides to go into clandestine operations—which is no woods for babes. Neither Egil Krogh nor David Young, who headed the plumbers, had relevant experience in this line of work. Their immediate superior, John Ehrlichman, had no investigatory experience. Liddy, who had worked for the FBI, and Hunt, who had worked for the CIA, did have relevant experience. But many instances are known where individuals can render valuable service within a large professionalized organization and yet be helpless or harmful when working without professional supervision and organized support. In the plumbers' unit, Liddy and Hunt plainly lacked the competence, restraint, and judgment to be found (one hopes) in the organizations that had previously girdled their exuberance.

A former aide to a different President believes that all White House staffs, becoming impatient with the regular line agencies of government, are from time to time tempted to get into operations themselves. They hardly ever do so, however, partly because of what he called "the danger of involving the President." He was talking about possible interventions far less dangerous to the presidential reputation than burglary. Why, then, was the Nixon White House so incautiously willing to bypass the regular agencies and place its honor in the hands of people who knew so little about what they were doing?

SHOULD BUREAUCRATS OBEY?

The decision was almost certainly influenced by an attitude of distrust toward the whole federal bureaucracy. This was one of the areas where members of the Nixon circle felt most sorry for themselves. One expert on government structure remembers a long meeting of Nixon staff men at San Clemente devoted to the question of how to make the bureaucracy more obedient.

A familiar management problem is involved here, as anybody knows who has taken over the top spot in a corporation, or a division, or even a small office. He is likely to have found there men and women who took their own responsibilities seriously and who are entrenched by their specialized competence. A wise executive does not try to command the servile obedience of such people. His responsibility for coordinating their efforts and changing the over-all direction of the organization can only be achieved through the patient arts of leadership. He has to talk, to listen, to persuade and be persuaded.

But from the first the Nixon inner circle seems to have misunderstood the nature of the difficulty. It saw bureaucratic resistance as arising from political philosophy. No doubt, most civil servants are Democrats and maybe even "liberals." But this is not as important a truth as the Nixon people thought it. Presidents Kennedy and Johnson also had trouble with the bureaucracy. A Nixon official who has been most effective in his leadership of civil servants is Secretary of the Treasury George Shultz, whose own political philosophy happens to be most remote from the presumed liberalism of the bureaucrats. Shultz talks and listens to his experts. Shultz does not withdraw into injured and persecuted silence because they won't obey him. In short, Shultz follows a pattern widespread among managers of corporations who anticipate resistance from their experts. They do not perceive it as disloyalty or hostility. They know that dealing with such resistance is just what they are hired to do.

WHEN THE BIG SCENE WAS BUNGLED

But the Nixon Administration, with some distinguished exceptions, had never been notable for strong, independent personalities, secure enough to listen to the experts below and speak candidly to the chief above. The White House staff, the citadel of the beleaguered city, seems to have been chosen more for its zeal to protect the boss than for ability to serve him with information and argument. This criterion owed part of its origin to the tragic flaw, and it resulted in disaster at a crucial decision time.

Classic tragedy moves toward a point of "recognition," the scene where the flaw in all its horror is revealed to the audience and the dramatis personae. In the Watergate sequence, that point was reached in the summer of 1972 after the arrests, after the disclosure that large sums of money had been "laundered" in Mexico. Clearly, these were no ordinary burglars. They had backing at high levels.

If at that point the President or his former Attorney General had publicly recognized that a serious error had occurred, Watergate would never have grown to anything approaching its ultimate proportions. Such a public recognition would have been painful, but it almost certainly would not have cost Nixon either the election or the respect of several millions of Americans who lost confidence in him this year.

Nixon and the men around him bungled the recognition scene. Or to put the same thought in business terms, they failed to face the hard decision to cut their losses. . . . As a group, the White House staff contained too few men of the caliber and courage to make Nixon face the situation that the public, Nixon's audience, had long since recognized. . . .

THE PRESS IS UNFAIR

The press is unfair to Nixon in a sense more fundamental than he knows. It has been unfair to all recent Presidents. It is unfair to businessmen, labor leaders, and everybody else responsible for carrying out action in a world whose complexity makes for dull writing. The inadequacy of the press in explaining to the public the actual working of government processes may be one of the most serious defects in contemporary democracy. Compared to this problem, the additional fact that many influential journalists don't much like Richard Nixon pales toward insignificance.

The Nixon White House diminishes its chances of constructive coverage by its attitude of pained withdrawal from the media. The exceptions demonstrate this general point. Henry Kissinger, who talks frequently and (relatively) frankly with reporters, manages to get through the media to the public. Nixon himself, on the rare occasions when he endures face-to-face contact with the media, handles press conferences with verve. His San Clemente press conference of August 22 [1973] was one of the few effective White House moves in the long Watergate sequence.

Nixon's relations with Congress also have that hurt and withdrawn look. Before he came to office, Congress was already becoming restless under what many of its members considered the undue power of the executive branch. Nixon was bound to have trouble with Congress, no matter what its political coloration might have been. But Nixon seems to have taken congressional opposition as a personal affront. In its day-to-day contact with individual Congressmen, the Nixon White House has been less active, less persuasively communicative than previous Administrations, including Eisenhower's. In public Nixon has, as a President must, often summarized what was wrong about the record of Congress and what was right about his own record. But in his relations with Congress he has not, as they say in Seville, worked close to the bull.

WHY WE REMEMBER HANNIBAL

Deplorable tendencies in Congress, in the bureaucracy, and in the media are easier to denounce than to overcome. A President, nevertheless, will be appraised by how much headway he makes against such objective difficulties. Hannibal is remembered for actually crossing the Alps, not for whatever Carthaginian maledictions that he, frustrated in Gaul, might have hurled at the "unfair" gradients confronting him.

The flaw that mars Nixon's style in domestic affairs becomes the more glaring when it is limned against his foreign policy successes. In dealing with Red China and the Soviet Union he has brilliantly demonstrated that he can rise above self-pity. He has studied these offshore adversaries so long and so intently that he can handle the problems they represent much more coolly, objectively, and effectively than he handles the onshore problems represented by Daniel Ellsberg or Larry O'Brien or the federal bureaucracy or the *Washington Post*. Nixon isn't thrown off stride by Peking's or Moscow's "dirty tricks." It never seems to occur to him that Brezhnev or Mao is "unfair." He manages his relations with them like a manager, not with the mien of a wounded deer.

Excessive self-pity is, of course, an emotional and moral flaw. It is often found entwined with an inaccurate cognitive picture of reality. Individuals or groups marked by such a flaw may be handicapped in practical affairs, even in those activities that are put in such specialized pigeonholes as politics or economics or management.

Machiavelli taught the world that politics, for instance, has rules of success that are independent of moral strictures. But he never taught that men who act in politics are to be considered unbound by moral law. Twenty years ago Professor Charles Singleton in a memorable lecture called "The Perspective of Art" pointed to a passage in Machiavelli's *Discourses* as a corrective to the popular view of what the Florentine believed. Machiavelli, in one of those typical passages about what a ruler must do to grasp and hold power, gives an example of some morally horrible but politically effective policies carried out by Philip of Macedon. Then Machiavelli says: "Doubtless these means are cruel and destructive of all civilized life, and neither Christian nor human, and should be avoided by everyone."

Now that politics is clearly recognized as an independent art, any practitioner faces a double hurdle. What he does must be good as politics, but must not be bad as morals. The point is even clearer in the relation of morals to economics. When Alfred Sloan, [the managerial genius of General Motors], learned that unsold cars were piling up, he shut down the production lines. As a compassionate man, he regretted the consequent unemployment and suffering. But in the economic circumstances his decision was not immoral. On the contrary, once he knew the facts any other decision would have been economically, managerially, and morally irresponsible.

Allen Dulles, when he was head of the CIA, once told a group of journalists that anyone entering upon his job must leave all moral considerations outside the door. This dangerous proposition is an example of the vulgar misreading of the Machiavellian view. The head of the CIA works in circumstances that ordinary citizens do not encounter. Circumstances change cases, and the head of the CIA may morally do things which an ordinary citizen would have no compelling occasion and no moral right to do. But the head of the CIA must nevertheless weigh the morality of any such act by whatever standards are approprite to the circumstances.

John Ehrlichman in his testimony indicated that he could think of circumstances involving, say, the threat of nuclear attack, in which a President could justifiably order a burglary. But does this mean that a President, by invoking the name of national security, can order *any* burglary? A weighing of circumstances becomes critical in government morality, as indeed it is in private morality. It is not only managerially shocking but morally shocking that so serious an offense as the Beverly Hills break-in was undertaken in circumstances that did not come within miles of requiring it.

MELANCHOLY EXAMPLE

The moral standards of political life are, indeed, often more strict than those of private life. "Dirty tricks" that may be merely tasteless in undergraduate elections are seriously offensive when plotted by people on a White House staff. All that useless Dick-Tuckery revealed by the Ervin committee is one of the most appalling aspects of the Watergate disclosures. Another, and more melancholy, example is brought to mind by Spiro Agnew's resignation. Many people may not regard an ordinary citizen's failure to report taxable income as one of the graver moral offenses. But when a Vice President of the United States is exposed as having done that, we are all—quite logically— horrified.

In the Watergate sequence, self-pity blinded the participants to dangers that were political, managerial, legal, and moral. As their retribution unfolds, the rest of us may from time to time ask whether our own legitimate resentment against our share of the injustices that all men experience might not be making us so sorry for ourselves that we mismanage our practical affairs.

15 | The Dialogues of Richard Nixon as a Drama of the Antihero

Arthur Miller

It is fitting for the playright Arthur Miller to comment on Richard Nixon because more than one observer has compared Nixon to Willy Loman, the central figure in Miller's Death of a Salesman. *In the first part of this selection Miller views the tapes as a drama and explores them for clues to Mr. Nixon's character. In the second half he provides an interesting explanation of why Nixon, despite himself, finally let it all hang out. He points out how Nixon's inability to examine and admit imperfection in his God-like self image was the key to his undoing. Although disavowing psychohistory, Miller's analysis is richly suggestive for those who prefer such an approach.*

Let us begin with a few meaningless statements. The President is the chief law-enforcement officer of the United States. He also represents what is best in the American people, if not in his every action then certainly in his aims. These assertions were violated by Lyndon Johnson, John Kennedy, Dwight Eisenhower, and Franklin Roosevelt, not once but many times in each case. Johnson fabricated the Tonkin Gulf hysteria. Kennedy set the country on the rails into Vietnam even as he espoused humanistic idealism. Eisenhower lacked the stomach to scuttle Nixon despite his distaste, if not contempt, for Nixon's unprincipled behavior. Roosevelt tried to pack the Supreme Court when it opposed him, and stood by watching the destruction of the Spanish Republic by Fascism because he feared the outrage of the Catholic hierarchy if he supported a sister democracy. And so on and on.

When necessity dictates, our laws are as bendable as licorice to our

Reprinted with permission from *Harper's*, September, 1974, pp. 13-20. Copyright © 1974. Initially it was titled "The Limited Hang-out."

Arthur Miller is the author of many dramatic works including *Death of a Salesman, View from the Bridge,* and *The Crucible.*

Presidents, and if their private conversations had been taped an awful lot of history would be different now.

Yet Nixon stands alone, for he alone is without a touch of grace. It is gracelessness which gives his mendacity its shine of putrescence, a want of that magnanimity and joy in being alive that animated his predecessors. Reading the Presidential transcripts, one is confronted with the decay of a language, of a legal system; in these pages what was possibly the world's best hope is reduced to a vaudeville, a laugh riot. We are in the presence of three gangsters who moralize and a swarming legion of their closely shaved underlings.

Let us, as the sayings goes, be clear about it—more than forty appointed cohorts of Richard Nixon are already either in jail, under indictment, or on the threshold of jail for crimes which, as these transcripts demonstrate, the President tried by might and main to keep from being discovered. The chief law-enforcement officer could not find it in his heart to demand the resignation of even one of them for betraying the public trust. Those whom public clamor forced to depart were given sad Presidential farewells and called "fine public servants."

This, to me, is the unexpectedly clear news in these transcripts— that, had he had the least civic, not to say moral, instinct, Richard Nixon could have been spared his agony. Had he known how to be forthright, and, on discovering that the direction of the Watergate burglary came, in part, from his own official family, stood up and leveled with the public, he would have exalted his partisans and confounded his enemies, and, with a tremendous electoral victory in the offing, he would have held an undisputed national leadership. Nor is this as naive as it appears; it seems believable that he need not have literally given the order to burgle Ellsberg's psychiatrist, was surprised by it, in fact. If, as also seems likely, he gave the nod to an intelligence operation against the Democrats at some previous meeting, it would not have been the first such strategy in political history, and he could have assumed the responsibility for that while disclaiming the illegal means for carrying it out. The nut of it all is that, even on the basis of self-survival, he marched instinctively down the crooked path.

THE PARADOX OF POWER

So we are back with Plutarch, for whom character is fate, and in these transcripts Richard Nixon's character is our history. But to ask why he could not come forward and do his duty as the chief law-enforcement officer is to ask who and what Nixon is, and there is no one we can ask that question. All one can really affirm is that these transcripts show certain attributes which now are evidentiary. Like a good play these dialogues spring from conflict surrounding a paradox: his power as President depends on moral repute, at bottom; therefore, one would expect him to go after any of his associates who compromised him. Instead, something entirely different happens. He sits down with Haldeman and Ehrlichman and proceeds to concoct a double strategy: first, to convince the public that he was totally ignorant of the crimes, which is an intelligent decision, and, second, to make it appear that he is launching an outraged investigation of the facts in order to reveal them, when actually he is using his discoveries to keep his associates' infractions concealed. The latter objective is impossible and therefore stupid, and in short order he finds himself in possession of guilty knowledge, knowledge an honest man would have handed over to the requisite authorities. So the crux is always who and what he is. Another man need not have been swept away by events.

In the face of the sheer number of his appointees and their underlings who turn out to be unprincipled beyond the point of criminality, the issue is no longer whether he literally gave the orders for the burglary and the other crimes. The subordinates of another kind of man would have known that such despicable acts were intolerable to their patron and leader simply by their sense of his nature. That more than forty— thus far—are incriminated or in jail speaks of a consistency of their understanding of what this President was and what he stood for. Many of his staff members he barely knew personally, yet all of them obviously had caught the scent of that decay of standards emanating from the center, and they knew what was allowed and what was expected of them. The transcripts provide the evidence of the leader's nature, specifically his near-delusionary notion that because he was "the President" he could not be doing what it was clear enough he was, in fact, doing.

At one point he and Haldeman and Ehrlichman are discussing the question of getting Mitchell to take the entire rap, thus drawing the lightning, but they suddenly remember John Dean's earlier warning that the two high assistants might well be indictable themselves.

> NIXON: We did not cover up, though, that's what decides, that's what's [sic] decides . . . Dean's case is the question. And I do not consider him guilty . . . Because if he—if that's the case, then half the staff is guilty.
> EHRLICHMAN: That's it. He's guilty of really no more except in degree.
> NIXON: That's right. Then [sic] others.
> EHRLICHMAN: Then [sic] a lot of . . .
> NIXON: And frankly then [sic] I have been since a week ago, two weeks ago.

And a moment later, Ehrlichman returns to the bad smell:

But what's been bothering me is . . .
NIXON: That with knowledge, we're still not doing anything.
So he knew that he was, at a minimum, reaching for the forbidden fruit—obstruction of justice—since he was in possession of knowledge of a crime which he was not revealing to any authority. . . .

PARTISAN IDEOLOGY AS RATIONALIZATION

There is a persistent note of plaintiveness when Nixon compares Watergate with the Democrats' crimes, attributing the press's outcry to liberal hypocrisy. The Democratic party is primarily corrupt, a bunch of fakers spouting humane slogans while underneath the big city machines like Daley's steal elections, as Kennedy's victory was stolen from him in Chicago. Welfare, gimme-politics, perpetuate the Democratic constituency. The Kennedys especially are immoral, unfaithful to family, and ruthless in pursuit of power. Worse yet, they are the real professionals who *know* how to rule with every dirty trick in the book. A sort of embittered ideology helps lower Nixon into the pit.

For the Republicans, in contrast, are naive and really amateurs at politics because they are basically decent, hardworking people. This conviction of living in the light is vital if one is to understand the monstrous distortions of ethical ideas in these transcripts. Nixon *is* decency. In fact, he is America; at one point after Dean has turned state's evidence against them, Haldeman even says, "He's not un-American and anti-Nixon." These men stand in a direct line from the Puritans of the first Plymouth Colony who could swindle and kill Indians secure in the knowledge that their cause was holy. Nixon seems to see himself as an outsider, even now, in politics. Underneath he is too good for it. When Dean, before his betrayal, tries to smuggle reality into the Oval Office—by warning that people are not going to believe that "Chapin acted on his own to put his old friend Segretti to be a Dick Tuck on somebody else's campaign. They would have to paint it into something more sinister . . . part of a general [White House] plan"—Nixon observes with a certain mixture of condemnation and plain envy, "Shows you what a master Dick Tuck is."

This ideology, like all ideologies, is a pearl formed around an irritating grain of sand, which, for Nixon, is something he calls the Establishment, meaning Eastern Old Money. "The basic thing," he says, "is the Establishment. The Establishment is dying and so they've got to show that . . . it is just wrong [the Watergate] just because of this." So there is a certain virtue in defending now what the mere duty he swore to uphold requires he root out. In a diabolical sense he seems to see himself clinging to a truth which, only for the moment, appears nearly criminal. But the *real* untruth, the real immorality shows up in his mind very quickly—it is Kennedy, and he is wondering if they can't put out some dirt on Chappaquiddick through an investigator they had working up there. But like every other such counterattack this one falls apart because it could lead back to Kalmbach's paying this investigator with campaign funds, an illegal usage. So the minuet starts up and stops time after time, a thrust blunted by the realization that it can only throw light upon what must be kept in the dark. Yet their conviction of innocent and righteous intentions stands undisturbed by their knowledge of their own vulnerability.

And it helps to explain, this innocence and righteousness, why they so failed to appraise reality, in particular that they were *continuing* to act in obstruction of justice by concealing what they knew, and what they knew they knew, and what they told one another they knew. It is not dissimilar to Johnson's persistence in Vietnam despite every evidence that the war was unjust and barbarous, for Good People do not commit crimes, and there is simply no way around that.

Yet from time to time Nixon senses that he is floating inside his own psyche. "If we could get a feel," he says, "I just have a horrible feeling that we may react. . . ."

HALDEMAN: Yes. That we are way overdramatizing.
NIXON: That's my view. That's what I don't want to do either.
[A moment later] Am I right that we have got to do something to restore the credibility of the Presidency?

And on the verge of reality the ideology looms, and they scuttle back into the hole—Haldeman saying, "Of course you know the credibility gap in the old [Democratic] days." So there they are, comfortably right again, the only problem being how to prove it to the simpletons outside.

Again, like any good play, the transcripts reflect a single situation or paradox appearing in a variety of disguises that gradually peel away the extraneous until the central issue is naked. In earlier pages they are merely worried about bad publicity, then it is the criminal indictment of one or another of the secondary cadres of the Administration, until finally the heart of darkness is endangered, Haldeman and Ehrlichman and thus Nixon himself. In other words, the mistake called Watergate, an incident they originally view as uncharacteristic of them, a caper, a worm that fell on their shoulders, turns out to be one of the worms inside them that crawled out.

So the aspects of Nixon which success had once obscured now become painfully parodistic in his disaster. He almost becomes a pathetically moving figure as he lifts his old slogans out of his bag. He knows now that former loyalists are testifying secretly to the grand jury, so he erects the facade of his own "investigation," which is nothing but an attempt to find out what they are testifying to, the better to prepare himself for the next explosion; he reverts time and again to recalling his inquisitorial aptitude in the Hiss case, which made him a national figure. But now he is on the other end of the stick, and, after a string of calculations designed to cripple the Ervin Committee, he declaims, "I mean, after all, it is my job and I don't want the Presidency tarnished, but also I am a law-enforcement man," even as he is trying to lay the whole thing off on Mitchell, the very symbol of hardline law enforcement, the former Attorney General himself.

THE DRAMA AS FARCE

Things degenerate into farce at times, as when he knows the Ervin Committee and the Grand Jury are obviously out of his control and on the way to eating him up and he speaks of making a "command decision." It is a sheer unconscious dullness of a magnitude worthy of Ring Lardner's baseball heroes. There are scenes, indeed, which no playwright would risk for fear of seeming too mawkishly partisan.

For example, the idea comes to Nixon repeatedly that he must act with candor, simply, persuasively. Now, since John Dean has been up to his neck in the details of the various attempts to first discover and then hide the truth, should Dean be permitted by the President to appear before a grand jury, eminently qualified as he is as the knower of facts? The President proceeds to spitball a public announcement before Ehrlichman's and Ziegler's sharp judgmental minds:

> NIXON: Mr. Dean certainly wants the opportunity to defend himself against these charges. He would welcome the opportunity and what we have to do is to work out a procedure which will allow him to do so consistent with his unique position of being a top member of the President's staff but also the Counsel. There is a lawyer, Counsel . . . [it starts breaking down] not lawyer, Counsel—but the responsibility of the Counsel for confidentiality.
> ZIEGLER: Could you apply that to the grand jury?
> EHRLICHMAN: Absolutely. The grand jury is one of those occasions where a man in his situation can defend himself.
> NIXON: Yes. The grand jury. Actually, if called, we are not going to refuse for anybody called before the grand jury to go, are we, John?
> EHRLICHMAN: I can't imagine (unintelligible).
> NIXON: Well, if called, he will be cooperative, consistent with his responsibilities as Counsel. How do we say that?
> EHRLICHMAN: He will cooperate.

NIXON: He will fully cooperate.
EHRLICHMAN: Better check that with Dean. I know he's got certain misgivings on this.
ZIEGLER: He did this morning.
NIXON: Yeah, Well, then, don't say that.

Refusing himself his tragedy, Nixon ends in farce. After another of many attempts at appearing "forthcoming" and being thwarted yet again by all the culpability in the house, he suddenly exclaims, "What the hell does one disclose that isn't going to blow something?" Thus speaketh the first law-enforcement officer of the United States. Excepting that this government is being morally gutted on every page, it is to laugh. And the humor of their own absurdity is not always lost on the crew, although it is understandably laced with pain. They debate whether John Mitchell might be sent into the Ervin Committee, but in an executive session barred to the public and TV and under ground rules soft enough to tie up the Old Constitutionalist in crippling legalisms.

NIXON: Do you think we want to go this route now? Let it hang out so to speak?
DEAN: Well, it isn't really that . . .
HALDEMAN: It's a limited hang-out.
DEAN: It is a limited hang-out. It's not an absolute hang-out.
NIXON: But some of the questions look big hanging out publicly or privately. [Still, he presses the possibility.] If it opens doors, it opens doors . . . .

As usual it is Haldeman who is left to interpolate the consequences.

John says he is sorry he sent those burglars in there—and that helps a lot.
NIXON: That's right.
EHRLICHMAN: You are very welcome, sir.

(Laughter), the script reads then, and along with everything else it adds to the puzzle of why Nixon ordered his office bugged in the first place, and especially why he did not turn off the machine once the magnitude of Watergate was clear to him. After all, no one but he and the technicians in the secret service knew the spools were turning.

WHY DOES A MAN BUG HIMSELF?

As a nonsubscriber to the school of psychohistory—having myself served as the screen upon which Norman Mailer, no less, projected the lesions of his own psyche, to which he gave my name—I would disclaim the slightest inside knowledge, if that be necessary, and rest simply on the public importance of this question itself. Watergate aside, it is a very odd thing for a man to bug himself. Perhaps the enormity of it is better felt if one realizes that in a preelectronic age a live stenographer would have had to sit concealed in Nixon's office as he exchanged affections with a Haldeman, whom he admired and whose fierce loyalty moved him deeply. At a minimum, does it not speak a certain contempt even for those he loved to have subjected his relationship with them to such recorded scrutiny? Can he ever have forgotten that the record was being made as he laughed with friends, heard their personal troubles and perhaps embarrassing secrets? What manner of man can so split himself? How could he have made this jibe with any notion of honor? And again, why didn't he turn the damned thing off once he saw where Watergate was leading him? It seems to me that the very heart of his perplexing nature is in this question. Is it conceivable for an Eisenhower, a Truman, a Kennedy, a Roosevelt to have done this? It doesn't seem so, and the reason is interesting—these men, different as they were, possessed a certain spontaneity which could not have borne the weight of knowing they were speaking into a microphone from morning to night, and spontaneity is a form of grace that Nixon lacks.

One can imagine two purposes for Nixon taping his own life. A secret record would help in case he needed it to confound political enemies who might distort what he told them. But this has a paranoid implication. It means that he must have felt himself utterly alone, surrounded by enemies. Secondly, the transcripts show him as wishing to go down in history as the great peacemaker, and his public speeches demonstrate that he relies heavily on his peacemaking role to justify the highest place in history. The pre-Watergate rationale can very possibly have been a desire to monumentalize himself, an emotion by no means unprecedented in leaders. But to offer one's every relationship to this monument is to live, in effect, as though one were already dead. In the act of being permanently taped he becomes his own subject, his own feminine, while at the same time he controls or masters whoever is sitting obliviously before him. He partakes secretly of that godhead which remembers everything and thereby holds control. Taping his life is the conception of a man desperate for reassurance as to his power, and it was to that power that Nixon offered up himself and his associates, friend and foe alike, day after day.

The transcripts make it easier to understand why he should so doubt his innate potency, his authority. Ehrlichman and Haldeman interrupt him at will as though he were an equal or less, cutting across his statements so frequently that I am sure a count would show he has more broken speeches by far than anyone in those pages. He is almost never addressed as "Mr. President," or even as "sir," except by Henry

Petersen, whose sense of protocol and respect, like—remarkably enough
—John Mitchell's, stands in glaring contrast to the locker-room famil-
iarity of his two chief lieutenants. He can hardly ever assert a policy
idea without ending with, "Am I right?" or, "You think so?" It is not
accidental that both Ehrlichman and Haldeman, like Colson, were so
emphatically rough and, in some reports, brutal characters. They were
his devils and he their god, but a god because the Good inhabits him
while they partake of it but are his mortal side and must sometimes
reach into the unclean.

STALLING ADMISSION OF GUILT

To turn off the tapes, then, when an elementary sense of survival
would seem to dictate their interruption, would be to make an admission which, if it were made, would threaten his very psychic existence
and bring on the great dread against which his character was formed—
namely, that he is perhaps fraudulent, perhaps a fundamentally fearing
man, perhaps not really enlisted in the cause of righteousness but
merely in his own aggrandizement of power, and power for the purpose
not of creativity and good but of filling the void where spontaneity and
love should be. Nixon will not admit his share of evil in himself, and
so the tapes must go on turning, for the moment he presses that STOP
button he ends the godly illusion and must face his human self. He can
record his own open awareness that he and his two bravos are quite
possibly committing crime in the sun-filled, pristine White House itself,
but as long as the tapes turn, a part of him is intrepidly recording the
bald facts, as God does, and thereby bringing the day of judgment
closer, the very judgment he has abhorred and dearly wants. For the
hope of being justified at the very, very end is a fierce hope, as is the
fear of being destroyed for the sins whose revelation and admission
will alone crown an evaded, agonized life with meaning. The man
aspires to the heroic. No one, not even his worst enemies, can deny
his strength, his resiliency. But it is not the strength of the confronter,
as is evidenced by his inability to level with John Mitchell, whom he
privately wants to throw to the wolves but face to face cannot blame.
It is rather the perverse strength of the private hero testing his presumptions about himself against God, storming an entrance into his
wished-for nature which never seems to embrace him but is always an
arm's length away. Were he alive to a real authority in him, a true
weight of his own existing, such a testing would never occur to him.
There are leaders who take power because they have found themselves,
and there are leaders who take power in search of themselves. A score

of times in those pages Nixon refers to "the President" as though he were the President's emissary, a *Doppelgänger*.[1] Excepting in official documents did Roosevelt, Eisenhower, Kennedy, even Truman, so refer to himself? Surely not in private conversation with their closest friends. But to stop those tapes would mean the end of innocence, and in a most cruelly ironic way, an act of true forthrightness.

If such was his drama, he forged the sword that cut him down. It was a heroic struggle except that it lacked the ultimate courage of self-judgment and the reward of insight. Bereft of the latter, he is unjust to himself and shows the world his worst while his best he buries under his pride and the losing hope that a resurrected public cynicism will rescue his repute. For it is not enough now, the old ideology that the Democrats are even more corrupt. The President is not a Democrat or Republican here, he is as close as we get to God.

And if his struggle was indeed to imprint his best presumptions upon history, and it betrayed him, it is a marvel that it took place now, when America had discovered the rocky terrain where her innocence is no more, where God is simply what happens and what has happened, and if you like being called good you have to do good, if only because other nations are no longer powerlessly inert but looking on with X-ray eyes, and you no longer prevail for the yellow in your silky hair. The most uptight leader we have had, adamantly resisting the age, has backhandedly announced the theme of its essential drama in his struggle —to achieve authenticity without paying authenticity's price—and in his fall. The hang-out—it is a marvel, is unlimited; at long last, after much travail, Richard Nixon is one of us.

NOTES

1. [double]

16 The Outsider on the Inside: Richard Nixon's Seventh Crisis

Garry Wills

Recently Wills noted the irony in Richard Nixon's constant references to the Alger Hiss case during staff conversations about the Watergate crisis. Although Nixon seemed blind to the possibility, Wills suggested that in the Watergate matter Nixon was actually playing the role of Hiss. Wills asserted, "By feeling the need to re-enact his life's high moments, mixed as they were with bitterness, Nixon remained the underdog fighting power—even when he had all the power he could wish." In this essay Wills elaborates on that theme. He shows how Watergate differed from the confrontations mentioned in Nixon's Six Crises *where an enemy existed to counterattack. The need for such a justifying adversary, the author argues, led Nixon to view Daniel Ellsberg as another Hiss. The President thereafter could pursue the politics of resentment with which he felt most comfortable.*

How did it happen, so soon after culminating triumph? Where were his skills, which even foes had come to respect? Why has the master of crises lost the art of crisis management? Nixon himself thinks he is at his best in moments of strain; if so, this should be his golden hour. Why isn't it?

One reason is that Nixon has been robbed of a satisfying crisis just when he needs it. For crisis, as he defines the term, is not just any old trouble—it is the purifying attack of evil men, which one must undergo, abandoned by allies, making a lonely decision, and then counterattacking. The scenario is written and explained in "Six Crises." Things that do not fit that pattern (e.g., Nixon's first California campaigns, or his relations with Senator Joseph McCarthy) are omitted. They were plain troubles, not crises.

Garry Wills is the author of *Nixon Agonistes: The Crisis of the Self-Made Man.*

Crisis is a spiritual category in Nixon's mind, a political "dark night of the soul" testing men, making them worthy. "The finest steel goes through the hottest fires." Thus crisis has a definite ritual shape, its stages well marked:

(1) One must be attacked, and seem defeated—and that fits his current ordeal.

(2) One must withdraw, and undergo purifying disciplines (mainly of lonely study and sleeplessness)—Nixon has done this at least twice . . . closing himself off at Camp David, preparing his response.

(3) One must make the decision from which all later acts will follow—and here the scenario, as currently played, gets muddled; for the lonely "Yes" said in the soul's night is denied the President. In all his six canonical crises, the decision was his alone—should he drop the Hiss case, should he resign from Eisenhower's ticket, give in to pressures to be an acting President, return home after the first South American riot, stalk off from Khrushchev, cancel further debates with Kennedy? He could undertake his disciplines of choice undistracted by others' preferences. But not now. The decision is largely out of his hands. Will his loyal troops stay loyal; will they protect him; or involve him; exonerate, or implicate? He has to wait, like the rest of us. The ordeal of decision is undergone, without the release of having decided. The unresolved air of even his most complete later statement is admitted: "My own information on those others matters is fragmentary and to some extent contradictory. Additional information may be forthcoming of which I am unaware. . . . As more information is developed, I have no doubt that more questions will be raised. To the extent that I am able, I shall also seek to set forth the facts as known to me with respect to those questions." It is hard to hold dark-night sessions for one's soul if you are also listening for other shoes to drop next door.

(4) Once the decision is made, one can counterattack. Any harm caused one's foe (whether Hiss or Kennedy, Acheson, or Khrushchev) is the result of his prior aggression—Acheson's on the subject of Hiss, or Kennedy's on the subject of Cuba. Besides, the purity of Nixon's response is demonstrated by the ordeal of self-punishment undergone before he punishes the enemy. This was always massive retaliation time for Nixon, turning the tables on his attackers—going after Stevenson's fund, or Kennedy's hawkishness, or Khrushchev's boorishness in debate. But now the counterpuncher's arms are tied. Where is the enemy, and how is one to isolate him? The structuring of crisis allowed Nixon in the past to shift the onus onto others—he was the defender, after others had attacked. In that sense, he had a talent for getting kicked, spat on, or insulted. If he was not very likable, one could sympathize with him when mistreated. All his most loyal

followers think of him as a man above all *wronged*. All his strength came from that weakness. But this time his very friends have wronged him; and he must protect their odd ways of protecting him, lest their protection be, in this extremity, withdrawn. That rules out the nuclear response—he is not lobbing a bomb into the men's room at the Kremlin, but into back rooms at the White House. He must raze part of the structure to keep his own part standing. While the press tries to make the whole White House a free-fire zone, poor Nixon is forced to make the liberal offer out of "Fail Safe": If I blow up part of my own country, will you let the rest survive?

(5) The aftermath of crisis is very important to Nixon—the time when he must stick by the decision, not losing his nerve, not lapsing into carelessness after the straining soul's long night. One can endure this aftermath within the expected rhythm of definable crisis—though even then it is the hardest part of the ordeal. But how is he to cope with a shapeless non-crisis, with an aftermath endlessly prolonged because deferred, once a sterile decision process has been undergone without decisiveness? With choice diffused among others and one's rhythms all thrown off, with the satisfactions of counterattack denied him, Nixon is bound to be disoriented.

Besides, he has been deprived of his crisis managers. If he had been asked, around inauguration time this year, what crises have succeeded the canonical first six, he would probably have answered: the Cambodia incursion, imposing Phase I controls, mining Haiphong harbor, and the B-52 raids of last Christmas. They all fit the pattern. In each of them he made the lonely choice and suffered through criticism while striking back at his foes; and, in each case, he won eventual vindication in his own eyes. But Haldeman and Ehrlichman were there, isolating him for the big decision, comforting him afterward, going with him through the prepared scenario. They made the crises run on time. And they are gone.

But the need for an enemy remains. No wonder Nixon cast wistful glances toward Ellsberg. But it is absurd to equate (as some have) one man breaking the law in response to what he believes is some higher law, and a crew of men in power breaking the law to prove there is no higher law than the law. Ellsberg was denying jurisdiction to an authority that had lost legitimacy in one area. Nixon's supporters were exercising jurisdiction, breaking laws to establish the law's legitimacy. It will be hard to get an audience's emotional juices running through the surreal baffles of this equation. Nixon used stolen "pumpkin papers" to get Hiss; and he looked patriotic and efficient. But his aides did not steal the papers. Using a psychiatrist's purloined records to get Ellsberg—and then not getting him, after all—looks not only low but idiotic. Best forget Dr. Dan.

THE USES OF ENEMIES

Nixon's need for a justifying opponent is dramatically revealed in the public's readiness to distrust him. Before the televised April [1973] speech, a majority of those with any opinion at all told pollsters they believed Nixon knew about Watergate before the event. After the speech, some polls showed a rise in that statistic. Despite reverence for his office, despite the huge election returns last fall, despite the pettiness of the act, a large number of the people who voted for Nixon believed him capable of a mean and silly crime. That is an astonishing fact—though I doubt that it astonished Nixon. He has never fooled himself about his personal appeal. He offered an expertise once in office and he put himself in office by being less despised than the alternative. His mode was, of necessity, the mobilization of resentment against that alternative. Men may not like him, but they like what he is doing (i.e., they like the ones he is getting to be got). One runs *against,* by Nixon's code. He felt he lost in 1960 because he was thrown on the defensive over Eisenhower's Administration. He cheerfully admitted in 1968 that he had the advantage against Humphrey because, as an outsider, he would be on the attack. It was massive retaliation time for Ramsey Clark, as "soft on crime" (i.e., "nigger-lover"). The target was chosen with Nixon's old undoubted skills. Of all who were then in the Administration, Clark could best be taken as a symbol of concern for the poor, the imprisoned and the wronged. Lyndon himself was too tough in other ways—one could not "pansify" him. (Besides, he was neutralized at his ranch during most of the campaign—better not to rouse him). Humphrey had no real authority in the Administration, and was trying to be tough on crime. Robert Kennedy was dead, so out of rhetorical reach. George McGovern had not yet effectively skewered himself for the sacrifice to his own and others' ambitions. Ramsey Clark it had to be—and Nixon "socked it to him." Nixon is at his best when expressing resentment, and he did it well in 1968.

But what of 1972? That would be 1960 all over again, his hands tied, having to take the positive side of a debate. He remembered that great campaign line, "Those who have had a chance for four years and could not produce peace, should not be given another chance." The scurrying of various plumbers, buggers and saboteurs looks silly in retrospect, so much wasteful vain effort. But that is not the way it looked, ahead of time, to a man who fears the insider's role. Nixon could not know, until later in the game, that McGovern and Eagleton would be better at splitting and sinking the Democratic party than any Republican saboteurs on earth.

And Nixon was not thinking in one-shot terms of the single election remaining to him. He had a constituency to maintain and expand, day by day—his recent setbacks with Congress show how a President is crippled without public confidence. Furthermore, he meant to build a permanent "new majority" for the party as his principal domestic achievement. His first steps in this direction were impressive. He almost *invented* the Silent Majority of Middle Americans. He was absorbing the old Democratic South, welcoming converts to the party without losing the old-timers, pleasing fat cats and hardhats equally. He was thinking in terms of a new coalition to last as long as Franklin Roosevelt's combination of various minorities.

But Roosevelt's minorities were economically deprived; and he dealt with a time when blacks and whites needed work too badly to fear and hate each other in electoral terms. And the break-up of that coalition began when first economic needs were substantially met—when labor unions were bourgeoisified; city machines began disintegrating; the suburbs filled up with workers, and the old city neighborhoods with blacks.

If the politically viable "left" addressed itself to economic needs, the "right" has always been more concerned with status—with acceptance, with maintaining small-town values against "Eastern Establishment" eggheads and godless reformers. The rise of the sixties "counterculture" —with its dirty words and flaunted sexuality—made the union man stop worrying about his paycheck while he inquired into his daughter's virtue. Enter Nixon, the scourge of pot and pornography. Enter Agnew, the scourge of long-haired flag-burners. Enter, at least for a while, the New Majority.

A NEGATIVE STRATEGY

Nixon's mandate was clear, and congenial to him: He was to be against the "counterculture"—upholding the first culture, but in a "counterinsurgent" way, since prior Administrations were felt to be equivocal toward the kids. (The Kennedys helped invent the kids, back in the days of the Peace Corps and civil rights). So Nixon's first strategy was negative; not only to be, retroactively, against the Kerner Commission, the Coleman Report, the Merhige decision—but to oppose the reports handed to his own office by the Scranton Commission, the Heard and Shapp Commissions (all of them speaking in the mushly voice of permissiveness).

Thus Nixon got the best of both worlds. He held the nation's highest office, yet could talk like a critic of power. He came to the weak old "establishment" like Green Berets to rescue Thieu; an outsider, propping up the regime, not taking blame for its weakness, fighting hard against the "insurgent" guerillas. Nixon conducted our first counterinsurgent Presidency. Friendly to the real corporations, he used neopopulist rhetoric on the "monopoly" of thought exercised by his TV critics and the academy. He enhanced his own vast powers by attacking Walter Cronkite's despotism. He fostered a police mentality by calling the "peace forces" helpless before crime forces. He portrayed himself as defending apple-pie values almost singlehandedly against kids, professors, Panthers, priests and Eric Sevareid. The act worked so well even the Democrats tried to think up a neopopulism of their own, an ethnic politics based on status resentments ("We Poles need recognition, too") rather than economic need.

But if an economic coalition can be dispersed by rising prosperity, status resentment is diluted by growing respectability. If an underdog President succeeds, he stops being an underdog. It was one thing to cry, "Foul" when two Supreme Court nominees were rejected in a row. But that gets harder after four have been accepted. Besides, all visible symbols of the enemy are almost gone—no more burning of flags, or bras, or campus buildings. The P.O.W.'s are home—Nixon's critics cannot be accused of abandoning them. The resisters and deserters do not have much hope of coming home; and an amnesty not granted cannot be resented. When the President ends our part in the war on Hanoi, he can no longer attack those calling for its end. With the fading of insurgents, counterinsurgency should also disappear. The counter-counterculture makes no sense without a counterculture. All we have left, in that case, is the first culture. The landslide President becomes Upper Dog, and his Adminstration is itself the Establishment.

Such a posture is untenable for Nixon. The true outsider can never be an insider. He likes to tell people how he wakes up with the thought, "I must tell such-and-such to the President"—only to remember he is President. The office is still to be gained, rather than held. The achiever gets up each morning to achieve all over again. He must rise each minute, if only by an inch—or fall back, helpless, toward the bottom; a bottomless fall. And the rungs of his ladder are necessary resentments. Hostility may be cooling under the hardhats; but Sweeney still agonizes in the White House: *"You don't see them, you don't—but I see them: they are hunting me down, I must move on."*

THE POLITICS OF RESENTMENT

No matter how others feel, Nixon retains his outsider's resentment. He is something of an athlete at this. Whenever the fresh spontaneous voice breaks through his stiff control, it is bitterness speaking:

Item: When Supreme Court nominee Clement F. Haynsworth Jr.

was rejected by the Senate, Nixon blew up at "the press," and substituted a man with white supremacism in his past.

Item: When the Senate showed resistance to the Carswell nomination, Nixon fired off a hasty letter (drafted by Charles Colson) saying the Senate meant to frustrate the President's constitutional responsibility.

Item: When Carswell was rejected, Nixon read an angry statement blaming the act on "malicious character assassination" caused by hatred of the South: "I understand the bitter feeling of millions of Americans who live in the South about the act of regional discrimination that took place in the Senate yesterday."

Item: When students rioted against his Cambodian invasion, Nixon lashed out at "those bums" as "the luckiest people in the world, going to the great universities"—always his tone when contrasting his own hard youth with that of pampered Establishment types. He called their concern over Vitenam insincere: ". . . storming around on this issue. You name it. Get rid of the war, there will be another one."

Item: He admitted making an ugly situation worse when, near San Jose State College, he flashed a V-sign at protesters "because this really gets them."

Item: He intruded himself into the legal process against Lieutenant Calley, participating in the outburst of resentment at his conviction.

Item: He intruded himself into the Charlie Manson trial, pronouncing that man guilty before the jury's findings, blaming the press again; and contrasting its attitude with the role of John Wayne in the movie "Chisum," the story of a man who takes the law into his own hands to kill off an outlaw menace. . . .

Nixon's other movie hero is revealing, as few things can be in a man whose nonpolitical needs and preferences have always been ascetically trimmed away. He likes what he should or must, without rebelling. His cultural world is bounded by Mantovani, Billy Graham, Allen Drury and the Redskins. But suddenly, in a time of deep self-realization for him—in a palpable crisis, certified as such by all the rules—he committed a definite *liking*. He liked "Patton." His mind, restless and starved when it spends five minutes away from political effort or talk soothed itself with repeated viewings of that film in the period when he most needed strength, in the "aftermath" of his choice to invade Cambodia.

His critics indulged a bit of massive retaliation on their own part when they heard of this preference—as if Nixon was reveling in bloodthirstiness and borrowed manhood while bombs dropped and rockets shot up. These people cannot have been paying attention to the movie. "Patton" was not about male aggressions satisfied. It was the story of an unappreciated dissenter, a man rejected (and by Eisenhower!)

despite his great contributions. Nixon was not reveling in vicarious assertion, but in shared rejection. He was stiffening his spine with the one sure medicine for it—resentment of his critics, and self-pity.

BEING VICTOR AND VICTIM

Since this is his own personality's tropism, we should not wonder if those he sifts for his inner communings share it. Indeed the men closest to him had no other discernible quality to recommend them. When they spoke, it was in hyperboles of rejection—Haldeman saying Nixon's critics were traitors; Mitchell saying the Senate would not have accepted one of the Twelve Apostles for the Supreme Court if he came from the South; Pat Buchanan arguing that Cronkite has poisoned the very airwaves against King and Country. The whole contradiction of "underdog power" lies in the Agnew-Buchanan war upon the press—for Buchanan argued equally that the people were with Agnew against TV commentators, yet that commentators had poisoned the minds of the people. If Nixon could be elected by a landslide, after Cronkite's long reign on the screen, then TV liberals' power must be not only ineffectual but self-defeating. The right thing for Buchanan to do is encourage liberalism's electronic euthanasia. But the President somehow has to be both the victor *and* the victim, to fit his own expectations and the role he has used all his life; and those around him were attuned to just these needs.

Such fears grew oddly more real and frantic as objects and occasions for them disappeared. Since Nixon and those around him knew he was still wronged and mistreated, an F.B.I. or C.I.A. insensitive to the threats must be fools of the Establishment. William Buckley argues that the right approach to E. Howard Hunt was to stress how little one can rely on conventional channels of protection, once "the Establishment" has narcotized those channels. Proof? Jack Anderson stole documents and got the Pulitzer Prize. No matter that the Pulitzer Committee is not identical with the F.B.I. If Ramsey Clark could cut down even J. Edgar Hoover's wiretapping activities in 1966; if Presidential commissions all gave permissive advice; if an Establishment figure like Richard Helms could run the C.I.A.; then who—in the end—could you trust to be unindoctrinated? Only Haldeman? Only Ehrlichman? And whom could they trust? Only Liddy? Only Hunt? And even then one must tap one's friends. (The poison had reached Kissinger.) If the campuses were quiet, Nixon could not just take credit for this silence. The enemy is still pursuing, more stealthily. One must be equally devious, find foreign influence and funds, bare the psychic twist in Ellsberg, get the evil secret of the Panthers.

And so his friends went to work, responding to fine signals from that violated sensibility. He had to be protected from his enemies, 24 hours a day; and he had to have enemies to be protected from. Only thus could he lead, or gain confidence; hold together his coalition of fears and grievances. He huddles over sustaining fires of grievance, even when grievances have to be conjured up—as air-conditioning keeps the White House artificially cold so Nixon can squirrel himself against the fireplace, shutting out the cold blasts of contempt and evil design he knows are out there. Others may think there is no enemy. But his old bruises ache to signal each change in political weather. It is only a matter of time before the press, or some other evil monster strikes. "I know who they are really after," he told the Cabinet after his two chief aides resigned. The bitterness is still there—flaring out at Charles Percy, at visible posting of F.B.I. agents in the White House, at requests for his record of visitors. But now the bitterness does not find a useful public channel, to mobilize in others a supportive hate of Commies or the press. He needs, above all, a useful public enemy.

Yet it was just that need that brought him to this fix. Knowing their man well, his aides served well in the hunt for public threats on a dwindling traitors' market. They certainly tried their best with Ellsberg—and with Edward Kennedy, with Muskie; with Humphrey and McGovern. The anti-Establishment Administration, still counter-insurgent in victory, staged a bloodless coup against itself, stealing votes in an election it had already, easily, won. This is the perfect expression of our outsider's inability simply to possess, to find peace inside. Richard Nixon, through whatever relayed hints or needs apparent to his friends, had to steal the White House from Richard Nixon. In Milton's words (from "Samson Agonistes"): "Oh lastly overstrong against thyself!"

17 | Preface to the Psychological Study of Richard Nixon

Paul J. Halpern

Even before Watergate, students of politics had devoted more time to probing the mind of Richard Nixon than any president in recent memory. He has been compared to an endless stream of historical and fictional characters. There have been "old" Nixons, "new" Nixons, "split personality" Nixons, "Freudian" Nixons. A variety of metaphors, analogies, and theories have tried to define the essence of the man. In this selection Halpern applies some of the concepts of depth psychology to analyze aspects of the behavior of Mr. Nixon. He presents an adaptive approach and argues that despite their costs, Nixon's actions need not be interpreted only in terms of theories of self-punishment. He also suggests what more can be learned from the recent comparison of Richard Nixon and Woodrow Wilson.

Journalist Lou Cannon, an astute observer of Richard Nixon, recently wrote: "From his first political utterance, Nixon has always seen himself in terms of some historical figure other than himself. He wanted to be a Lincoln, an Eisenhower—most of all a Woodrow Wilson—and he has usually been most comfortable when clothed in the oratorical robes of some dead President."[1] With regard to his desire to emulate Woodrow Wilson, Nixon finally got his wish—but not in the way he probably conceived of it. Students of politics are comparing his self-destructive handling of Watergate with President Wilson's equally disastrous management of his fight to get Senate approval of the League of Nations Treaty. In a widely-read study political scientist James David Barber has concluded that Wilson and Nixon shared the same basic type of presidential personality which seeks political power to compensate for low self-esteem and an ego damaged in childhood.

An original essay.

Paul J. Halpern is Assistant Professor of Political Science, University of California, Los Angeles.

Professor Barber suggests that as a consequence of its motivations, this type tends to become rigid and sticks to a failing policy when its power is challenged in areas of personal importance.[2]

Woodrow Wilson is important to the psychological study of Richard Nixon not only because one must come to terms with Professor Barber's theories and Nixon's idolization of President Wilson, but also because Wilson is the subject of the most highly regarded psychological biography yet written about an American president. It is *Woodrow Wilson and Colonel House: A Personality Study* by Alexander and Juliette George, which provides much of the theory that inspired comparisons between Nixon and his Democratic idol.[3]

The work of the Georges is useful in providing conceptual models for subsequent psychobiographies of presidents. So far it has been the Georges' specific substantive theories about Woodrow Wilson's needs to exercise political power that have received most attention from students of Richard Nixon. However, a much more important contribution of the Georges, at a broader level of generalization, is their elaboration of how over time an individual's mind or ego goes about handling emotions and thoughts that make it feel uncomfortable or guilty, and anxious or depressed. The essence of depth psychology is the study of unconscious feelings and the defenses used by people to keep certain of these feelings from disturbing their conscious mind.

Psychoanalytic theory tells us that beginning in childhood there are feelings of love and hate which we do not always express or even hold in our consciousness because of fear and ultimately because we develop a conscience that disapproves of many of these thoughts and feelings. Without our being aware of it our defense mechanisms function to repress these feelings about family members. Later we transfer these feelings onto external objects or persons as we develop rationalizations that the conscience finds acceptable for the expression of such feelings. Sometimes called "ego defenses," the defense mechanisms employed by people to ward off uncomfortable feelings vary in their success and specific content from individual to individual and from time to time. In the words of the Georges: "Modern psychologists generally agree that unacceptable thoughts and feelings anxiously dispatched from awareness do not obligingly depart once and for all. Rather, they establish themselves elsewhere within the mind and continue to direct behavior, frequently in highly disruptive fashion."[4]

RECENT WRITINGS

Richard Nixon's role in the various Watergate scandals has certainly demonstrated the need for in-depth personality studies of the former president. However, some of the recent popular literature about Mr. Nixon that was inspired by his handling of the Watergate matters has suffered from a lack of perspective. Revisionist Nixon commentators have called his entire public career a failure and have made no attempt at least to indicate his strengths and explain why even a critical press has at times granted him successes.

Assessments of his personality have often ignored the pro-Nixon literature that stems from interviews with his old friends (other than Haldeman and Ehrlichman) and that indicates a more complicated person than the caricature sometimes found in the press.[5] Psychoanalytic name-calling has sometimes replaced serious study. Some psychological interpretations of Nixon have focused so narrowly on his conduct in the Watergate affairs that they provide explanations inconsistent with what we know about the man from his pre-Watergate career. There is also a possibility that revelations about the President's emotional state during his last days and weeks in the White House will be generalized backward in time to explain why he became involved in the Watergate scandals to begin with (or his entire career), an approach frought with methodological dangers.

The self-defeating nature of Nixon's treatment of Watergate-related problems has led some observers of a psychoanalytic bent to argue that Nixon had an unconscious desire to fail, was filled with self-hate, and that "only the presidency could give him the power to experience punishment and humiliation equal to his profound feelings of worthlessness."[6] Although plausible in the abstract, such an argument has yet to be presented with the intellectual rigor necessary to make it plausible in this case. Finally, some of the recent literature on Nixon engages in crude psychological reductionism by attempting to explain substantive presidential policies solely in terms of the action of Richard Nixon's defense mechanisms. Because the multiple causes of policy decisions are often rooted in the interaction between a president's political attitudes and the political situation he faces, a clearer picture of how his emotional life affects his personality and his politics may often be found by examining his political and personal styles. In the case of Richard Nixon, understanding his relationship with his White House chief of staff, H. R. "Bob" Haldeman, may be as rewarding to the study of this president as the focus on the friendship with Colonel House was to the study of Woodrow Wilson by Alexander and Juliette George.[7]

It is not surprising that the literature about Richard Nixon generated during the Watergate period suffers from some of the excesses that we have outlined. Now that he has departed from public life (if not the public consciousness), hopefully Richard Nixon will be viewed with greater detachment by serious observers of political personality, and more attention will be devoted to explaining the whole career, not just Watergate. A recent poll of some prominent historians by the *Los Angeles Times* disclosed that few of them felt that as a president Nixon's place in history was likely to recover from the Watergate scandals.[8] It is possible, however, that like his hero Woodrow Wilson (and Presidents Andrew Jackson, Theodore Roosevelt and Harry Truman), Nixon will eventually become one of those historical figures subject to constant revisionist interpretations and academic controversies. What effect the future evaluations of his administration will have on psychohistorians is unclear. But he remains a subject of fascination for the present generation of scholars and nonscholars alike who (in the words of Richard Poirier) have pondered his mysteries like Ahab and his crew in *Moby Dick* wondering about the great white whale while in his pursuit.[9]

At the moment what seems to be lacking most in the popular accounts of Richard Nixon's career is an understanding of how the very developments in personal and political style that he made over the years in response to the threat of personal anxiety and political failure (the very behavior patterns that we now condemn) have also been partly responsible for his political successes and his emotional and physical durability. The pre-Watergate psychological literature on Nixon is much better on this point. From the perspective of personality theory, the interesting question is not whether Mr. Nixon's emotional health deteriorated along with his physical health during his last months in the White House, but how he was able to remain *relatively* healthy for such a long period of his adult life. In short, what is missing is an appreciation of the irony in the Nixon history and an understanding of why he refused to abandon his decision-making style and Watergate policies despite their enormous political costs.

CHILDHOOD

In trying to unravel the mysteries of Richard Nixon's personality, psychobiographers have focused on three components of psychological studies: (1) the description of those behavioral traits that the writer believes are tied to underlying personality needs, (2) the presentation of a theory of personality dynamics, and (3) speculations about the origins of the personality in childhood and in the cultural milieu of the child.[10] The handling of the childhood period is often the most controversial because in biography it is usually based on conjecture without the benefit of the extensive personal contact a psychoanalyst has with a patient. Critics of psychobiography, however, fail to note that even a practicing analyst has to engage in a certain amount of speculation about the relative importance of events a patient may describe. In the case of Richard Nixon psychobiographers do not always agree about the specific kinds of unconscious feelings he had toward his parents and his brothers or the relative significance and intensity of these feelings. But a general consensus is present that the events of Nixon's childhood were not conducive to the growth of a sense of security in a young person. In the words of James David Barber, "No President of the 20th century experienced such an incredible series of hard knocks in childhood as Richard Milhous Nixon did."[11]

The second born of five sons, Nixon was nearly killed in a fall at the age of three. In the next year he had a serious case of pneumonia. Later he suffered from motion sickness, hay fever, and a case of undulant fever. When Richard Nixon was twelve years old, a younger brother who was his favorite died after contracting tubercular meningitis. At about this time his mother left home for two years to be with an older brother who had tuberculosis and was hospitalized in Arizona. This brother also died of the disease when Richard was in his teens. The Nixons were poor and often struggled to make ends meet. Nixon's mother had to work and was often absent from home when he was young. Perhaps of greatest importance, Richard Nixon's father, Frank, was a man who has been variously described as loud, quarrelsome, aggressive, unpredictable, moody, competitive, a strong believer in corporal punishment for children, and one who suffered from ulcers. By contrast, Richard Nixon's mother, Hannah, with whom he apparently was close, displayed a very different sort of personality and was quiet, kind, a religious Quaker, self-controlled, the peacemaker, and generally a woman of strong character as was her own mother.

Psychological studies of Nixon suggest that he is ambivalent about aggressive impulses because, as one commentator has put it, Nixon is a man torn between his mother's dislike of "warfare" and his "father's sharp competitiveness."[12] Noting he was a quiet, day-dreaming, and serious youth rarely given to emotional outbursts, biographers assert that under his mother's influence, Nixon developed a strong conviction that it was not right in general to lose one's temper. Such an attitude also helped him avoid beatings by his father. The problem, so the argument goes, is that due to the difficult nature of his childhood and his father's aggressive personality, Nixon had his share of hostile and aggressive feelings toward family members even if such feelings could not always be directly expressed or consciously felt. Urged on by the example of his mother, Nixon resolved this conflict by learning to control his emotions at the conscious level. This process became a key to his self-esteem and emotional stability. The very act of conquering his impulses helped compensate for their troublesome and anxiety-producing nature.

This line of reasoning about the origins of Nixon's admitted concern with emotional control may be accurate but it has an aura of inevitability that is misleading. As Nixon's younger brother Don has pointed out,[13] not all the Nixon children reacted to their environment by exercising rigid self-control. Why Richard Nixon took this route may remain a puzzle.

COPING

Managing the conflict between feelings and conscience (regardless of its substantive content or historical origins) has been a preoccupation for Nixon throughout his life. It has used up much time and energy. This "emotional self-management" (to use David Barber's phrase) certainly affected his personality. His shyness and uneasiness in personal encounters, his lack of spontaneity, his desire to be left alone, his indecisiveness about firing employees, his constant denials of aggressive intent in the midst of argument, his basic self-consciousness and his suspiciousness about journalists, psychiatrists, and others whose job it was to observe human behavior and speculate about motives, his verbal slips, his secrecy, his lack of humor, his post-crisis let-downs, and even the elaborate crisis perspective itself may all be attributed to Richard Nixon's drive to maintain rigid control over his emotional life.

Nixon's ways of coping with emotions are not limited to denial and repression. As he became older the young Nixon found socially and personally acceptable outlets for his aggressiveness and competitiveness, including sports, debating competitions, achievements in school, and eventually politics. His staying power (despite setbacks in progress) in sports, in politics, and even in courting his wife need not be seen as a neurotic effort at self-punishment but rather as the healthy reluctance of an ego to give up activities that provide it with an opportunity to release pentup emotional feelings. Indirectly, his entry into political life was due to his failure after law school to land a job in the lucrative, intellectually exciting, and combatative world of Wall Street lawyers, a career that offered fewer emotional rewards than presidential politics when he finally entered it as a retired politician and at too advanced an age to become a professional litigation attorney on a daily basis. He accidently found in politics a profession that would give him chances to see the faraway places he dreamed of when hearing train whistles as a child. It would also allow him to unleash his aggressive and hostile feelings in causes of national and international significance which provided noble rationalizations for his conscience. It is no wonder Nixon willingly tolerated the inconveniences which stemmed from the fact that (in his own words) ". . . I am shyer than the usually extrovert politician ought to be. This seems to be an inborn trait which I cannot change or alter."[14]

Richard Nixon could not change his "inborn traits" because he was afraid to take a look at their causes. This is not an uncommon attitude. Nixon even shared it with his idol, Woodrow Wilson, who also believed in self-control and hard work as the most important virtues. Garry Wills has suggested that the similarities in temperament of the two presidents may be related to Nixon's idolization of Wilson[15] although Nixon stresses more substantive causes. The following description of Wilson by Alexander and Juliette George could be applied to Nixon:

> If ever he was aware of his hostility toward his father, he seems to have banished it from consciousness and to have lived in fear of the possibility of ever stumbling upon the knowledge. All his life long, he shrank from reflecting about his inner motivations. The very idea of such self examination made him uneasy. He once wrote in a letter that he had always had an all but unconquerable distaste for discussing the deep things that underlie motives and behavior. He believed the solution to personal difficulties was rigorous self-discipline.[16]

Nixon's concern with self-control has not prevented angry outbursts which have characterized his entire public career and have puzzled the reporters who covered his pre-presidential days when he was more accessible and his uneasiness in interpersonal relations was visible. That an essentially private man should respond with subtle and sometimes not so subtle aggressiveness against those who are making him feel uneasy should not come as a surprise. Once shyness is recognized as the core of his personality, much of the anger becomes an understandable consequence of the stresses coming from such a public career. What remains largely a mystery are the origins and psychological meaning of his shyness. Roy Day, Nixon's first campaign manager, recalled to Lou Cannon that when Nixon first ran for Congress he "was so shy that he had to be advised to look women in the eye when he spoke to them."[17] Students of the mind tell us in general that shyness is due to a fear of the emotions that might be exhibited if the shy person were more engaging and to the humiliation that might result. Those given to speculation about the roots of Nixon's public manner should keep in mind that during his political career he was shy with men as well as women.

Whatever its causes Nixon's preoccupation with self-control has not been limited to preventing encounters that would be a public embarrassment or hurt his political fortunes. He has demonstrated the same attitude toward minor physical ills, such as his hay fever (which he has tried to disguise), and towards totally private encounters. A few years ago comedian Jackie Gleason told a reporter for the ZNS news service that in the mid-1960s he spent an eight-hour period drinking with Nixon and that when their drinking session ended, "Nixon stood up and walked out of the room 'as straight as a soldier.' " Other Nixon stories tell of similar feats of personal discipline. One commentator has even argued that the most extraordinary aspect of Nixon's famous "last press conference" after an electoral defeat in 1962 was not his loss of control but his constant ability to regain a semblance of control during the long tirade against the assembled journalists in the Beverly Hilton Hotel in Los Angeles.

A NEW STYLE

Reporters changed their early judgment that Nixon's performance at this press conference was the death blow to his political career. However, their initial assessment in a sense may have been correct, for it was the changes he made in political style as a result of the disastrous event that led Nixon to his isolation in the White House, his dependence on Haldeman, and ultimately to Watergate. The "last press conference" confirmed Nixon's suspicions that emotions should be kept under control in public and spontaniety will only get one into trouble. In *The Resurrection of Richard Nixon,* Jules Witcover notes, "From the moment of his disastrous 'last press conference,' the man embarked on a determined effort never again to inflict damage on himself through lack of self-discipline."[18] In addition, when his career in electoral politics resumed in 1968, Nixon emerged with a new working style that featured a minimum of interpersonal contact, avoidance of the press, tight control over the staging of public contacts, and an end to spontaneity in political interactions. These tendencies were sometimes evident in his previous behavior but now they were to be followed rigidly.

The man who helped design the 1968 campaign that implemented this style, the man most responsible for enforcing it on the candidate as well as the public was H. R. Haldeman, a close observer of Richard Nixon's personality. Haldeman's strategy of how best to market Nixon in the 1968 presidential campaign has been well chronicled in the books written about that election.[19] But the new working style was intended to have effects on the candidate as well as the electorate.

By shielding Nixon from personal contacts, by delegating many decisions that the candidate found agonizing to make (with resulting poor
judgment in previous campaigns), by limiting his public appearances,
Haldeman hoped to conserve Richard Nixon's energy, increase his
efficiency as a campaigner, and reduce his anxiety which so often had
adverse effects on previous campaigns. Haldeman's biggest contribution, however, was in making sure Nixon followed this new working
style as they traveled around the country. As became abundantly clear
once he was in the White House, Richard Nixon's temperament made
it difficult for him to turn down personal requests that his intellect told
him should be declined. Haldeman knew this and became the enforcer.
The results were spectacular. Shrewd journalists like Theodore White
and Jules Witcover, who saw glimpses of the relaxed Nixon of the
mid-1960's when he was not in the public limelight and observed how
successful he was in using the working style of 1968, tended to think
a "new" Nixon had emerged—that the personality itself had changed
rather than simply its ways of adapting. As White eloquently put it:

> None has shown himself, in the way to power, so susceptible
> to strain, yet apparently learned better how to cope with strain
> within himself. Richard Nixon has roved across the entire map
> of the United States geographically, emotionally, spiritually,
> above all, politically, seeking his own lodestar. But no passage
> of this public wandering has been more impressive than the
> transformation of the impulsive, wrathful man of the 1950's,
> so eager for combat and lustful for vengeance, to the man in the
> White House, cautious and thoughtful, intent on conciliation.[20]

The political strategy of Nixon's brain trust in New York and his
basic lack of personal popularity almost lost him the election. But
Haldeman's efforts on the road not only resulted in good public
relations but probably increased Nixon's self-esteem since he was
confronted with fewer anxious moments. When he entered the White
House in 1969, Nixon installed Haldeman as his chief of staff, initially
an administrative post with responsibilities over the President's daily
schedule. Since Nixon "had never managed anything larger than a
Navy cargo depot [during World War II],"[21] it was unclear what he
would be like as chief executive. Gradually, as it became evident that
Nixon's personality was no more suited to the demands of the presidency
than it was to those of electoral politics, the working style of the 1968
campaign took over the White House—personal isolation, minimum
contact with the press, and Haldeman as enforcer. In their book,
Nixon in the White House, Rowland Evans and Robert Novak present
evidence of President Nixon's susceptibility to emotional appeals by
Cabinet members, his inability to engage in personal confrontations,

his reluctance to fire government or party employees he wanted ousted, and his continuing uneasiness in personal relationships. Subsequent studies have confirmed these observations. In fact, in those rare interviews granted to members of the press (Haldeman having orchestrated their timing to the President's good moods), Richard Nixon himself explained that his object was to make decisions without allowing emotions temporarily to cloud his judgment:

> The major weakness of inexperienced people is that they take things personally, especially in politics and that can destroy you. . . .
>
> Years ago, when I was a young congressman, things got under my skin. . . . But now when I walk into this office I am cool and calm. I read the news summary and get both sides. That's important because there are so many emotional issues these days, such as the war and busing and welfare.
>
> I probably am more objective—I don't mean this as self serving—than most leaders . . . when you're too subjective, you tend to make mistakes. . . .
>
> When I came into office, I'd been through enough—those shattering defeats in 1960 and 1962, and then those eight years "in the wilderness," the way De Gaulle and Churchill were.
>
> The result was I was able to confront tough problems without flapping. I don't flap easily. An individual tends to go to pieces when he's inexperienced. . . .[22]

Obviously, he did not always exhibit these qualities as President. Word of his occasionally angry moods seeped from the White House even before the Watergate tapes. But the hiding of Nixon's emotional moments was not the only point of the system of isolation. His quoted remarks are not just public relations. Nixon was sincerely concerned about the subtle ways in which other people's emotions affected his decision-making capabilities. The above quoted passage does tell us something about what was on his mind and behind his White House decision-making process. Mr. Nixon was not striving for "objective" decisions in the sense of their being "value-free" or unrelated to his sense of priorities. He was trying to insulate himself from what he perceived to be his own weaknesses. To substitute for personal contacts, the President put emphasis on paperwork. In discussing the Nixon approach, the *Wall Street Journal's* John Pierson has said, "The trouble with a memo is that it fails to convey the passion of the young or the depth of their disenchantment with 'the system'."[23] However, from the President's viewpoint, "now it's not true that I don't feel emotional or pay attention to what others feel. But the most important thing I can do is make decisions for the long run."[24] Apparently, a system that was good for his peace of mind was also considered best for the national interest.

Despite this cold, calculating attitude toward White House decision-making, Nixon's personal behavior toward members of the White House staff appears to have involved much kindness and considerateness. The most arrogant of presidents in his attitude toward other institutions, Nixon seems to have been the least arrogant of presidents within his own house. Stories of great kindness on the part of Richard Nixon are also told by his longtime personal friends. It is unfortunate that Mr. Nixon's personal conduct was so split between loyal followers on the one hand and opponents on the other. In a revealing remark to CBS News, Senator Barry Goldwater stated:

> I think probably most of the trouble he has is the fact that he's never been able to be one of the boys. Now, I've seen him, on occasion, sort of let his hair down. And there's no more delightful man in the world, no more communicative a man, than Richard Nixon is when you catch him in those rare moments when he isn't measuring every single word he says or every gesture he makes.

Although Mr. Nixon's lack of spontaneity has been criticized, his role-playing and acting is something every politician must do at times. To some politicians tact and diplomacy come naturally and we say they have a "political personality." Senator Howard Baker seems to be an example *par excellence*. Other politicians dislike role-playing and are less willing to engage in it. We call them "outspoken" and "color-ful." They are often our heroes but rarely our presidents. Senator Goldwater himself is an outstanding example of what can happen to a politician who is too spontaneous when he runs for the highest office. Being able to "play the game well" in public appearances—to say the right thing—is a big asset for a politician. Mr. Nixon has gained some political benefits from his tendency to rehearse every word. At the personal level, however, it has prevented him from being a very attractive person. The kind of guarded speech that most politicians use only in public and for political purposes, Mr. Nixon seems to use on all occasions and for personal reasons.

SHARING POWER

Reporters figuratively referred to Theodore Sorensen as President Kennedy's alter ego. In the case of the Haldeman-Nixon relationship, such a description was more literally true. Perhaps this is why there is so little deference shown on the Watergate tapes. Haldeman was not so much an extension of Nixon's own character, as he was a replacement for the part of Nixon's personality that the President found weak —being tough in direct personal confrontations. In every administration there is a top assistant to the President who acts as a buffer, takes on unpleasant tasks, and serves as a scapegoat for political criticism. In Haldeman's indelicate words, "Every President has a 'son-of-a-bitch,' I'm his." The difference, however, was that in Nixon's case, Haldeman served this function not only for administrative and political reasons but also because the President was incapable of doing it himself and he knew it. Nixon could stand up to a Krushchev in a kitchen debate, once provoked, but Nixon himself described this as a great crisis. In the White House he could hardly bring himself to fire Walter Hickel, his secretary of the interior, even though he detested the man, because Hickel shrewdly insisted on being fired personally by the President.

A disadvantage of having Haldeman serve as gatekeeper and enforcer in Nixon's White House is that he often took seriously commands that Nixon's longtime friends feel they would have ignored or did ignore. As one former Nixon aide noted, "Haldeman protects Richard Nixon against everybody's bad ideas except for Richard Nixon's."[25] It is not surprising that the type of personality who shared the President's view of the world would carry out his orders without question.

The relationship with Haldeman is a useful focal point for comparing Richard Nixon and Woodrow Wilson. These two men had some similarities as chief executives. Both were accidental presidents in some sense, both were personally hated by the opposition, both were sensitive to criticism and concerned about the loyalty of aides, both showed contempt for the Congress, and both had a top advisor who served emotional as well as political functions. James David Barber has suggested that both had a drive for power as their primary motive force, a drive that ultimately destroyed their careers. If Nixon had a preoccupation with power, it was somewhat different than Wilson's, at least as the Georges portray it. In those areas that took on meaning for him (certain issues fused with moral content), Wilson was primarily concerned with the *exercise* of power. He would monopolize decision-making in these areas and was suspicious of any aides who interfered. The downfall of Colonel House as a confidant of Wilson's was partly due to his decision to accept a presidential appointment involving the exercise of power.

By contrast, Nixon does not appear to have been jealous of the power exercised by his top assistants in foreign or domestic affairs. He seemed more concerned with the *occupation* of power than its personal exercise. Perhaps this is why a commentator has suggested that respect was the value Nixon most sought.[26] A concern for the occupation of power would also help explain Nixon's campaign tactics. Whatever his attitudes toward power, Nixon did not "draw the line" on policy matters and refuse to compromise when it was tactically necessary. The Georges suggest that Wilson became rigid in policy debates because he used substantive issues with moral content as his rationalization for aggression against his personal enemies. He needed the issues to justify to himself his expression of hostility. Nixon, on the other hand, only had trouble exhibiting aggressive or hostile feelings in direct personal confrontations. For this he needed Haldeman. However, he was quite capable of "screwing his enemies" behind their backs without relying on public issues. Thus, he could be more flexible in public policy matters when this was absolutely called for, regardless of whether the issue was war in Cambodia, bombing in Vietnam, or obeying court orders on Watergate scandals.[27]

Of course, like Wilson, Nixon needed some kind of rationalization for his aggressiveness. He found it in a conspiracy theory of his opponents, a theory that so many observers have characterized as paranoid in its implications. Students of personality have suggested that such feelings are a projection of his own hatreds onto others, a device allowing him an opportunity to hate in return. According to his conspiratorial notion, Nixon's adversaries in the "Eastern Establishment" institutions were allying with powerful liberal elements in Congress and the press in an attempt to destroy his political career—an effort he traced back to their supposed resentment at his success in destroying the career of Alger Hiss. Just as Woodrow Wilson appreciated Colonel House for his constant bolstering of Wilson's belief in his rationalizations, so too, did Richard Nixon probably find comfort in the confirmation Haldeman and his associates provided that his rationalizations were justified.

DEFEAT

Nixon's rigidity was in his inability over the years to break away from this conspiratorial view, especially after Watergate began to unfold and his political survival became dependent on firing all those involved and trusting the public to forget the matter or to forgive him. This solution to his Watergate problems would have worked for any number of months. Instead he took the highly risky approach that eventually destroyed him. Given the emotional functions Haldeman was performing for him, one can understand Nixon's reluctance to part with his chief of staff even if there was not the possibility (which there was) that he might then be implicated in illegal activities by a former employee. But the most important reason Nixon could not dispose of his conspiratorial views was that they performed the same function in his personality that Wilson's morally-laden policy issues performed in his character. They rationalized aggression whatever the ultimate causes of that aggression were in his past. Without a rationale acceptable to his conscience, Richard Nixon would have been overwhelmed with anxiety long before his Watergate troubles.

The reasons why his conscience found a conspiracy theory satisfactory are unclear. Nixon's resentments of the "Eastern Establishment" go back to his professional rejection by Wall Street law firms after doing well in law school, his cultural rejection by the bureaucrats he worked with in the Office of Price Administration, his political rejection after exposing Hiss, and his social rejection by elements of New York society when he finally became a Wall Street lawyer. This may help explain the content of his remarks about the "establishment," but it still leaves unanswered the question of why he developed such an intense feeling of "we versus them" toward political opponents.

The interpretation of Richard Nixon's behavior that has been presented here has stressed the adaptive aspects of human personality. Nixon's political career and personal style are viewed from the perspective of an individual ego looking for ways to reduce anxiety and maintain its equilibrium. The particular methods of resolving internal conflict consciously and unconsciously evolved by Nixon had their costs. Ultimately his reputation, his health, and his political career were seriously damaged. In this sense his conduct was self-defeating. Another interpretation of Nixon's downfall asserts that in some sense the self-destructiveness was intentional. In other words at the unconscious level Nixon wanted to punish himself because of strong guilt feelings stemming from deep-seated and unconscious hatreds generated in childhood. One version of this theory notes that Nixon's self-destructive Watergate troubles came after he had achieved his greatest success—reelection to the highest office in the land by a landslide vote. Questioning the coincidence of these two events, this approach suggests that Nixon may have had guilt feelings about such a success and political success in general because it represented a triumph over the achievements of his father. More generalized versions of the self-punishment interpretation highlight the self-defeating aspects of Nixon's behavior throughout his career and assert that (whatever the reasons) Nixon has always been trying to punish himself. Having achieved the presidency through political luck, he simply failed on a bigger scale than previously.

In dealing with these notions one must distinguish the general concept of guilt from the more specific idea of career failure as a means of self-punishment. Guilt is a universal concept. Unquestionably Richard

Nixon had his share of unconscious guilt that shaped his personality and affected his behavior in everyday life. This is entirely consistent with the interpretation which stresses adaptation, in fact, it is part of it. The idea of self-punishment through career failure is more complicated. It is possible to explain Nixon's downfall without it. To this author it seems unlikely that a man so ill-suited to a public life and whose ambivalence about aggression was so evident in his daily life would have to resort to career failure to satisfy any longings for self-punishment.

NOTES

1. Lou Cannon, "The Forces that Forged the Future: 'He Didn't Want to Stay in Yorba Linda'," *The Fall of a President* (New York: Dell, 1974), p. 64.

2. James David Barber, *Presidential Character: Predicting Performance in the White House* (Englewood Cliffs, N.J.: Prentice-Hall, 1972), chaps. 1-4, 10-12. Also see Garry Wills, *Nixon Agonistes* (New York: New American Library, 1971), pp. 394-396.

3. Alexander L. George and Juliette L. George, *Woodrow Wilson and Colonel House: A Personality Study* (New York: Dover, pb. ed., 1964). Some of the theoretical framework is explained in "Research Note" on pages 317-322 and in Alexander L. George, "Power as a Compensatory Value for Political Leaders," *Journal of Social Issues*, 1968, pp. 29-49.

4. Alexander L. George and Juliette George, p. 11.

5. Notable exceptions in recent work are Cannon, "The Forces That Forged the Future . . . ;" and Richard Tanner Johnson, *Managing the White House* (New York: Harper and Row, 1974), pp. 208-209.

6. Frank Fox and Stephen Parker, "Why Nixon Did Himself In: A Behavioral Examination of His Need to Fail," *New York Magazine*, September 9, 1974, p. 28.

7. A problem with examining such relationships is the decline in letter writing that has occurred in the twentieth century. At least in this case the White House tapes exist although much more material would be needed for a thorough study.

8. Jack McCurdy, "Scholars' Opinions Bode Ill for Nixon's Place in History," *Los Angeles Times*, October 20, 1974, part II, p. 1.

9. Richard Poirier, "Will the Real Richard Nixon Please Stand Up?" *New Times*, July 28, 1974, p. 19.

10. This three-fold distinction is from Fred I. Greenstein, *Personality and Politics* (Chicago: Markham, 1969), pp. 65-86.

11. James David Barber, "President Nixon and Richard Nixon: Character Trap," *Psychology Today*, October, 1974, p. 113. In addition to the work of Barber, psychobiographies dealing extensively with Nixon's youth include Bruce Mazlish, *In Search of Nixon: A Psychohistorical Inquiry* (New York: Basic Books, 1972) and Eli S. Chesen, *President Nixon's Psychiatric Profile* (New York: Wyden, 1973).

12. Bruce Mazlish, p. 97.

13. Richard Tanner Johnson, p. 201.

14. Lou Cannon, p. 50.

15. Garry Wills, p. 395-396.

16. Alexander and Juliette George, p. 11.

17. Lou Cannon, p. 41.

18. Jules Witcover, *The Resurrection of Richard Nixon* (New York: Putnam, 1970), p. 34.

19. Theodore H. White, *The Making of the President 1968* (New York: Atheneum, 1969); Joe McGinniss, *The Selling of the President 1968* (New York: Trident, 1969).

20. Theodore H. White, p. 434.

21. James Macgregor Burns, "The Nixon Tightrope," *Life,* April 2, 1971, p. 51.

22. Saul Pett, "Nixon, With Brief Look Back, Prepares for Four More Years," *Los Angeles Times,* January 14, 1973, p. 20.

23. John Pierson, "Presidential Isolation Is Part of the Job," *Wall Street Journal,* June 5, 1970 as reprinted in Nelson W. Polsby, ed., *The Modern Presidency* (New York: Random House, 1973), p. 223.

24. Saul Pett, p. 20.

25. Suzannah Lessard, "Nixon and His Staff: The View from Their Own Mirror," *Washington Monthly,* May, 1972, p. 56. See also William Safire, "On Temper," *New York Times,* August 23, 1973, p. 37, and Lou Cannon, pp. 63-64.

26. Alexander L. George, "Assessing Presidential Personality," *World Politics,* January, 1974, p. 264.

27. Bernard Brodie, "The President's 3 Surrenders," *Los Angeles Times,* November 6, 1973, part ll, p. 7.

18 | Democratic Character and the Presidency

Edwin C. Hargrove

In reviewing the character traits of recent presidents Hargrove raises some important questions about the relationship of personality and political skill. Realizing personal needs are often the driving force that make for skilled, power-seeking politicians, he suggests that we may have to revise our conceptions of the presidency if we want presidents with healthier personalities. Because liberals assumed that chief executives would use the highest office for purposes they approved, power-seeking politicians were considered to make the best presidents. The author employs the typology of presidential character developed by James David Barber to show how low self-esteem had adverse effects on the political leadership of Presidents Johnson and Nixon. Hargrove concludes with an analysis of how democratic leadership style will help produce better public policy.

. . . In the heyday of Lyndon Johnson this writer developed the thesis that personal insecurity and political skill were linked. The creative politician was depicted as the man who required attention and needed to dominate and therefore had developed skills of self-dramatization and persuasion that would serve those needs. The thesis was applied to American Presidents. The two Roosevelts and Wilson were pictured as men especially in need of attention and power, and skill and creativity were said to be related to a perpetual striving to serve these goals. Whereas Presidents lacking such needs were also

From Edwin C. Hargrove, "The Crisis of the Contemporary Presidency," (pp. 17-25) in *Choosing the President,* James David Barber, Ed., © 1974 by The American Assembly, Columbia University. Reprinted by permission of Prentice-Hall, Inc., Englewood Cliffs, N.J.

Edwin C. Hargrove is Chairman and Professor of Political Science, Department of Political Science, Brown University. He is author of *The Power of the Modern President* and *Presidential Leadership: Personality and Political Style.*

seen as without abilities—with Taft, Hoover, and Eisenhower as instances. They were pictured as almost too healthy to be good leaders.[1]

The view of the presidential office and the skills required was that presented by Richard Neustadt.[2] The Presidency was seen as institutionally weak in power and each President had to start from scratch in developing political resources. A sensitivity to power and power relationships was therefore essential. Coalitions of support within and outside of government had to be built up out of the perspectives of others who had power in their own right, independent of the President. The argument went further than Neustadt's in asking what kinds of personalities had such power skills.

This thesis assumed that Presidents were guided by moral purpose and it was frankly biased in the direction of the liberal, power-maximizing Presidents. It was assumed that purpose would purify power. To be fair to oneself the argument was made that such power-striving, if rooted in personal needs, could lead to self-defeating eruptions of personality such as Theodore Roosevelt's in 1912, Wilson's rigidity in the League fight, and FDR's plan to pack the Supreme Court. However, it was assumed that institutional checks and balances were sufficient to control such behavior. The price was worth paying because strong political leadership was required. Lyndon Johnson seemed the ideal President in this scheme of things. His voracious needs and insecurities provided the fuel for his great abilities in the service of genuinely liberal values in which he deeply believed. How much of this position needs to be taken back now that we have had a longer and fuller look at LBJ? And does the experience of Richard Nixon as President add to the difficulty?

"POLITICAL MAN"

The formulation reflected the liberal optimism of the time that power would be used for the right purposes. Therefore, there was insufficient inquiry into possible variations in the personal needs for attention and dominance of creative leaders. The hypothesis about the relation between needs and skills was taken from Harold Lasswell but optimistic conclusions were drawn from the inference—something Lasswell did not do. Lasswell drew a distinction between "political man" and "democratic character." The former sought a political life in order to bolster low estimates of the self. Early feelings of deprivation would be overcome by political successes. A prominent type of "political man" was the "agitator" who taught himself to play on the emotions of audiences, whether large or small, and direct their attention and affection toward himself. The "democratic character" on the other hand had successfully passed through the developmental crises of life, and had no such insecurities and needs. He had "outgrown" politics, and in a society conducive to the development of "democratic character" there would be no "political men."[3]

Lasswell did not solve the problem of what to do about selecting leaders until that ideal time. So this writer adapted the model of "political man" to the requirements of democratic leadership, aware that a price might have to be paid. The experience of Johnson and Nixon has increased that concern greatly. The tragedy of each Presidency has been that the basic insecurities of the man, which were one basis for the talent that had been developed, were also the principle reason for failure. The negative effects upon the Presidency have been great.

We do not need to question Johnson's strong desire to do good when we point out that it was always joined to a compulsion to rule others. Those who worked closely with him felt that this compulsion was rooted in an uncertainty and insecurity about the self which seems to have had two dimensions. There was the cultural insecurity of being from Texas, of not having gone to Harvard and feeling ill at ease with intellectual and Eastern "establishment" figures. But there was also a much deeper uneasiness that showed in his sensitiveness to criticism and the demand for absolute loyalty from subordinates and associates.

His insecurities were less apparent in Congress because the setting was more provincial and his power was limited. He worked well in bargaining situations where he knew he could not dominate by fiat, and the Senate of the nineteen-fifties was his element. He continued the same style of broker for a consensus in his first year as President— especially in his leadership of Congress, in which he employed the forcefulness of his personality upon its members and yet respected congressional prerogatives.

However, within his own official family a different Lyndon emerged, the one who had always been a bully to his staff. He demanded total loyalty within and lashed back at criticism from without. His excessive reaction to criticism of the Dominican Republic intervention forecast what was to come on Vietnam. As the war grew more frustrating he created an artificial world within the government about the reality outside which led to a public credibility gap. He refused to believe he might be wrong until the very last. Even if we believe his Vietnam policy to have been correct, Johnson's psychology was one of defensiveness and rigidity. He responded with fury to all threats to his self-esteem. The consequences affected not only policy but the entire atmosphere of his administration. The Presidency as an authoritarian force emerged into full view.

President Nixon's troubles stem from deep strains in his character as well. One need not believe that he was an active participant in the Watergate affair to give him responsibility for the atmosphere in the White House which produced Watergate.

Nixon's entire career has been a painful series of efforts to overcome a deep uncertainty about himself. The obsession with facing a "crisis" well reflects a fear that he might fail to meet the test. The persistent theme of a Uriah Heep—such as self-pity and the identification of all his problems with "enemies"—reveals a man who cannot relax in a happy love of self. The awareness that he tires easily and needs time and seclusion to make up his mind shows us a man doubtful of his inner resources.

Behind the Watergate tragedy we see an isolated President who created a White House staff defensive and protective of the President and full of contempt for his "enemies." We had the incredible paradox of people in positions of national power who felt weak and defensive in regard to national "establishments" like Congress, the bureaucracy, the media, and the major universities. The morality tale of Watergate is a pathetic unraveling of the presidential personality.

The great danger is that a President who feels threatened by events or harassed by "enemies" will precipitate a crisis in order to shore up his own inner doubts and confound his opposition.

"DEMOCRATIC CHARACTER"

Yet Theodore and Franklin Roosevelt enjoyed attention and power and needed office and a full political life to realize themselves. How do they differ from Johnson and Nixon? The answer seems to be that despite their insecurities and strong needs these two men sought a life in politics as a self-actualizing quest. They were not so much insecure as needing fulfillment. They were at their happiest when in the saddle, and in fact Teddy Roosevelt's aberrations came when he was out of office and desperate to get back in. John Kennedy was similar to these two in the self-affirming character of his leadership but his needs and drives were not so intense nor were his skills as fully developed.

James David Barber, writing after the experience of Johnson and Nixon, and therefore free of any temptation to idealize the power-seeker, has given us the clue to the differences between these kinds of Presidents. Franklin Roosevelt, Truman, and Kennedy were happy, integrated, self-respecting, and expansive people who were capable of growth and learning. Their energies were directed outward toward achievement, not bound up in defensive postures. Roosevelt in particular shared the characterization of Lasswell's "political men" in their political needs and skills. But they also possessed "democratic character."[4]

Woodrow Wilson, Hoover, Johnson, and Nixon brought a negative cast to their careers according to Barber. Ceaseless striving for place, power, and deference could never be satisfied because the lack of self-esteem that needed strengthening was insatiable. Political style took on a compulsive quality. And sharp threats to self-esteem and position were often met in rigid and ego-defensive ways.

Not all persons who have confidence in themselves and politics are skillful political leaders. Dwight Eisenhower had a basic self-respect and stability which was a source of strength to him as President, but he lacked the personality needs which might have made him a complete politician.[5] John Kennedy fell somewhere between the two Roosevelts and Eisenhower on such a need skill scale.

However, we cannot expect to get brilliant "political men" who are also "democratic characters" very often. A great many extraordinarily able political leaders are not "democratic characters" but "active-negatives," to use Barber's term, who desperately need office and power and can do great harm with power if unchecked. We must particularly be on guard against such people and this is not easy since "active-positives" and "active-negatives" often appear the same to observers on the surface. This is particularly the case in an entrepreneurial political culture in which the politician who would succeed must develop self-dramatizing and power-maximizing skills to a great degree.

Of course individuals do not embody the characteristics of "ideal types." Johnson had an "active-postive" expansive and joyful side to his personality and leadership. Who can deny that Woodrow Wilson was a great President with an enormous gift for moral leadership despite a tragic flaw in his character? We cannot expect to be able to predict what kind of President an individual will be by placing him within a typology. But these crude beginnings in linking character to style should at least make us sensitive to what we wish to avoid. In the immediate future we are likely to emphasize character over great political skill. Truman, Eisenhower, and Kennedy will be our models. They were not great political craftsmen but were rather "democratic characters" who were teaching themselves to be "political men."

Perhaps we have made too much of a sensitivity to power relations as the key to success as President. By putting such a high priority on the ability to manipulate others we make ourselves prey to the "active-negatives" who are good at this. The experiences of Johnson and

Nixon show that a heightened sensitivity by the President to his personal power position may actually blind him to the kind of learning and listening required by his official power position.[6] And the positive achievements of all Presidents, and especially the master of tactics like FDR, were not really based upon tactical skill at manipulating others. Rather the basis of influence and achievement was the ability to appeal to others in terms of shared values.[7] There are many bases of power and most important among them is the affirmation of future possibilities in terms of common values. The "active-positive" leader is more likely to lead in this way and these are the qualities of leadership that we must look for.

Democratic Style of Authority

The fruits of "democratic character" are in a style of authority which encourages others to express themselves freely and which promotes discussion processes in which there is a maximum possible variety of viewpoints on both normative and factual questions. Clearly there are limits in time, energy, and world view as well as political constraints on such a style and process but it is the basic posture that we demand. We need leadership which will be a catalyst for initiatives and ideas and which will learn from this process. At the end of the day a President must decide for himself and then find ways to persuade others to support his view. But there is a greater likelihood of his decisions being "good" in terms of his own objectives if he has an open style of authority.

Of course there is not a perfect relationship between democratic character and a democratic style of authority. Skill at organizing discussion processes is not necessarily related to character, and even the most skillful President can make a mess of things. Nor will a democratic style guarantee an accurate presidential view of the world or of American society. No President can completely transcend the stock of commonly shared cultural biases nor perhaps should he. Also, under some conditions a secretive authoritative style in a President is necessary. But, on the whole, openness makes for better decisions, and institutions in which all actors feel free to speak out are better than ones bound up in hierarchy, deference, and fear.

CASES

The numerous foreign policy crises of the nineteen-sixties stimulated a search by political scientists for the conditions which produce policy mishaps in which the decision-makers fail to see basic factors in a situation which will ensure failure, judged in terms of their own objectives. In this sense a "good" decision is one which manifests an understanding of the real situation. This is a limited perspective because a group of men could see a situation accurately and yet act in ways we would condemn because our moral standards would differ. But, the model is useful for analyzing the decision process.

The crucial variable in achieving a "good" decision in the sense defined above is presidential style of authority. Theoretical conclusions from experiments with laboratory small groups are confirmed by current history. An authoritarian leadership style saps the initiative of the group and screens out information. A democratic leadership style, which is not so permissive that authority is lost, liberates the energies of a group and permits creativity of response to new situations.

Glenn Paige was the first to develop a theoretical framework for looking at decisions in this way.[8] He developed a model of the properties of a crisis decision out of his study of the United States intervention in Korea. When faced with an unexpected crisis the small group which the President brings together for decision is likely to make a "high consensus decision" in which support for the President and group solidarity will be strong. The President will set the limits of possible option by the cues he gives the group. In this case, President Truman made it clear from the beginning that American action against aggression was essential and this inevitably led to a military commitment. In such a group the picture of the world which its members bring is likely to continue to prevail against new information in the short run. And in the moment of crisis little heed is paid to external critics.

Paige does not regard the Korean decision as a bad one but he does point out the dangers in such a decision process. Conformity and group solidarity can rule at the expense of new ideas. Excessive deference to the President can prevail and potential dissent be stifled. Information contrary to the group consensus can be unconsciously screened out. He urges that special pains be taken to build in adversary processes through the use of staff and that an effort be made to solicit external criticism.

The dynamics of such a decision group are obviously capable of great variety depending upon presidential style. The Bay of Pigs invasion and the Cuban missile crisis illustrate Paige's basic insights. In the first case John Kennedy did not encourage the members of the decision group to criticize the assumptions or information supplied by the Central Intelligence Agency nor did he support the efforts of Senator Fulbright and Arthur Schlesinger to challenge the consensus. The President encouraged his associates to close ranks behind a decision that was poorly presented and inadequately scrutinized. The execution of the decision proved this to be so, for much of the intelligence provided was simply wrong. Of course the even greater failure on the part of the President was not to raise the question of the morality of the action.

In the second case Kennedy acted deliberately out of the experience of the first. He had already changed decision styles within his government to promote adversary debate by using McGeorge Bundy as a staff catalyst in this regard and pushing his brother Robert and Theodore Sorensen to be devil's advocates. He was fortunate in having a brother who was completely secure with the President and not afraid to speak out and who could therefore legitimize courage for others. Thoroughly open discussion characterized the executive committee during the missile crisis. The result was a high consensus decision but one of a higher level of synthesis than the Korean decision because it had emerged from a more intense and searching consideration of alternatives.

Of course, Kennedy ruled out a nonmilitary response at the beginning. Had the decision been for an air strike resulting in a nuclear exchange, we would not be praising it. Adlai Stevenson's plea for a strictly political response was ridiculed by some members of the group. The efforts of Secretary McNamara in the same direction stopped when he saw they would not carry the President. But the point is clear, that Presidential style is the critical variable in setting the tone and limits much of the content of group discussion.

COUNTERING CONFORMITY

Irving Janis postulates that there is a strong tendency toward working conformity in small groups. The mechanisms for uncovering and challenging unexamined premises are often lacking.[9] Dissenters are likely to be ignored or ejected. What seems like vigorous debate is usually about instrumental questions rather than basic assumptions. In short, everything about presidential decision-making is likely to serve the President ill unless he self-consciously takes deliberate steps to ensure variety, dissent, conflict and make clear to his advisers that he values honesty above all else. Even then, he may have a hard time getting others to approach him on equal terms. The personal ambition of advisers and plain speaking to the leader are often not compatible unless he rewards frankness.

Alexander George has suggested that the President set a staff "custodian" to watch over the quality of advice and debate, but one must stress the point that only the President can communicate his intentions to others and must do this by his personal relationships with them. No "custodian" can do that for him.[10]

Chester Cooper describes how Lyndon Johnson would poll his principal foreign policy advisers one at a time on questions to do with the conduct of the war. He would go around the table and elicit an "I agree, Mr. President" from each one. Cooper imagined a fantasy in which he would stand up and announce with a flourish, "Mr. President, gentlemen, I most definitely do not agree." But when his turn came he always heard himself saying, "Yes, Mr. President, I agree."[11]

One forms a strong impression from the accounts of Vietnam decision-making that Johnson initially gave his advisers cues that precluded any serious consideration of withdrawal or a political settlement in 1965 and that he promoted a subsequent hardening of commitment to the policy of intervention until 1968 when a series of shocks penetrated his reality world and caused him to pull back. It was largely due to the courage of new and old advisers, especially Clark Clifford, that this change occurred. But even that might not have happened had it not been for the Tet offensive and the candidacies of McCarthy and Kennedy.[12]

All of this suggests that a presidential style of authority which sets undue limits on discussion is likely to reinforce all the other factors in government that make for policy mishaps: the timidity and conformity of advisers, lack of sensitivity to external critics, failure to examine the assumptions behind prevailing policies, and adherence to bureaucratic routine. A democratic style of authority therefore is not a weak or permissive posture. It is the insistence by a President that he be well served. He must be tough, ask hard questions, break up comfortable alliances and, above all, encourage those who work with him to strive for fresh views and to have the courage to speak out. Clearly we are in the realm of subjective judgment when we start to say that a given President should have cast his net more widely in a given case or cases. We may simply disagree with his decision and wish that he had given greater weight to our values. It is also true that all Presidents set limits to the ideas they will entertain and that no President likes an adviser who is consistently critical or difficult.

But, we can make a general evaluation of a man's style of inquiry and discourse and here Presidents differ greatly. Theodore and Franklin Roosevelt were superb at reaching out for information from a variety of sources and at encouraging them to provide it. Dwight Eisenhower and John Kennedy had open, inquiring styles but each was limited by the uniformity of his key associates and advisers, in contrast to FDR, for example. However, Kennedy's capacity for growth as evidenced by his initiatives for civil rights and an end to the Cold War in 1963, neither of which were characteristic of the strident cold warrior and cautious politician of 1961, stands in clear contrast to the imperious style of Johnson and the crabbed isolation of Nixon.

There are always intellectual and normative limits to the scope of presidential discourse but we must ask—is a President trying to learn and encouraging others to do so? And the negative cases convince us of the importance of the question. . . .

NOTES

1. Erwin C. Hargrove, *Presidential Leadership, Personality and Political Style* (New York: MacMillan Co., 1966).

2. Richard E. Neustadt, *Presidential Power, The Politics of Leadership* (New York: John Wiley & Son, Inc., 1960).

3. Harold P. Lasswell, *Power and Personality* (New York: W. W. Norton, 1948.)

4. James D. Barber, *The Presidential Character, Predicting Performance in the White House* (New York: Prentice-Hall, 1972).

5. Barber classifies Eisenhower as a "passive-negative" but I do not agree with that interpretation. [There are two dimensions in the Barber scheme: the active-passive scale reflecting the degree of activity of the President and the positive-negative scale based on whether his overt emotional reactions to the job show enjoyment or unhappiness. From these dichotomies Barber creates a four-fold typology of active-positive, active-negative, passive-positive, and passive-negative.]

6. Alexander L. George, "The Case for Multiple Advocacy in Making Foreign Policy," *American Political Science Review*, Vol. LXVI, no. 3 (Sept. 1972), pp. 751-785.

7. Peter W. Sperlich, "Bargaining and Overload: an Essay on Presidential Power," in Aaron Wildavsky, ed., *The Presidency* (Boston: Little, Brown & Co., 1969).

8. Glenn D. Paige, *The Korean Decision, June 24-30, 1950* (New York: Free Press, 1968).

9. Irving L. Janis, *Victims of Group Think* (Boston: Houghton Mifflin Co., 1972).

10. George, pp. 751-785.

11. Chester L. Cooper, *The Last Crusade, America in Vietnam* (New York: Dodd, Mead & Co., 1970).

12. Townsend Hoopes, *The Limits of Intervention* (New York: David McKay Co., Inc., 1969); David Halberstam, *The Best and the Brightest* (New York: Random House, 1972); Cooper, op. cit.

Selected Bibliography: Watergate, Richard Nixon, and the Nixon Administration

WATERGATE, IMPEACHMENT AND RESIGNATION

Books

Anderson, Jack, with George Clifford. *The Anderson Papers.* New York: Ballantine Books, 1974.

Bernstein, Carl, and Robert Woodward. *All The President's Men.* New York: Simon and Schuster, 1974.

Chester, Lewis, Cal McCrystal, Stephen Aris, and William Shawcross. *Watergate: The Full Inside Story.* New York: Ballantine Books, 1973.

Dobrovir, William A., Joseph D. Gebhardt, Samuel J. Buffone, and Andra N. Oakes. *The Offenses of Richard M. Nixon: A Guide To His Impeachable Offenses.* New York: Quadrangle, 1974.

Evans, Leo, and Allen Meyers. *Watergate and the Myth of American Democracy.* New York: Pathfinder Press, 1974.

Harward, Donald W., editor. *Crisis In Confidence: The Impact of Watergate.* Boston: Little, Brown, 1974.

Jenness, Linda, and Andrew Pulley, editors. *Watergate: The View From The Left.* New York: Pathfinder Press, 1973.

Lurie, Leonard. *The Impeachment of Richard Nixon.* New York: Berkeley Publishing Co., 1973.

Magruder, Jeb Stuart. *An American Life: One Man's Road to Watergate.* New York: Atheneum, 1974.

McCord, James. *A Piece of Tape.* Washington: Washington Media, 1974.

Mosher, Frederick C., et al., *Watergate: Implications for Responsible Government.* New York: Basic Books, 1974.

Myerson, Michael. *Watergate: Crime In The Suites.* New York: International Publishers, 1973.

Roberts, Charles, editor. *Has The Presidency Too Much Power?* New York: Harper's Magazine Press, 1974.

Saffell, David C., editor. *Watergate: Its Effects On The American Political System.* Cambridge, Mass.: Winthrop, 1974.

Sego, Michael A., editor. *The Issues of Watergate.* Cleveland: Regal Books, 1973.

Shannon, William V. *They Could Not Thrust The King: Nixon, Watergate and the American People.* New York: Collier Books, 1974.

Staff of the New York Times. *The End of A Presidency.* New York: Bantam Books, 1974.

Staff of the Washington Post. *The Fall of A President.* New York: Dell, 1974.

Sussman, Barry. *The Great Cover-up: Nixon and the Scandal of Watergate.* New York: New American Library, 1974.

Articles

Barber, James David. "The Presidency After Watergate," *World Magazine,* July 31, 1973, pp. 30-32.

Bensman, Joseph. "Watergate: In the Corporate Style of Life," *Dissent,* Summer, 1973, pp. 279-280.

Bickel, Alexander M. "Watergate and the Legal Order," *Commentary,* January, 1974, pp. 19-29.

Branch, Taylor, G. Gordon Liddy, E. Howard Hunt et. al. "American Character: Trial and Triumph," *Harper's,* October, 1974, pp. 39-76.

Broder, David, James David Barber, James MacGregor Burns, Thomas E. Cronin, Alexander L. George, Fred I. Greenstein, and Aaron, Wildavsky. "The Presidency After Watergate: A Symposium," *The Washington Post,* September 16, 1973.

Burlingham, Bo. "Paranoia in Power," *Harper's,* October, 1974, pp. 26-37.

Chomsky, Noam, "Watergate: A Skeptical View," *New York Review of Books,* September 20, 1973, pp. 3-8.

Epstein, Edward Jay. "Did the Press Uncover Watergate?" *Commentary,* July, 1974, pp. 21-24.

Fallows, James. "Crazies by the Tail: Bay of Pigs, Diem, and Liddy," *The Washington Monthly,* September, 1974, pp. 50-58.

Geyelin, Philip. "Washington Dateline: Impeachment and Foreign Policy," *Foreign Policy,* Summer, 1974, pp. 183-190.

Holles, Everett R. "Klein Says Nixon Became Captive of Deceitful Men," *The New York Times,* August 25, 1974, p. 33.

Hughes, Emmet John. "A White House Taped," *The New York Times Magazine,* June 9, 1974, p. 17 ff.

Kurland, Philip B. "The Issues Beyond Watergate," *Wall Street Journal,* December 12, 1973.

McCarthy, Mary. "Watergate Notes," *The New York Review of Books,* July 19, 1973, pp. 5-8.

.... "The Watergate Solution," *The New York Review of Books,* April 4, 1974, pp. 6-19.

Morgenthau, Hans J. "The Aborted Nixon Revolution," *The New Republic,* August 11, 1973, pp. 17-19.

Osborne, John. "The Unmasking of a President: Nixon Postscript," *The New Republic,* September 7, 1974, pp. 10-14.

Peters, Charles. "Why the White House Press Didn't Get the Watergate Story," *The Washington Monthly,* July-August, 1973, pp. 7-15.

Reichley, James A. "Getting at the Roots of Watergate," *Fortune,* July, 1973, p. 91 ff.

Sale, Kirkpatrick. "The World Behind Watergate," *The New York Review of Books,* May 3, 1973, pp. 9-16.

St. George, Andrew. "The Cold War Comes Home," *Harper's,* November, 1973, pp. 68-81.

Trevor-Roper, Hugh. "Nixon—America's Charles I?", *Spectator,* August 11, 1973.

Schneier, Edward, Murray L. Weidenbaum, Herbert Marcuse, Ithiel de Sola Pool, Robert Nisbet, and Stuart A. Umpleby. "Controversy: Social Scientists Speak on Watergate," *Society,* September-October, 1973, pp. 19-28.

Waskow, Arthur I. "Impeachment Is Only a Crossroads," *The Nation,* February 9, 1974, p. 174 ff.

Whalen, Richard J. "The Downfall of an Arrogant and Ignorant Elite," reprinted from *The Washington Post* in *The Los Angeles Times,* May 13, 1973, pt. 4, p. 1.

Wildavsky, Aaron and Nelson W. Polsby. "The Legitimacy of the Presidency," *The Washington Post,* October 28, 1973, p. Cl.

Government Documents: Public Editions

U. S. Congress, House of Representatives, Committee on the Judiciary. *Articles of Impeachment.* Hearings, 93 Congress, 2nd session, February 5, 1974–July 30, 1974 (40 volumes).

.... *Articles of Impeachment.* House Report 93–1305, 93rd Congress, 2nd session, (August 20) 1974.

.... *Statement of Information,* Book I. Events Prior To The Watergate Break-In, December 2, 1971–June 17, 1972. Hearings, 93rd Congress, 2nd session, 1974.

.... *Statement of Information,* Book II. Events Following The Watergate Break-In, June 17, 1972–March 22, 1973. Hearings, 93rd Congress, 2nd session, 1974.

.... *Statement of Information,* Book III. Events Following The Watergate Break-In, June 20, 1972–March 22, 1973. Hearings, 93rd Congress, 2nd session, 1974.

.... *Statement of Information,* Book IV. Events Following The Watergate Break-In, March 22, 1973–April 30, 1973. Hearings, 93rd Congress, 2nd session, 1974.

.... *Statement of Information,* Book V. Department of Justice— ITT Litigation, Richard Kleindienst Nomination Hearings. Hearings, 93rd Congress, 2nd session, 1974.

.... *Statement of Information,* Book VI. Political Contributions by Milk Producers: The 1971 Milk Price Support Decision. Hearings, 93rd Congress, 2nd session, 1974.

.... *Statement of Information,* Book VII. Surveillance Activities and Campaign Activities. Hearings, 93rd Congress, 2nd session, 1974.

.... *Statement of Information,* Book VIII. Internal Revenue Service. Hearings, 93rd Congress, 2nd session, 1974.

.... *Statement of Information,* Book IX. Watergate Special Prosecutors—Judicial Committee's Impeachment Inquiry, April 30, 1973–July 1, 1974. Hearings, 93rd Congress, 2nd session, 1974.

.... *Statement of Information,* Book X. Tax Deductions For Gifts of Papers. Hearings, 93rd Congress, 2nd session, 1974.

.... *Statement of Information,* Book XI. Bombing of Cambodia. Hearings, 93rd Congress, 2nd session, 1974.

.... *Statement of Information,* Book XII. Impoundment of Funds —Government Expenditures on President Nixon's Private Properties at San Clemente and Key Biscayne. Hearings, 93rd Congress, 2nd session, 1974.

.... *Statement of Information,* Appendix II. Papers in Criminal Cases Initiated by the Watergate Special Prosecutor's Force, June 27, 1973–August 2, 1974. Hearings, 93rd Congress, 2nd session, 1974.

.... *Statement of Information on Behalf of President Nixon,* Book I. Events Following the Watergate Break-In, June 19, 1972–March 1, 1974. Hearings, 93rd Congress, 2nd session, 1974.

.... *Statement of Information on Behalf of President Nixon,* Book II. Department of Justice—ITT Litigation. Hearings, 93rd Congress, 2nd session, 1974.

.... *Statement of Information on Behalf of President Nixon,* Book III. Political Contribution by Milk Producers Cooperatives: The 1971 Milk Price Support Decision. Hearings, 93rd Congress, 2nd session, 1974.

.... *Statement of Information on Behalf of President Nixon,* Book IV. White House Surveillance Activities. Hearings, 93rd Congress, 2nd session, 1974.

U. S. Congress, Senate, Joint Committee on Internal Revenue Taxation. *Examination of President Nixon's Tax Returns for 1969 through 1972.* Senate Report 93–768, 93rd Congress, 2nd session, 1974.

.... Select Commitee on Presidential Campaign Activities. *Presidential Campaign Activities of 1972,* Books 1–9. Watergate and Related Activities, Phase I: Watergate Investigation. Hearings, 93rd Congress, 1st session, 1973.

.... *Presidential Campaign Activities of 1972,* Books 10–13. Watergate and Related Activities, Phase II: Campaign Practices. Hearings, 93rd Congress, 1st session, 1973.

.... *Presidential Campaign Activities of 1972,* Books 14–17. Watergate and Related Activities, Milk Fund Investigation. Hearings, 93rd Congress, 1st and 2nd sessions, 1973–1974.

.... *Presidential Campaign Activities of 1972,* Books 18–19. Watergate and Related Activities, Use of Incumbency-Responsiveness Program. Hearings, 93rd Congress, 2nd session, 1974.

.... *Presidential Campaign Activities of 1972,* Books 20–24. Watergate and Related Activities, The Hughes-Rebozo Investigation and Related Matters. Hearings, 93rd Congress, 1st and 2nd sessions, 1973–74.

.... *Presidential Campaign Activities of 1972.* Legal Documents Relating to the Select Committee Hearings. Appendix to the Hearings, 93rd Congress, 1st and 2nd session, 1973-74.

.... *Presidential Campaign Activities of 1972:* The Final Report. Senate Report 93-981, 93rd Congress, 2nd session, July 12, 1974.

Government Documents: Commercial Editions

The Senate Watergate Report. The Final Report of the Senate Select Committee on Presidential Campaign Activities (The Ervin Committee). Vol. I. New York: Dell, 1974.

Staff of the New York Times. *The Watergate Hearings: Break-In and Cover-Up. Proceedings of the Senate Select Committee on Presidential Campaign Activities.* Viking, 1973.

.... *The White House Transcripts. Submission of Recorded Presidential Conversations to the Committee on the Judiciary of the House of Representatives by President Nixon.* New York: Viking, 1974.

Staff of the Washington Post. *The Presidential Transcripts.* New York: Delacorte Press, 1974.

The Staffs of United Press International and The World Almanac. *The Impeachment Report. A Guide to Congressional Proceedings in the Case of Richard M. Nixon President of the United States.* New York: New American Library, 1974.

RICHARD NIXON: POLITICAL BIOGRAPHY AND PERSONALITY

Books

Allen, Gary. *Richard Nixon: The Man Behind the Mask.* Belmont, Mass.: Western Islands, 1971.

Alsop, Stewart. *Nixon and Rockefeller: A Double Portrait.* Garden City, N.Y.: Doubleday, 1960.

Barber, James David. *The Presidential Character.* Englewood Cliffs, N.J.: Prentice-Hall, 1972.

Chesen, Elis. *President Nixon's Psychiatric Profile.* New York: Wyden, 1973.

Chester, Lewis, Godfrey Hodgson, and Bruce Page. *An American Melodrama: The Presidential Campaign of 1968.* New York: Dell, 1969.

Costello, William. *The Facts About Richard Nixon: The Unauthorized Biography of Richard Nixon. The Formative Years 1913–1959.* New York: Viking, 1960.

de Toledano, Ralph. *Nixon.* New York: Holt, Rinehart and Winston, 1956.

.... *Man Alone: Richard Nixon.* New York: Funk and Wagnalls, 1969.

English, David, and the staff of the London Daily Express. *Divided They Stand.* Englewood Cliffs, N.J.: Prentice-Hall, 1969.

Hess, Stephen and David Broder. *The Republican Establishment: The Future of the G.O.P.* New York: Harper and Row, 1967.

Keogh, James. *This Is Nixon.* New York: Putnam, 1956.

Kornitzer, Bela. *The Real Richard Nixon: An Intimate Biography.* Chicago: Rand McNally, 1960.

Mazo, Earl. *Richard Nixon: A Political and Personal Portrait.* New York: Harper & Row, 1960.

..............., and Stephen Hess. *Nixon: A Political Portrait.* New York: Popular Library, 1968.

Mankiewicz, Frank. *Perfectly Clear: Nixon from Whittier to Watergate.* New York: Quadrangle, 1973.

Mazlish, Bruce. *In Search of Nixon: A Psychohistorical Inquiry.* New York: Basic Books, 1972.

McGinniss, Joe. *The Selling of the President, 1968.* New York: Trident Press, 1969.

Nixon, Richard M. *Six Crises.* Garden City, N.Y.: Doubleday, 1962.

Spalding, Henry D. *The Nixon Nobody Knows.* Middle Village, N.Y.: Jonathan David, 1972.

Voorhis, Jerry. *The Strange Case of Richard Nixon.* New York: Popular Library, 1973.

Wills, Garry. *Nixon Agonistes: The Crisis of the Self-Made Man.* Boston: Houghton Mifflin, 1970.

White, Theodore H. *The Making of the President 1960.* New York: Atheneum, 1961.

.... *The Making of the President 1968.* New York: Atheneum, 1969.

Witcover, Jules. *The Resurrection of Richard Nixon.* New York: Putnam, 1970.

Woodstone, Arthur. *Nixon's Head.* New York: St. Martin's Press, 1972.

Articles

Barber, James David. "President Nixon and Richard Nixon: Character Trap," *Psychology Today,* October, 1974, pp. 113-118.

.... "The Question of Presidential Character," *Saturday Review of the Society,* October, 1972, pp. 62-66.

Fox, Frank, and Stephen Parker. "Why Richard Nixon Did Himself In: A Behavioral Examination of His Need to Fail," *New York Magazine,* September 9, 1974, pp. 26-32.

George, Alexander L. "Assessing Presidential Character," *World Politics,* January, 1974, pp. 234-282.

Goodwin, Richard N. "How History Will View 'The Candidate'," *Rolling Stone,* September 12, 1974, pp. 8-9.

Jackson, Donald. "The Young Nixon," *Life,* November 6, 1970, pp. 54-66.

Miller, William Lee. "An American Failure Story," *Commonweal,* September 6, 1974, pp. 476-478.

Muller, Rene J. "The Fictional Richard Nixon," *The Nation,* July 6, 1974, pp. 6-11.

Poirier, Richard. "Will the Real Richard Nixon Please Stand Up?" *New Times,* June 28, 1974, pp. 18-27.

Rogin, Michael, and John Lottier. "The Inner History of Richard Milhous Nixon," *Trans-action,* November–December, 1971, pp. 19-28.

Safire, William. "On Temper," *The New York Times,* August 23, 1973,
    p. 37.

Wills, Garry. "The Hiss Connection Through Nixon's Life," *The New
    York Times Magazine,* August 25, 1974, p. 8 ff.

THE NIXON WHITE HOUSE: DECISION-MAKING AND EVALUATION

Books

Brandon, Henry. *The Retreat of American Power.* Garden City, N.Y.:
    Doubleday, 1973.

Brown, Clifford W., Jr., and the Ripon Society. *The Jaws of Victory.*
    Boston: Little, Brown, 1974.

Cohen, Richard M., and Jules Whitcover. *A Heartbeat Away: The
    Investigation and Resignation of Vice President Spiro T. Agnew.*
    New York: Viking, 1974.

Drury, Allen. *Courage and Hesitation: Notes and Photographs of the
    Nixon Administration.* Garden City, N.Y.: Doubleday, 1971.

Evans, Rowland, and Robert D. Novak. *Nixon in the White House:
    The Frustration of Power.* New York: Random House, 1971.

Gardner, Lloyd C., editor. *The Great Nixon Turnaround: America's
    New Foreign Policy in the Post-Liberal Era.* New York: Franklin
    Watts, 1973.

Gartner, Alan, Colin Greer, and Frank Reissman. *What Nixon is
    Doing to Us.* New York: Harper and Row, 1973.

Johnson, Richard Tanner. *Managing the White House.* New York:
    Harper and Row, 1974.

Kalb, Marvin, and Bernard Kalb. *Kissinger.* Boston: Little, Brown,
    1974.

Keogh, James. *President Nixon and the Press.* New York: Funk and
    Wagnalls, 1972.

Moynihan, Daniel Patrick. *The Politics of a Guaranteed Income: The
    Nixon Administration and the Family Assistance Plan.* New
    York: Random House, 1973.

Novak, Michael. *Choosing Our King: Powerful Symbols in Presidential
    Politics.* New York: Macmillan, 1974.

Osborne, John. *The First Two Years of the Nixon Watch.* New York:
    Liveright, 1971.

.... *The Third Year of the Nixon Watch.* New York: Liveright,
    1972.

.... *The Fourth Year of the Nixon Watch.* New York: Liveright,
    1973.

.... *The Fifth Year of the Nixon Watch.* New York: Liveright,
    1973.

Osgood, Robert E., *et al. Retreat from Empire? The First Nixon Administration.* Baltimore: Johns Hopkins University Press, 1973.

Polsby, Nelson W., editor. *The Modern Presidency.* New York: Random House, 1973.

Rather, Dan and Gary Paul Gates. *The Palace Guard.* New York: Harper and Row, 1974.

Schlesinger, Arthur M., Jr. *The Imperial Presidency.* Boston: Houghton Mifflin, 1973.

Whalen, Richard J. *Catch the Falling Flag: A Republican's Challenge to his Party.* Boston: Houghton Mifflin, 1972.

White, Theodore H. *The Making of the President 1972.* New York: Atheneum, 1973.

Wise, David. *The Politics of Lying.* New York: Random House, 1973.

Articles

Banfield, Edward C., Nathan Glazer, Michael Harrington, *et. al.* "Nixon, The Great Society, and the Future of Social Policy: A Symposium," *Commentary,* May, 1973, pp. 31-61.

Brzezinski, Zbigniew. "The Deceptive Structure of Peace," *Foreign Policy,* Spring, 1974, pp. 35-55.

Cormier, Frank. "Nixon Prefers Solitude in Deciding Issues," *The Los Angeles Times,* November 16, 1972, pt. 7, p. 1.

Duscha, Julius. "The White House Watch Over TV and the Press," *The New York Times Magazine,* August 20, 1972, p. 9 ff.

Horner, Garnett. "Transcript of Interview With President Nixon," *The Washington Evening Star and Daily News,* November 9, 1972, p. A-7.

Johnson, Haynes. "Nixon Secretive Yet Revealing President," *The Washington Post,* January 20, 1973, p. 3.

Lessard, Suzannah. "Nixon and His Own Staff: The View from Their Own Mirror," *The Washington Monthly,* May, 1972, pp. 53-59.

Pett, Saul. "Nixon, With Brief Look Back, Prepares for Four More Years," *The Los Angeles Times,* January 14, 1973, p. 1.

Plumb, J. H. "Nixon as Disraeli," *The New York Times Magazine,* February 11, 1973, p. 12 ff.

Szulc, Tad. "Behind The Vietnam Cease-Fire Agreement," *Foreign Policy,* Summer, 1974, pp. 21-69.